William S. Hart

WILLIAM S. HART

PROJECTING THE AMERICAN WEST

Ronald L. Davis

UNIVERSITY OF OKLAHOMA PRESS : NORMAN

ALSO BY RONALD L. DAVIS

A History of Opera in the American
West (New York, 1965)

Opera in Chicago (New York, 1966)

The Social and Cultural Life of the
1920s (New York, 1972)

A History of Music in American Life
(New York, 1982)

(with Paul Boller) Hollywood Anec-
dotes (New York, 1988)

Hollywood Beauty: Linda Darnell
and the American Dream
(Norman, 1991)

The Glamour Factory: Inside
Hollywood's Big Studio System
(Dallas, 1993)

John Ford: Hollywood's Old Master
(Norman, 1995)

Celluloid Mirrors: Hollywood and
American Society Since 1945
(Fort Worth, 1997)

Duke: The Life and Image of John
Wayne (Norman, 1998)

La Scala West: The Dallas Opera
Under Kelly and Rescigno
(Dallas, 2000)

Van Johnson: MGM's Golden Boy
(Jackson, Miss., 2001)

John Rosenfield's Dallas: How the
Southwest's Leading Critic Shaped
a City's Culture (Dallas, 2002)

Published with the assistance of the National Endowment for the Humanities, a
federal agency which supports the study of such fields as history, philosophy, liter-
ature, and language.

Library of Congress Cataloging-in-Publication Data

Davis, Ronald L.
      William S. Hart: projecting the American West / Ronald L. Davis.
         p.   cm.
      Filmography: p.
      Includes bibliographical references and index.
      ISBN 0-8061-3558-1 (alk. paper)
         1. Hart, William Surrey, 1864–1946.   2. Motion picture actors and
actresses—United States—Biography.   I. Title.

PN2287.H3D38 2003
791.43'028'092—dc21
[B]

                                                                    2003041008

1   2   3   4   5   6   7   8 9   10

For Santiago,

El chico grande,

who taught me about living

Contents

Illustrations

Preface

For silent picture fans William S. Hart became a cherished symbol of the romantic old West. For Hart himself, the untamed West was the real West, and he never tired of saying that his childhood on the plains and prairies of America's closing frontier had taught him the truth about the nation's westward experience. "I spent my boyhood out there when some of the earliest pioneers were yet living," he said in 1921, at the crest of his career, "and I had direct from them much of the history of their early struggles. I have read, too, everything I can find on Western subjects, for it has been my ambition to try to reconstruct all that early history on the screen."

Hart vowed to make motion pictures that were authentic mirrors of frontier life and to capture all the "fascinating and colorful charm" of those unruly times. It was the picturesque, action-packed, alluring side of the frontier West that Hart chose to remember and that he portrayed. He never lost his nostalgia for the "redman, the buffalo, and those stalwart types of men who packed guns in the open." Preserving the flavor of incidents he had glimpsed as a child became Hart's mission.

The actor exaggerated his knowledge of the West, and his exposure to life on the frontier was more as a circumspect tourist than as a longtime resident. Hart's family was constantly on the move, and he developed an intimate acquaintance with few of the places they lived. Even so his memory was selective. Hart's knowledge of Plains Indians was far more superficial than he liked to pretend. "I learned to hunt and track with the wisdom of my red friends," he said. "We used to sail primitive Indian iceboats on the upper Missouri River" and "my early . . . relationship with the Sioux Indians enabled me to learn their tribal traits and history nearly as well as I know our own."

As his career progressed, the actor buttressed his childhood experiences in the West not only with reading but also by cultivating relationships with flashy representatives of the late frontier era, most notably Charles M. Russell, Wyatt Earp, and Bat Masterson. He also had brushes with Al Jennings, Charles Siringo, and Buffalo Bill Cody and counted Will Rogers among his best friends. This distinctive clique added vigor and validation to Hart's pose as a westerner, and he surrounded himself with an aggregation of Indian rugs and handicrafts, antique guns, cowboy accoutrements, buffalo robes, and a remarkable collection of western art.

Bill Hart began acting at an early age and struggled for years to earn a modest living. He suffered the indignities that most members of his profession did in an era when itinerant actors were considered pariahs in respectable circles. Young Hart had the responsibility of supplementing his family's income, and constant travel allowed him little opportunity to establish lasting relationships. The youth developed an insular temperament and appeared most comfortable with work and fantasy. He trained on the stage in Shakespearean tragedies and nineteenth-century melodramas, and he internalized theatrical excesses and a tragic stance until they framed his concept of life. Even though Hart had a paternity suit filed against him at the height of his fame, he was a moralist to the point of prudery. His good bad men on the screen were more opportunistic than evil, and the reformation his characters underwent by the final reel made his Westerns as much morality plays as action thrillers.

Hart began making movies in 1914, shortly after the American frontier had reached its final phase. Western outlaws still operated in the first decade of the twentieth century, and the last big cattle roundups took place around 1907. Geromino, the great Apache chief, was still a prisoner at Fort Sill, Oklahoma, in 1909. When Hart arrived in California, scores of cowboys who had worked the open range were drifting into Hollywood, hoping to find jobs in the infant movie business, where they could play cowboy when making a living in the dying Cattle Kingdom was no longer possible.

To today's audiences, except for the few rabid silent picture buffs who respect an earlier generation's tastes in entertainment, William S.

Hart's movies appear overdone and sometimes laughable. The old cowboy star's acting, with its emphasis on semaphoric gestures and undulating glances, is difficult for modern filmgoers to take seriously. To them, much of Hart's "realism" seems artificial and quaint.

But Hart holds an honored place in cinema history, and his work is esteemed by western history scholars for its visual accuracy. Despite all the caricature and stale action, Hart's films contain a look and an ambience of the frontier West, and their central character is both renegade and visionary. If Hart's concept of the West was skewed, it is a view that popular culture has held in high regard.

Cowboy stars who came after Hart (Tom Mix, Buck Jones, Ken Maynard, Charles Starrett, Sunset Carson, Gene Autry, Roy Rogers, and the rest of the Saturday matinee idols) emphasized nonstop action and showmanship in their movies, with little or no transformation of character. Hart's good bad men came to grips with moral issues, made decisions, and suffered the consequences. Not until the classic Westerns of John Ford, beginning with *Stagecoach* in 1939, and the adult Westerns that came on the heels of *The Gunfighter* (1950), *High Noon* (1952), and *Shane* (1953), did the genre reach maturity.

For a generation that had never ridden in an airplane, received its news in a belated fashion, and moved at a generally slower pace than we in the twenty-first century, Hart's silent Westerns offered excitement, lessons in righteous behavior, and stirring entertainment. Enveloped in darkness and riveted to the screen, with no distracting sound to lessen the visual impact, audiences—particularly those in the vast rural areas—thrilled at a reconstruction of a recent past that had crossed into lore. In darkened movie houses filled with music befitting the drama, unsophisticated audiences found in William S. Hart a hero they could revere. They could return to their mundane lives assured that good triumphed over evil and that even the bad were capable of redemption.

Hart stands on the divide between fact and fiction. His films, like his life, were a combination of myth and reality. Many of the people Hart knew—Earp, Masterson, Russell, Jennings, Siringo—helped to shape the public's romantic image of the late frontier West, and they, too, were men whose careers blended myth and reality. If Hart approached filmmaking as a realist, it was as a sentimental realist. His yarns were the type western cronies fancied and spun among themselves. Like Charlie Russell, Hart fell in love with the West at an early age and made it his career. He not only became a symbol of the frontier legacy, he convinced himself that he was a true westerner with a unique knowledge of the frontier's role in American history. Like Frederick Jackson Turner, Hart regarded the westward experience as the central force that shaped the national character. But Hart's West was laced with righteousness, high drama, and an abiding nostalgia that reflected secret longings of his puerile personality.

I decided to write on William S. Hart for two major reasons. Despite Hart's prominent reputation in film history, no previous full-length life story of the actor exists aside from his autobiography, *My Life East and West*, which is a saccharine read and not an altogether reliable source. In the Seaver Center for Western History Research at the Natural History Museum of Los Angeles County, however, there are some one hundred thirty boxes of William S. Hart papers, and that cache of material seemed to offer the makings for a solid biography. Unfortunately, most of the data contained in the Seaver collection deals with Hart's later life and career. *My Life East and West* remains the primary source on his early years, apart from scattered newspaper items. Of necessity, the first three chapters of *William S. Hart: Projecting the American West* rely heavily on the actor's published memoir. Try as I did to locate supplemental data, the discouragements were many.

Early in my research, however, I had a stroke of luck. One evening while eating dinner in Los Angeles with producer Walter Seltzer and his wife, Mickey, I mentioned that I was thinking about writing a biography of William S. Hart. Mickey Seltzer voiced immediate surprise. Her reaction was soon explained when she told me that her mother, Jane Novak, a silent picture actress and one of Hart's leading ladies, had once been engaged to Hart. I interviewed Mickey a few days later, and she loaned me a stack of photocopied love letters Hart had written her mother in 1921.

Emotionally involved by the time I finished taking notes from Mickey Seltzer's collection of letters, I had little choice but to proceed with this biography, although I was aware early in the research that the result would be an uneven book. The actor was a conscientious letter writer, so documenting the latter part of his career was partial compensation for the meager sources on his early years. His boyhood years and early adulthood remained difficult to trace, and in many instances voids were impossible to fill because of the peripatetic nature of his family. Thanks to the Aurora Public Library I was able to re-create Hart's months in the Fox River Valley of Illinois through letters that came into the press at the time *My Life East and West* was published.

After going through the one hundred thirty boxes of William S. Hart's papers (some twenty of which consist of canceled checks), I still had trouble getting a handle on the actor's personality. Somehow we did not connect to the degree I had with subjects of other biographies I had written in which oral history played an important role in my research. Between Christmas and New Year's Eve in 1998, I drove to Durango, Colorado, to visit my friend Harry Carey, Jr., one of the few people still alive who knew Hart personally. Within twenty minutes he gave me what I thought was the key to Hart's personal makeup. "Bill Hart was always 'on,'" Carey said. "He was a ham actor who had learned his craft in melodrama. He talked in the declamatory way he'd learned during his years on the stage." Suddenly all the letters I had read that were written by Hart made sense, and the pieces began to form a character.

Like any author, I owe thanks to a host of people who helped make this book possible. My gratitude goes first to Mickey Seltzer, Harry Carey, Jr., Joe McNinch, and Diana Serra Cary, who supplemented archival research with personal recollections of Hart. John Cahoon in the Seaver Center of the Natural History Museum of Los Angeles County was a paragon of patience and guidance during my weeks there. Zandra Stanley at the William S. Hart Museum in Newhall, California, gave me a private tour of the Hart home that placed the silent cowboy star's reclusive personality during his old age in a setting so powerful that I felt I had actually touched the man. Mary Ann Pirone at the Aurora Public Library supplied me with the data I needed to amplify Hart's boyhood in the Fox River Valley.

Barbara Hall, head of special collections at the Margaret Herrick Library of the Academy of Motion Picture Arts and Sciences, is a model of professionalism, as well as an engaging lunch partner. The entire staff of the Herrick Library makes doing research there a pleasure. Ned Comstock in the film and television archives of the University of Southern California remains a researcher's dream. Ned is not only efficient and knowledgeable, but he remembers who is working on what project and stays in contact. My thanks extend to the staffs of the Library of Congress, the American Film Institute in Los Angeles, the theater section of the New York Public Library, the Columbia University Oral History Archives, the Nebraska Historical Society, the Huntington Library, Haden Library at Arizona State University, and Rita Forrester in the local history department of the public library in Newburgh, New York. Also helpful in Newburgh was local historian Patricia Favata, who called me with additional information after I returned to Dallas.

Without my personal support system, it is unlikely that this book would ever have reached completion. Among that team are Judy Bland, who doubles as my secretary, Jane Elder, Tony and Ghada Colom, Brenda Cooper, Dana and John Pickett, Gail Alpert, Mary Jo and Bob Harding, Suzy Ruff, Robert Richmond, Sally Caldwell, Steve Simonson, and Bill Wylie. Marilynn Hill and Charles Cooper spent part of the summer of 1999 with me in Los Angeles, where we worked hard on our respective biographies, laughed our way through breakfasts and dinners, and bonded into a surrogate family that continues. Finally, I must give special recognition to Santiago Nambo, who has been my steadfast friend in work, travel, and play, and allowed me undisturbed time to do the writing I enjoy. It is appropriate that this book is dedicated to him.

WILLIAM S. HART

Boyhood

Although William S. Hart became the prototype of the tough, gun-toting westerner in silent pictures, he was born in Newburgh, New York. His birthdate is a matter of conjecture, since the town's health department did not keep records until 1869. Accounts agree that Hart was born on December 6, but the year reported varies from 1862 to 1876. Most likely the date was 1864, for that is the year listed for Hart's birth on records of the postal service, where the future cowboy star worked as a youth, and it jibes with census data indicating that his family lived in the Fox River Valley of Illinois in 1870 before he was old enough to attend school.

Newburgh, on the west bank of the Hudson River a few miles north of West Point, was not an incorporated town until 1865. By then the community's diversified manufacturing interests had entered a period of prosperity stimulated by the Civil War, and the surrounding farms were doing a lively trade in milk, butter, and fruit. Still, most of Newburgh's streets remained ungraded, and the town's population was concentrated in a compact area. Civic boosters liked to point out that General George Washington had made Newburgh his headquarters during the latter part of the American Revolution, and landscape architect Andrew Jackson Downing was a lifelong resident of the community.

William S. Hart (the middle initial stood for Surrey, not Shakespeare, as some writers have maintained) was the third child and the first son of Nicholas and Roseanna McCauley Hart. Roseanna's parents had emigrated to America from Northern Ireland when she was three

3

years old. The girl grew into a hardworking, nurturing woman, whom her famous son described as a person "of gentle upbringing and refinement." Nicholas was born in Liverpool and raised in the English Midlands. Quick-tempered and a good talker, Nicholas arrived in the United States as a young man, proud to be descended from a line of barristers. It is unlikely that Nicholas was a graduate of Oxford, as has been claimed, and to call him an engineer, as Bill Hart later did, would be an exaggeration. Throughout most of his son's boyhood, Nicholas worked as a miller, more given to dreams and wanderlust than to achieving financial success, and he was never able to provide his family with more than a scant living.

Roseanna grew up in Newburgh and met her husband there. At the time of their first son's birth, they were living in a brick house close to the freight yard. The future cowboy actor was born at 45 Front Street, near the river and the docks. Much of the town's business activity—the factories, the wholesale houses, the telegraph office, the coal and lumber yards—stood along Front and Water Streets, since that location gave them ready access to both the steamboat landings and the railroads.

Although Newburgh's economy was flourishing at the time of Bill Hart's birth, his family benefited little from the prosperity. Dreaming of the perfect site for a flour mill that would earn him a fortune, Nicholas Hart decided to gather his brood and head west when his son was only a few months old. The Illinois Federal Census of 1870 states that Nicholas Hart, age thirty-seven, was living in Oswego Township, and the Edwards Aurora Census two years later confirms the presence of the Hart family. Bill's two sisters, Mary Ellen and Frances, were both old enough to attend school.

Bill Hart's first recollection was of Oswego, where the family lived near the Parker grist mill on the Fox River. There were only two houses in the immediate vicinity, and the nearest farmhouse was a mile away. George Parker and his family lived in the house nearest the Harts, and Nicholas worked for Parker as head miller. Bill's earliest memory was of springtime, when the ice was breaking up on the river and making its way downstream in slabs. Bill remembered how he and his father were in a rowboat, taking supplies to some sawmill workers marooned on the opposite bank of the raging, ice-filled stream. The family's dog, a shepherd named Ring, spotted Nicholas and Bill from the shore, plunged into the water, and began swimming after them. Nicholas stopped rowing and managed to get the struggling dog inside the boat but not without hazard to his son and himself as they tossed about in the surging water. Bill recalled the episode in his autobiography in thrilling detail, almost as though he were acting the scene in a movie.

After the star's book was published in 1929, John Parker, son of the grist mill owner, remembered young Bill Hart, whom he called Willie, as "a round chunk of a boy" who used to show up at the Parkers' door with his sister Frances whenever John's mother baked cookies. Frances was "a very quick-spoken girl, much like her father," John Parker recalled, "while Willie was more deliberate, taking after his mother, and he was somewhat bashful." Nonetheless, Frances would push her little brother ahead to act as spokesperson in their quest for cookies, even though his halting words were not easily understood. "He says he likes cookies," Frances would interpret, causing Mrs. Parker to smile since she knew from experience what the children's mission was.

Nicholas Hart, as John Parker remembered him, was "a man of dominant character," of medium height and athletic build. He wore a well-trimmed sandy beard and glasses, usually colored, since he was having trouble with his eyes. A particle of steel from a mill pick had entered Nicholas's eye while he was working in Oswego, and the inflammation spread to the other eye. His sight grew so bad that the family feared he might be going blind. "Hart was one of those self-confident men," Parker said, "an expert in his line, very particular in his work and would brook no carelessness or negligence in others. He possessed a sharp tongue and never hesitated to speak his thoughts. He was bold and fearless, much like the characters his son portrayed in later years, and courageous in emergencies." John Scheets, who worked under Hart at the mill, remembered Nicholas as "an able miller and an expert millstone dresser. He became sort of a rover or itinerant mill worker, dressing stone and repairing mill machinery."

Parker confirmed a story that the star related in his autobiography regarding Nicholas's pursuit of some horse thieves who stole the mill team in the middle of the night. "Hart, clad in his night gown and armed with a butcher knife, chased the thieves until they abandoned the team up on the main road," Parker remembered.

Although Bill was too young to attend school in Oswego, he was developing into a self-reliant boy who seemed capable of taking care of himself. He often entertained himself in the vicinity of the mill and was well liked by the farmers who came from the surrounding countryside to get their wheat ground into flour. Mrs. Nellie Herren, who owned the farm on which the grist mill still stood in 1945, recalled that it was "a common sight to see eight or ten loads of grain waiting their turn."

The Fox River Valley was an idyllic place for a young boy with a taste for the outdoors. The river's current was swift near the mill, and workmen from the neighboring sawmill used long poles with hooks at the ends for pulling logs into the desired place. On weekends in the spring, summer, and fall, fishermen gathered along the banks, and in the winter ice was harvested from the river and stored in sawdust in a nearby icehouse for sale during the summer months. Bill, like most of the children in the area, liked to suck and chew on sugarcane stalks that he grabbed off wagons taking cane to a nearby sorghum mill to be boiled into molasses. Sometimes his mouth and chin were red with the juice.

When a misunderstanding arose between Nicholas and George Parker, Nicholas hastily resigned from the mill in Oswego and moved his family to Montgomery, a few miles away. Nicholas had ambitions of going farther west and starting a mill of his own in Iowa. He asked George Parker to allow his family to remain in the house in Oswego while he made a prospecting trip to the adjoining state, but the mill owner needed the dwelling for his successor. The argument that followed nearly destroyed a friendship, although in time the relationship was patched up.

Hart changed his mind about going to Iowa and accepted a position with the Hard flour mill in Montgomery. The family's house in Montgomery stood by itself, close to the mill, but there was a general store in between that sold candy. Nicholas's vision had become so impaired that he could not find his way to the mill alone and had to rely on Bill or one of his daughters to guide him. When Bill's turn came, he always stopped when they reached the store, which was a hint for his father to buy him a stick of candy.

Before long the family moved again, this time to Aurora, Illinois, also on the Fox River, where Nicholas took a job at the city mill. Aurora was larger than its neighboring villages and later virtually absorbed them. The Harts lived a half mile from the flour mill in Aurora, close to the C.B.&Q. railroad tracks, the train depot, and the riverbank. Within a few weeks Nicholas's eyesight proved so bad that the mill owners would not permit him to work for them any longer. Although Bill liked to say as an adult that his father was an expert at his trade and made a good salary, in truth the family lived in near-poverty throughout most of the boy's growing-up years.

In his memoirs the aging William S. Hart viewed his childhood as a grand adventure, particularly his years in the West. He remembered playing outlaw and pretending that the fence around his family's house was a robber's cave. He conjured happy visions of romping with various dogs and the excitement he felt braving the unsettled West. He recalled privation, but in mawkish terms. In Aurora the family was so destitute that the children found only two pennies and a handful of raisins in their Christmas stockings from Santa Claus. "We were satisfied," Hart wrote in his memoirs. "But how well I can remember . . . the drawn, pinched expressions of my father and mother!" Nicholas's failure to become a prosperous, independent miller marked Bill for the rest of his life, yet in later years he defended his father and glossed over his inadequacies as a breadwinner. To the aging star, his father was a restless, reckless man, ready to battle for his rights and the rights of others. "I only know my fond memories are those of my youth," Bill wrote John Scheets in 1929.

William S. Hart developed an early capacity for romanticizing his life, and even as a child he seems to have retreated into himself emotionally, preferring loneliness over intimate family ties. Although he talked about his family in idealized terms, he found ways of distancing himself from prolonged contact. Later, Lotta, his baby sister born during the time the family lived in the Fox River Valley, would be the embodiment of saintly innocence for Bill, but that was when he was spending most of his time on the road and particularly after Lotta's death. In his youth he viewed her far differently. "I would stick pins in my new baby sister to hear her cry," he admitted as an adult. The Harts' migratory life and precarious financial condition made their life sufficiently difficult that the boy's retreat into fantasy is understandable.

Faced with the possibility of blindness, Nicholas was obliged to travel alone to New York City for a series of operations. Eventually Dr. C. R. Agnew of the Manhattan Eye and Ear Hospital cut deeply enough into the miller's pupil, without impairing his vision, to find an infinitesimal particle of steel that was causing the trouble.

Roseanna waited with the Hart children in Aurora for her husband's return, strapped for money. "My mother used to tell us to mind her," Bill recalled, "because our father was not there to take care of us, and then she would read letters and cry a little." Roseanna seemed to cry a great deal during her marriage, for life on the western prairies never offered her the fulfillment or security that Nicholas had promised. By the time the family left Aurora, Roseanna had four youngsters to care for, Bill and the three girls, one of whom was a babe in arms.

With his eye problem solved, Nicholas returned to Aurora and, since he could not work in the mills for a while because of the dust, took a job as night watchman at a silverplate factory. But in pursuit of his dream of pushing farther west, he soon decided to move to Portland, Iowa. Roseanna and the children were left behind while Nicholas explored the possibilities in Iowa. Once he was established, he wrote his wife to gather their brood and join him in Portland. "I remember being set off on the prairie—no station, just a pole with an iron arm for a mail bag," Bill remembered. Nicholas was at the stop to greet them when they arrived. "We all laughed and we all cried," Bill said.

The family's new home was a one-room wooden house with a false front; the building had once been a trading post. The flour mill and river were just across the road. The only other structure anywhere near was a half mile away, and that was a one-room shack used as a schoolhouse. Young Bill spent a great deal of time in Portland swimming in the river and following a teamster who hauled flour to Mason City, fifteen miles away.

But once Nicholas had the millstones in shape for grinding and the mill in working order, he was ready to move on. Bill referred to his father as a "white gold" pioneer and said that he was known throughout the West as a finder of water power and a builder of flour mills. By nature Nicholas suffered from an itchy foot, yet in his admiring son's imagination he represented the courageous breed of men who settled the country's last frontier. "All pioneers were real men, big men," Bill wrote an acquaintance in Aurora in 1929, "and no band of pioneers were bigger or more real than those men that wore the dusty clothes of the miller."

The Harts moved next to nearby Rockford, Iowa, then a settlement of about one hundred people. They lived in another house close to another mill on yet another river. But the hotheaded Nicholas and the mill owner in Rockford soon squabbled, and for the testy Nicholas arguments usually led to a fight. Young Bill stood watching in tears as his father slugged it out with the mill owner. Thinking that his dad was in danger, the boy took him a large, double-edged ax he could barely lift. Nicholas won the fight without his son's help, but he also lost his job. For the third time in six months, the family uprooted.

They left Rockford on a bitter-cold winter night. The children were carried to the train station by men wearing long blue army overcoats. "There were three of them," Bill said, "big stalwart men that had fought under Grant. Fighting men always liked my father." The wind was blowing so strong when they left Rockford that the men, each with a child in his arms, had to walk backward. Meanwhile Nicholas protected Roseanna and their baby from the cutting blizzard.

This time the family settled in Minneapolis, already one of the great flour-milling centers of the country. The Harts found housing in two rooms over a saloon, just off Hennepin Avenue. The street was full of horses, oxen, and sleds loaded with cordwood, and the sidewalks were made mostly of planks. Indians walked the streets, some with baskets of goods on their backs, and lumberjacks were everywhere. The Harts were Episcopalian, and Bill remembered his father taking him to a little stone church in Minneapolis for services.

The family stayed in the city until springtime. Then Nicholas made a seventy-five-mile trip to Trimbell, Wisconsin, to inspect another mill site, talking Bill with him. They walked the last twelve miles of the journey, and Nicholas had to ask directions from a stranger they met on the way. Trimbell at the time consisted of only three houses and a store that doubled as a post office.

The mill there, owned by a half-breed Indian, was about two miles down the river. The Harts took up residence in a three-room house by the mill, near where the owner and his family lived. The owner's mother was a full-blood Sioux, and his sister was a girl about twelve years old. The girl took a liking to Bill and spoke to him in the Sioux language, which intrigued the boy, as did the sign language that the old woman used. In time Bill became so fascinated by the woman and the girl that he followed them as they went about their chores. Eventually he came to understand some of what they said, and the old woman talked to him as if he were an adult, telling him tales of Indian deeds and bits of Indian lore. "I can only think and live in the past," the woman said. "The white people have taken away all of the Indian's future." Bill made friends among the Sioux boys, accompanied one in particular as the lad hunted partridges in a thicket, and developed a respect for Indian ways that remained with him for the rest of his life.

In Trimbell, Roseanna gave birth to another son, aided in the delivery by her Sioux neighbor since no doctor was available. Bill liked having a baby brother and enjoyed tickling him with a feather to make him laugh, but the child lived only a short time. Bill remembered the baby's crib covered over with a blanket and the old Indian woman sitting beside the corpse all night, smoking. The infant was buried in a homemade coffin on a hillside overlooking the Mississippi River, near Red Wing, Minnesota.

When construction began on a flour mill on the Orinoco River in Minnesota, Nicholas was offered a six-month job installing its machinery and dressing the burrs. Not willing to be separated from his wife and children, Hart moved them to Orinoco, a five-day trip from Trimbell. They traveled to their temporary home in a prairie schooner pulled by three yokes of steers. "How I envied the driver," Bill said, "a strapping, curly-headed youth of about eighteen, as he curled his long-lashed bullwhip over his team." Young Bill trudged along behind the schooner on the journey. At night he slept under the wagon with his father and his young idol, while the three girls and his mother bedded down inside.

Orinoco, Minnesota, consisted of approximately fifty people who lived in a dozen houses. Bill acquired a dog named Prince and spent much of his time in Orinoco fishing. On one of his outings he stumbled onto a small Sioux village about four miles downstream from the mill where his father worked. The boy was surprised to learn that the Sioux did not like fish and only ate them in the winter when their food supply ran low.

Nicholas's work in Orinoco was not finished by the time winter set in, and he decided to send his family back to Trimbell without him. The return trip was faster than the going, as the wagon Roseanna and the children rode in was drawn by four spirited horses. Bill sat on the seat with the driver, a bewhiskered plainsman, and the lad enjoyed himself immensely and felt like the man of the family.

After their return to Trimbell, Roseanna and the Hart youngsters lived for a while in a one-room log cabin nestled in a tract of timber, about three miles from the half-breed's mill. Their nearest neighbor was a mile away through a dense woods. A cougar, smelling meat in the house, tried to get inside one night and tore some shingles off the roof. Even more frightening was the night Bill's dog went mad from rabies. "He was running amuck all over the room among sleeping children," Bill recalled. Somehow Roseanna got the beast out of the house without anyone being hurt. The next day Bill and his Indian friend tracked the dog in the snow until they were exhausted but never found him.

By the time Nicholas rejoined the family, snow was piled high. The Harts survived an unusually severe winter living in one of the three houses in Trimbell. As the ice on the river grew thick, Bill and his sisters had to scrape frost from the window panes to see outside. There was no work, so Nicholas read to the children from his collection of Charles Dickens's novels—*Oliver Twist, Nicholas Nick-leby,* and *Old Curiosity Shop.* With no income, things became so desperate for the family that Roseanna sent Bill to the store to trade her most prized possession, a silver caster, for flour, sugar, and tea.

When spring came and the streams began running again, the mill resumed operation. One night in early May, Nicholas got Bill out of bed and hurriedly sent him after the old Indian woman the family had come to respect. Roseanna was about to have another baby. By the time the boy got home, he had a new baby brother, whom his parents named Nicholas, Jr. But Roseanna did not respond to the Indian woman's treatment after the birth and grew seriously ill. The Harts soon moved to Prescott on the St. Croix River, where there was a doctor among the town's two hundred residents. Nicholas went to work as an extra hand in a flour mill in Prescott. But Roseanna's need for better medical facilities became so critical that she soon returned to Newburgh with the girls and the baby. Bill remained with his father and remembered putting his mother and siblings on a train in Hastings and watching from the station platform as the railroad cars sped out of sight.

Nicholas and Bill returned to Orinoco and boarded for a time at the Len Hanson Hotel. Lonely for his mother, sisters, and brother, young Hart filled much of his time riding horses and fishing. Since Nicholas was working at the mill all day and sometimes far into the night, Bill could largely do what he pleased. He sold most of the fish he caught and for a short time did odd jobs on a farm fourteen miles out of town. "I was doing a man's work in the fields, plowing all day," Hart said in his memoirs. During thrashing season, the boy drove a team that dragged straw away and lived with the farmers in tents. "I thought it pointed the way to becoming a cow-puncher and no school," he said.

Bill grew up with practically no schooling, and for years he did not even know the letters of the alphabet. In most places the family lived, schools were not available, which gave the boy ample opportunity to avoid formal education. He had no use for school and reveled in the lack of supervision he had enjoyed since his mother's departure. But Orinoco had a school, and Nicholas insisted that Bill must attend when classes began. To prepare his son, the father began teaching him the alphabet.

Bill preferred what he later called the "wonderland of the western outdoors" and the lessons to be learned from nature. As an adult Hart claimed that the frontier West shaped his personality and thinking. "The bigness of the West makes men quiet; they seldom talk unless they have something to say," he wrote in his memoirs. "The altitude clarifies their brains and gives them nerves of steel."

Once he got used to school, the experience was somewhat less painful than young Hart had expected. He met other boys nearly as untutored as he was, and his teacher in Orinoco, a rancher's daughter, could barely read and write herself. On the way to school one day Bill met a bear on the road, and that gave him an excuse not to go anymore. "My schooling was a failure," he admitted in 1917.

From a Sioux friend who lived in a nearby Indian village, Bill learned to hunt and track, use a bow and arrow, and shoot accurately with a rifle. He claimed to have become skilled at riding ponies bareback as well as with a saddle. During the winter, he and his Sioux companion sailed iceboats on the river, and in the summer he usually wore moccasins. Bill and his friend went for long swims in the river's cool water during summer afternoons and then sat on the bank and told stories. "In short," Hart later reflected, "I was a Western boy."

A rattlesnake bit him one day, and he credited an Indian woman's knowledge of cures with saving his life. Young Hart mastered Indian sign language and a little of the Sioux tongue, which he used to his advantage once he became a star. He came to admire the simplicity of the Indians' way of life and their regard for nature. "I always found them steadfast, loyal, and stoically grateful," Hart said in 1925. He remembered his Sioux neighbors as kind, straightforward, and honest.

When Nicholas received word that Roseanna was recuperating nicely under a doctor's care in Newburgh, he decided to resume his search for a mill site that could become his family's permanent home. He journeyed down into central Kansas, taking Bill with him, and checked out water power around Abilene, Ellsworth, Hays City, and Newton. "I did not care much for these places," Bill recalled. In Abilene, Nicholas and Bill stayed in a hotel over a saloon. Young Hart was awakened one morning by the sound of his father's loud, angry voice downstairs. Bill went to the top of the stairway and saw a man, whom he later discovered was named Three-Fingered Texas Jack, facing his father with his hand on a pistol. Nicholas shouted at the assailant, "My boy is sleeping in that bed with me, and you fellows try and pull any drinking bouts up there again and I'll beat hell out of the whole crowd." Bill remembered the lawlessness of the Kansas cattle towns and the southern drawls of the Texans who rode through the streets with their herds.

For a week Nicholas joined a group of cowboys driving cattle to Fort Robinson, with Bill tagging along. The beef was being sent by the government to feed some Indians there. Bill recalled that the trail had been traveled so heavily that the grass was grazed off. "I made quite a hit with this outfit," Hart boasted in his memoirs. "My father's horse was cutting up a bit and I traded with him."

Failing to find a suitable mill site in Kansas, Nicholas decided to try Dakota Territory. He and Bill's journey to the Black Hills took them through Julesburg, Colorado, and Sidney, Nebraska. Bill recalled seeing crowds of people in these towns, many speaking different languages and toting rifles or shotguns. "There were fathers and mothers with lots of children," he said. "Many of the people were cooking and living in the streets," which were clogged with soldiers, Indians, teamsters with bullwhips, cowboys, loose cattle, horses, mules, dogs, and prairie schooners. Furniture of all kinds was piled everywhere. "There were also young women wearing fancy short dresses covered with beads," Bill said, "with a pretty colored shawl over their shoulders and a flower in their hair."

After traveling east on the Union Pacific railroad and north by stagecoach, Nicholas and his son came into the Black Hills. Gold had recently been discovered in the region, and miners from all over the world had poured in, causing the Indians in the area to grow apprehensive and restless. In response to reports of depredations, the government had increased the number of soldiers in the territory, but hostilities continued.

Nicholas hoped to form a partnership with relatives of the half-breed he had known in Wisconsin and build a flour mill on one of the swift-running streams in the Black Hills. Once the mill was in operation, he intended to send for Roseanna and his other children. "My father did not tell me his plans until we reached Sioux City," Bill recalled, but the boy grew excited at the prospect of having his mother, sisters, and brother with him again.

In Sioux City, Bill and his father were on their way to buy some horses early one morning when they saw a sheriff and two gamblers stumble out of a saloon and begin shooting. Father and son stood frozen in the crossfire, while the sheriff shot the gamblers but suffered a severe wound himself. Badly shaken, Nicholas took Bill back to their lodging without buying any horses. "I knew the bad men of those days," William S. Hart would later claim. "I remember them perfectly. In those days the law was the law of guns."

Traveling by stagecoach, Nicholas and Bill continued on to Yankton in Dakota Territory. A French Canadian there supplied Nicholas with three saddle horses and two packhorses and escorted them northwest into the Indian country. After riding for two days they came upon a small army post. "After that," Bill remembered, "we saw no towns, no white people, no log houses, no settlements."

One morning the threesome came over a rise in the prairie and saw a herd of horses in the distance. Nicholas looked through a pair of field glasses, noted that the animals were either standing or grazing, and determined that they were a band of wild horses. As the encroachers drew nearer, they heard a yell, and suddenly Indians in war paint seemed to leap on the backs of every horse and start racing toward them. Bill claimed in his memoirs that he "gaily started to chatter Sioux" as the leader approached, much to the Indians' astonishment. "I was not a bit timid or afraid," he said. "I can remember vividly their smiles and their humorous looks, each to the other, at my kid talk."

Nicholas was apprehensive as the riders drew near but finally decided that the Indians constituted a hunting party that had left their reservation in search of food. When the Indians showed no signs of hostility, Nicholas told them that he wanted to see Red Cloud or one of their chiefs. The leader signaled for the whites to continue on their way, and the painted band rode off. "To me," Bill later wrote, "these men were Indians, and I played with Indians; they were my friends. . . . Indians always liked me."

Hoping to gain permission from a Sioux chief to establish a flour mill in the Dakotas, Nicholas worked his way north, following the west bank of the Missouri River. Bill remembered seeing very little game and no buffalo on the trip. He and his father passed several small Indian villages and came upon a larger one on the White River that consisted of thirty or forty lodges and some one hundred fifty people. None of the Indians they met gave them any trouble, and since winter was approaching, Nicholas decided to make camp a short distance from the White River settlement. "An hour after we arrived," Bill recalled, "I had forgotten all about mill-sites . . . and was playing with the Indian children as though I had lived there all my life."

Nicholas tried to explain to the Indians how a mill could operate on the water power that came from the streams that emptied into the Missouri and how grain could be planted, grown, and turned into flour that could be sent down the big river to market. But the Sioux were hunters, not farmers, and had trouble understanding. Planting meant plows, and plows reminded the Plains Indians of what the government agents tried to send them instead of rifles and blankets. While his father talked business in the council lodge, Bill played with the Indian children from early morning until twilight. "The boys had many games that I had never seen," he said.

With the onset of winter, Nicholas realized that he and his son must leave Dakota Territory or be snowed in. The Indians gave them a farewell party, at which Bill was allowed to sit by his father's side with the men. "I never shall forget the beautiful talk made by Lone Bear," Hart wrote in *My Life East and West*. "It told of the troubles of the white and the red people; how they were climbing the same mountain on opposite sides." One day, the chief predicted, the two races would reach the top of the mountain together, and there, "close to the roof of heaven," the Great Spirit would talk to them and their troubles would end.

As Bill and his father left the Indian camp, dogs were barking and Bill's playmates came out to see him off. "There were no words spoken on either side when we left," Bill said, "but it was felt to be a sad parting, and we had been there only a little over six weeks."

Nicholas had decided to return to Minnesota, a journey of about three weeks. He and Bill reached Rochester, Minnesota, by train, then hitched a ride with one of the mill teams to Orinoco. They arrived to find the Indians they had known there gone. By Christmas news came that Roseanna's health had been restored and that she, the two younger girls, and Bill's baby brother would be joining them in the spring. Meanwhile Bill was forced to attend school.

Since no house was available in Orinoco, Nicholas decided to build one. He did the work himself, with Bill serving as errand boy. Trees were cut, and a log cabin was constructed and rough furniture made. By April all was ready for the family, and Bill and his father eagerly awaited the stagecoach that would bring Roseanna and the children the final lap of their journey west.

"We saw the six-horse team coming splashing through the mud," Bill recalled. "My mother was hugging me. She had my little brother in her arms and she was crying." The eldest Hart girl, Mary Ellen, had been left in Newburgh with her grandmother so that she could receive better schooling. But the reunion was a glorious occasion nonetheless.

Ever the wanderer, Nicholas soon decided to make another move. He had received an invitation from his former half-breed partner in Wisconsin, asking him to go in with him on building a mill on the Zumbro River. Bill was dispatched with a letter saying that his father would accept the offer. The boy traveled by stagecoach for the first forty miles of the trip but had to walk the last twenty. "When the stage drove away and left me at the crossing of the trails," Bill recalled, "I did not feel so good."

A month later the family was established at Zumbro Falls. "It was hard to leave the little Orinoco log cabin," Bill admitted, and his mother suffered even more. Roseanna remained frightened by life in remote places and missed the amenities of Newburgh, where there were doctors and decent schools and civilized talk. In Zumbro Falls, the Harts took shelter in an old store with a false front, much like what they had lived in earlier in Portland. Nicholas, overseeing twenty

Indians, began supervising the building of a mill and a dam half a mile up the river.

There was no school within twenty miles, much to Bill's delight. For a few weeks he plowed fields for a nearby farmer, earning fifty cents a day and using fourteen-hundred-pound steers to pull the plow that broke the virgin soil. Hundreds of prairie chickens strutted to one side as he cut furrows through their flock, and young though he was, Bill realized that a primeval domain was nearing extinction.

Tension increased on the northern prairie, as greater numbers of armed soldiers were sent west by the War Department. "In our immediate country," Hart remembered, "while outnumbered by whites, there were enough Sioux to cause anxiety in the event of trouble." Word came in June 1876 that General George Armstrong Custer and his troops had been annihilated at Little Big Horn, several hundred miles west of Zumbro Falls. Nearly all of the Sioux men that Bill and his father had met on the White River, including Lone Bear, were dead. "The whole village had moved to the Big Horn country," Hart said as an adult. "They were a hunting party, with their women and children with them, and were in camp when attacked by the soldiers."

Roseanna hated the West, and the threat of Indian troubles made her life there unbearable. Before long she suffered a relapse. A doctor traveled many miles to attend her, but he informed Nicholas that his wife needed surgery. Otherwise her life was in danger. There was no choice but to send Roseanna and the children, including Bill to look after the women, back to Newburgh.

The mill in Zumbro Falls was not finished yet, and no money was coming in. Nicholas turned over his share of the enterprise to his half-breed friend, and after putting Roseanna and the children on a train headed for the East, he took off for the western Indian country again, hoping that he could earn a better living and gain more independence in the Dakotas.

Bill did not take kindly to living in the settled East. He continued to daydream about faraway outposts and the freedom he had enjoyed on the vanishing frontier. He missed romping with the Indian boys and tending the animals he had come to love. Although he left the old West as an early teenager, Bill Hart would spend the rest of his life romanticizing the life he had experienced there. "My youth had been spent in the open," Hart later wrote. "The breath of the prairies nourished me throughout my early boyhood years."

William S. Hart claimed to know and understand the Indians far better than he in fact did and in his later years would assume the stance of an expert. "If an Indian looks straight at you when he's talking, it's good," he wrote in *My Life East and West*. "If he looks past you, it is not so good." By 1927 he had added an innocent flirtation to his memories of the half-breed girl he had admired in Trimbell. He was only ten years old at the time, she was about fifteen. "I thought she was the most beautiful creature ever created," Hart said when he was a Hollywood star. In later years he embellished the wisdom and impact of the old Sioux woman he had known in Trimbell, turning her into a sage, a medical marvel, a primitive scholar, and a Socratic teacher. He boasted that his Sioux friends had given him the name Chanta Suta, meaning "Strong Heart," and said that his friendship with the Indians had done much to strengthen his character and deepen his understanding of fundamental truths. "In fact," he wrote in the foreword to *Pinto Ben and Other Stories*, "my early days of intimate relationship with the Sioux Indians enabled me to learn their tribal traits and history nearly as well as I know our own."

Hart professed to have encountered some of the frontier West's most famous characters—outlaws, cattle rustlers, horse thieves, gamblers, grizzled prospectors, rowdy cowboys, and veterans of the Seventh Cavalry. He liked to talk about hearing the death cry of starving wolves during brutal winter nights on the northern plains and how he became a crack shot with the rifle and the six-gun. As he grew older, these stories had been repeated so often that they took on deeper hues. Bill would eventually tell fan-magazine writers that he spoke Sioux better than English as a boy and that he had been on friendly terms with Sitting Bull.

Bill Hart saw enough of various aspects of frontier life to make an indelible impression on him. What he retained was more the color of the old West than a factual reality. To make a cinematic comparison, the West became William S. Hart's Rosebud, a delicious memory from childhood that lingered and shaped his destiny, much as the sled from Charles Foster Kane's boyhood dominated the subconscious of the dying tycoon in Orson Welles's movie. In Hart's mind he never completely left the West of his youth. He longed to go back—if only in fantasy. "My only regret is that our stay was so short up there on the prairie," Hart said in 1926.

Life in Newburgh was certainly not easy for teenage Bill. What money Nicholas managed to send the family went primarily for Roseanna's medicine and doctor bills. After their return to Newburgh, the Harts initially occupied a two-room apartment in a frame house on Washington Street, opposite St. George's Cemetery. Mary Ellen went to work in a soap factory, and Bill sold newspapers and shoveled snow off sidewalks to earn supplemental funds. He did not go to school because there was no money for books. The family was so poor that they soon had to move to cheaper quarters on Western Avenue.

Bill hated everything about Newburgh, which in the 1870s was a town of about seventeen thousand people. Eastern boys did not understand Hart's ways, thought him mannerless and uncouth, and laughed at his talk about Indians. Whereas boys in the East grew up playing baseball and football, Bill knew only Indian games. Fortunately he had developed into a husky youngster, and Nicholas had taught him how to box. After a few fights, Bill won the respect of his young Newburgh neighbors, but he preferred to remain apart from them.

Roseanna insisted that her son be baptized and attend services regularly in Newburgh's Episcopal church. For a time Bill was a choirboy at St. George's Church, and longtime residents of the town remembered him singing a solo at a Christmas service. His young acquaintances said that he sang like a girl, which led to more fights, but Bill generally managed to hold his own in these brawls because of his size.

The family's financial predicament became so severe that Nicholas was at last forced to abandon his dream of owning a mill and return to Newburgh to support them. The stories he told them of recent happenings in the Indian country were sad indeed. The War Department had ordered cavalrymen to follow Indian bands and force them onto reservations. "Old people, women, and children were being attacked in their tipis and shot down in the snow and brush as they tried to run away," Bill remembered his father saying.

Nicholas found a job in Newburgh breaking stones with a sledge-hammer, but the family's poverty persisted. Bill carried ice and worked as a teamster, but he recalled standing in front of Duncan's bakery during the winter, hungrily admiring the delicacies in the window and relishing in the heat that wafted up through a grate from the ovens in the basement. After Nicholas rejoined the family, the Harts lived in Cart Alley, a short dead-end street with stables for the horses and wagons of nearby store owners on one side and small frame houses on the other. The Harts lived on the second floor of one of the houses, above a mute cobbler.

Within a few weeks the restless Nicholas bid his wife and children good-bye and took off for Troy, northeast of the state capital, where there were flour mills. He soon heard of a mill in West Farms, a suburb of New York City, that needed a stone dresser, and he worked as a hired hand in Troy just long enough to earn the money he needed for railroad fare to West Farms. When the ice broke up in the spring, his family took a barge down the Hudson River to join him.

Bill claimed that in West Farms the family was prosperous and happy for a time. He attended school there, and after school hours his father taught him to dress millstones. Bill swam in the Bronx River during the summer and skated on the river in the winter. On Sundays the family attended Grace Church. Then Nicholas caught his hand in a conveyor at the mill, an accident that would have torn him apart had he not managed to yank his crushed arm free. Even so, the back of his hand was torn off, making it impossible for him to work for many weeks.

During his recuperation, the Harts' youngest son, Nicholas, Jr., died, and the family went into mourning. Bill remembered his mother awakening him night after night and telling him to go find his father. "I always found him with his mangled arm at the same place," Bill said, "my little brother's grave. His great heart was breaking!"

Roseanna's health did not improve, requiring the consultation of several doctors before another operation was deemed necessary. Roseanna remained in Women's Hospital in New York for several weeks. Funeral expenses, hospital bills, and Nicholas's prolonged unemployment combined to make it essential for Bill to find full-time work. For a while he was an errand boy for a butcher, but he gave up the job to become a helper on an express wagon. His duties required him to handle the horses and cart trunks into the city. The wagon passed Women's Hospital every day, and Roseanna would wave to her son as he drove by. "Once every week I was allowed to go in and see her," Bill recalled.

Later young Hart made fifty cents a day as a delivery boy on a Bronx River ice wagon, working from three o'clock in the morning until three in the afternoon. "I cleaned and fed my team while the wagon was being loaded," Bill said, "and we started for Harlem and Yorkville at about four o'clock each morning." Untrained and uneducated, the stripling had to take whatever work he could find.

When Roseanna was allowed to come home, she was still pale and weak. During Nicholas's recovery, the mill where he had worked was sold, and the new owners brought in their own crew, which meant that Nicholas was again out of a job. "So my father took the big leap," Bill said. "We moved to the big city, little dreaming that our Western hopes were never to be realized." For two years the family lived at the Everett House at Seventeenth Street and Fourth Avenue.

A block away from their new quarters was the Clarendon Hotel, which was under the same management as the Everett House. Bill became a messenger boy for both hotels. His duties required him to make two trips daily to the general post office for mail and run miscellaneous errands for the hotels' clerks and bartenders. For extra money he carried messages for guests. Business was good for him since only a few telephones had been installed at the time.

As a reward for his services, Bill sometimes received theater passes. The first play he saw was a melodrama, and the villains and the beautiful heroine in distress made a lasting impression on his fertile imagination. Bill loved the shows, and when he had no pass, he frequently paid fifteen or twenty cents to sit in the top gallery. Occasionally he was given tickets to grand opera. He saw Fanny Davenport, Annie Louise Cary, Tommaso Salvini, Etelka Gerster, and many of the other theatrical and operatic greats of the day, some of whom stayed at the Everett House. He delivered a bouquet of flowers to the legendary French actress Sarah Bernhardt on her opening at the Booth Theater, and she rewarded him with a pinch on the cheek.

Bill later claimed that he had only two ambitions in life. One was to attend West Point, probably because of the academy's proximity to Newburgh, although Hart liked to say that the notion stemmed from the forts and soldiers he had seen in the West. But since young Hart had virtually no formal education, West Point was out of the question for him.

His other ambition was to be an actor. "The stage idea just came," Bill said. He thought he might have a chance of becoming an actor since a gift for talk ran in the family. "My father was a wonderful orator," he recalled. "That's the best talent in the world to inherit for the stage. A great orator is necessarily a great actor. In his speech, his gesticulation, his graceful postures in delivery, you have the elements of acting."

Most of the acting Hart saw in his youth was of the declamatory style, in which celebrated performers exhibited themselves onstage in mesmerizing postures and vocalized in a bombastic manner. The broad, melodramatic approach was the vogue in nineteenth-century theater, and Hart would master that technique during his stage career and eventually internalize it in his private life.

The roving spirit seized Nicholas again, and he took off for Hall County, Georgia, where he found a position running a small flour mill. He then moved to Kansas City and worked there for a while. Meanwhile the family had to find cheaper rent and relocated on Diamond Street in New York. When Nicholas returned to the family, the Harts moved again, this time to 152d Street and Third Avenue. Somehow the girls managed to stay in school, but Bill had to keep working.

Since the lad was walking constantly, he developed a lively pace cutting through dark streets at night. He became so adept as a sprinter that he began pitting himself against horse cars. In time young Hart heard that contests were held in Madison Square Garden, and he decided to enter one. The yelling crowd and the glare of the lights distracted him, and he lost his first race. He began to train with some seasoned athletes and soon won a two-mile walk.

For several months Bill worked for the Collender Billiard Table Manufacturing Company, pumping water by hand from the cellar to a tank on the roof. The job was so strenuous that he exhausted himself. Fortunately a Broadway tailor with a liking for professional athletes noticed the youth and gave him a better-paying job as an errand boy.

Bill's reputation as a sprinter grew as he won several medals and cups. The Manhattan Athletic Club accepted him into its ranks, and he became a member of the Cherry Diamond Track Team and went to meets in Philadelphia, Chicago, and Montreal. For a seventeen-year-old boy, the attention was heady and welcome.

Another baby, a boy, was born into the Hart family but lived only a few hours. Nicholas eased his grief by taking off to the West again. For a brief time he ran a mill in Yankton, Dakota, but the financial situation of his family was so bad that he had to come home. Nicholas then found work as a janitor at an apartment house on West Fifty-sixth Street. His salary was sixty dollars a month, and the family was allowed to live in the basement without charge. The better neighborhood would be the Harts' home for three years. The girls continued their schooling, yet they were slighted by their classmates because they lived in a basement.

Bill worked for a period at a nearby riding academy, exercising horses in Central Park. He liked the job and loved the animals, but his determination to become an actor had taken root. He knew that to accomplish his aim the rough edges of his bumptious personality would have to be refined. He lacked culture and needed the education he had never had. Although Roseanna saw nothing but disappointment and futility in Bill's desire to go on the stage, Nicholas was supportive and advised him to take fencing and dancing lessons. Always eager himself for an excuse to travel, Nicholas told Bill that he should go to Europe, where he could observe centuries of art and meet learned people. "America is the flower of the human kingdom, the smile of the Sea," Nicholas told his boy. "But America is new."

Dreaming of a career in the theater, eighteen-year-old Bill Hart decided to heed his father's counsel and make a trip abroad. He had no money, so he worked his way to England on a cattle boat. "I guess I am the only actor who ever set forth on a mission of art acting as chambermaid to a shipload of long-horned Texas steers," Hart said years later. Tall and in excellent physical condition, young Hart planned to do odd jobs and supplement his income by winning footraces. He intended to see as much theater as possible in Europe, take in the museums of London and Paris, and absorb the learning and culture that had not interested him earlier. If he couldn't become a soldier and return to the West he loved, he would be an actor and travel wherever work was available. Europe, he felt, was the best place to acquire the background and polish that a successful actor needed.

Struggling Actor

On his first trip to Europe, Bill Hart walked from Liverpool to London. With his funds exhausted, he roamed the English capital in search of work and finally found a job as a delivery boy in a gun shop. During hours off, he visited art galleries, the Tower of London, and all the quaint, old places he could enter without paying a fee. He went to the theater and saw Henry Irving and Ellen Terry perform five times. "If I could have gotten in for a penny, I would have been there every night," Hart said.

Like his father, Bill was not inclined to stay in one place for long. He decided to save money for passage to Paris and later marveled at his nerve. "Here I was, an awkward, green, gawky, long-legged boy, all hands and feet, and not speaking a word of the French language," he told a Hollywood reporter. "Strange to say, I had no difficulty at all." In the France of the Third Republic he found work delivering goods to the English customers of a Parisian shopkeeper and supplemented his income by washing windows. He was up at daybreak every morning and in exchange for janitorial services, received fencing lessons at a private gymnasium.

Determined to absorb as much culture as possible, Bill went to the theater in Paris almost every night. He saw many of the great French stars of the day and saturated himself with contemporary acting. The actress who stood out in his memory was Agnes Sorel. "She was one of the most beautiful women who ever lived," Hart remembered. "You can imagine the effect she would have upon a lonely, clumsy, homesick [eighteen-year-old] boy. Looking down upon her from the galleries, she was installed in the place where I kept my ideals as an angel of light."

Hart returned to England and sailed for New York on the *Helvetia*. Lack of education still prevented him from securing the caliber of positions he would have liked, and theatrical agencies showed no interest in a gangly lad whose talk was bigger than any promise he showed. For several months he worked as a cashier at Caswell and Hazzard's Drug Store and attended dancing school with his sisters. "I believe it did me much good," Hart later said, although he looked more suited to a boxing ring than behind footlights.

At nineteen Bill passed a civil service examination and became a clerk in the New York general post office. He worked there for more than three years. He stayed in good physical condition and won races at the Manhattan Athletic Club track. With Bill earning better wages, one of the Hart girls working as a dressmaker, and another employed as a telegraph operator, the family's financial situation improved. Nicholas never adjusted to living in a big city and still entertained notions of returning to the West. When his girls complained that a man who sat on a neighboring stoop ogled them as they walked by, the irate father dashed out and walloped the offender.

Nicholas took a job as a maintenance man in a Manhattan office building, and the Harts moved to an apartment on Sixty-second Street, near Ninth Avenue. Bill had begun to feel a surge of late adolescent cockiness and started hanging out at such dubious places as Tom Gould's and the Haymarket. The twenty-year-old postal clerk was making a hundred dollars a month by then and had most of his evenings free. "It was a very narrow trail that I traveled," Bill said later. "It was tortuous and ran along the edge of a cliff that shunted off into a mighty deep chasm." Although young Hart did not drink liquor or smoke, he watched a friend at the post office become so enamored with a "lady of the evening" that the acquaintance started missing work and was eventually dismissed. Bill once spent a considerable sum of money himself taking some chorus girls to a horse show at Madison Square Garden. Nicholas noticed that his son was in danger of becoming a philanderer and sat him down for a talk. "Will,"

Nicholas said, "there is so little time in life; none of it should be frit-
tered away." Nicholas advised his son to save his money, return to
England, and make his bid for a stage career there. "With my father
to decide on a thing was to do it," Bill said, and within four months
he was on his way back to England, this time as a cabin passenger.

After returning to London, Bill found an instructor and paid five
pounds for a course in acting. He saw Mary Anderson and Forbes-
Robertson in *A Winter's Tale* at the Lyceum Theatre and determined
to concentrate on the skills that would help him enter the acting profession. But after a few weeks the youth grew so lonely and homesick that he threw his clothes into a bag, caught a train to Liverpool,
and boarded a steamship for home.

In New York, Hart began studying with F. F. Mackey, a retired
actor and respected teacher. "I am grateful that I fell into his hands,"
Bill later wrote. The strapping lad exercised regularly at Wood's Gymnasium and swam on the ocean side of Staten Island. "There was
nothing there but the station," he said, "no habitation whatever." With
no one to interfere, Bill did deep breathing exercises and spoke Shakespearean lines to the surf. "One day a dead man washed in on the tide
while I was swimming," he recalled. "The man had been shot through
the head. I never knew what became of the case."

After answering endless advertisements, the aspiring actor landed a
job in 1888 with Daniel E. Bandmann's theatrical company, earning
twelve dollars a week. "Everything I know about acting I learned from
the boss of that old barnstorming troupe," Hart later told a reporter.
"He was the finest stage technician I have ever known. He had an
absolute knowledge of the craft." Bandmann, who had played engagements with Henry Irving in London, spent vacations on his ranch in
Montana, and while the troupe waited for their star to join them,
Bandmann's leading lady, Louise Beaudet, supervised rehearsals.

With Grover Cleveland in the White House and the West struggling to recover from drought and the winter of 1887, William S. Hart
made his debut before an audience as Friar Lawrence in *Romeo and
Juliet,* by coincidence at the opera house in Newburgh. On tour
through the East, the company played the Shakespearean love story
at matinees and *Dr. Jekyll and Mr. Hyde* at night. In New York City,

the troupe opened at the People's Theater in the Bowery with Tom Taylor's *Dead or Alive*, which Bandmann renamed *Austerlitz*. Then the company took to the road again, journeying as far west as St. Louis.

Bill Hart at age twenty-five spoke in a voice that was soft and low. From time to time Bandmann called the young actor into his dressing room and, in a thick German accent, complimented him on his studiousness and the ability he demonstrated during performances. But the old actor neglected to raise Hart's salary, so the novice was forced to become adept at stalling hotel keepers for payment of bills and rustling cheap meals.

Bandmann's cast consisted mostly of beginners, and the company traveled with only a few antiquated side wings and a drop for scenery. In April 1889 the troupe played McVicker's Theater in Chicago, where a critic for the *Chicago Times* wrote, "Mr. W. S. Hart acted with dignity and intelligence the part of a young physician." After the Illinois engagement Bandmann returned to his ranch in Montana, leaving the rest of the troupe broke and stranded. Bill found himself in freezing weather, obliged to seek shelter under one of the Illinois Central's depot sheds. He took a job peeling potatoes for two weeks to earn enough money to get himself back to New York. Tough though the life of an itinerant actor was, he thrived on the adventure it offered.

Later in 1889 Bill was engaged by a company headed by actor Lawrence Barrett for a new play, *Ganelon*, that Barrett was producing. The expensive production was set in the Middle Ages, and Ganelon, played by Barrett, was a traitor who is run through by a Saracen chieftain's spear at the end of the fifth act. Such spectacles attracted large audiences in the late nineteenth century, and although few of them were worthy drama, they allowed Bill Hart to learn his craft.

As the Barrett troupe was preparing to leave New York, Hart saw the distinguished tragedian Edwin Booth (brother of presidential assassin John Wilkes Booth) at the ferry, preparing to go on the road as the star of another of Barrett's companies. Although *Ganelon* was a success in the cities where it played, Barrett became sick and in Baltimore received word that he needed to have an operation to remove a large growth from his neck. The tour ended after an engagement in Washington, D.C., although Barrett decided to play repertory the final two weeks there. Such plays as *Richelieu, The Merchant of Venice, Francesca da Rimini, Hamlet,* and *Julius Caesar* were advertised for presentation. "Here was a special cast for a new play, instructed to costume, study, rehearse, and give a performance of at least twelve plays on two weeks' notice," Hart recalled. "The performances were given, and they were highly creditable, too!" In *Hamlet* Bill was assigned numerous supporting roles, but he was relieved when the engagement ended.

Bill came back to New York and found quarters in an attic on Fourth Avenue, sharing sleeping accommodations with three other young actors. His father meanwhile had grown restless and was trying one last time to operate his own flour mill in the West. The husband of Bill's middle sister had gone to the far Northwest and sent his father-in-law a favorable report on the opportunities there. "So once more our family, filled with high hopes, moved westward," Bill said, although the struggling actor stayed behind to search for work. His family remained in the Pacific Northwest only a few months. When they returned to the East, Nicholas took a job in Brooklyn that included free rent, and Bill moved in with his parents and his two unmarried sisters for a short time.

Since Hart found memorizing dialogue difficult, Mary Ellen, his oldest sister, whom he called Mamie, frequently held the script and prompted him as he learned his lines. Sometimes they worked together on plays ten hours a day. Bill could obtain free tickets to most of the shows in New York, and he usually took Mamie with him when he went to the theater. Mary Ellen had completed her college education, was a bright young woman, and gradually became an excellent judge of drama. She often advised Bill in his choice of material, and he grew to be quite dependent on her.

For a time the budding actor played one-night stands with a stock company headed by Margaret Mather. The work was exhausting, and none of it lasted long. In 1890 Hart found a season's employment with Robert Downing's troupe, which included Dustin Farnum, another struggling actor whom Bill came to know well. Downing's repertoire consisted of seven or eight plays, but Hart's best role was Appius Claudius, a lascivious young aristocrat, in *Virginius*. The company opened in that play at the Grand Opera House in Philadelphia in December with mixed results. Bill got so carried away with his libidinous role that his wig became twisted over one ear and his patrician wreath was trampled in a skirmish with Virginius, who was trying to protect his daughter's virtue. As the curtain fell, Bill heard the stage manager yell at him, "What in hell is the matter with you?" Try though he did to achieve a modicum of sophistication, Hart was still the bumpkin he had been when he went to Europe.

Slowly Bill began to understand an actor's need for discipline. He became a serious reader of stage history, and with experience his timing and projection improved. In April 1891 the *Boston Trancript* reported in its review of *Virginius*, "Mr. W. S. Hart was quite effective as Appius Claudius." Although subtlety was never Hart's strength as a performer, vigor and power were. He grew to love his chosen profession, even though he seldom had more than a few dollars to show for his early efforts. As a member of traveling stock companies, he had to pay his own hotel bills and incidental expenses, supply his own costumes, wigs, and footwear, and cover his own railroad fare to wherever rehearsals began. Between jobs he studied and exercised to maintain an athletic appearance.

In the fall of 1891, with his beloved frontier all but gone, Hart was engaged by the Prescott-MacLean company as a leading man, earning forty dollars a week. His roles included Romeo, Antony, Iago, and Phasarius in Montgomery Bird's *Spartacus*, a play American audiences admired at the time because it idealized the fight for freedom. The troupe rehearsed in Lexington, Kentucky, then played small towns in Alabama and Georgia. In early October the company performed at the opera house in Springfield, Missouri, where the local press said, "Mr. Hart's rendition of Romeo was all but ideal."

A month later the players reached San Antonio. When the company performed *Spartacus* there, the press reported: "Mr. Hart is a really fine actor, who reads his lines well and who suits his actions to his words." *Spartacus*, in a less than magnificent production, was performed at the Union Square Theater in New York City in December

1891, whereupon the *New York Recorder* said that Hart "created a more favorable impression" than R. D. MacLean, the company's star. The critic went on to write that Hart, in Phasarius's reconciliation with his brother and subsequent death, "showed a strength of dramatic feeling and truth of impulse that carried the audience by storm." The rest of the cast was judged to be average.

Bill's notices in New York were good enough that he secured a leading man position the following season with a more noted company headed by Hortense Rhea (who billed herself as Madame Rhea in an attempt to gain greater respectability). Hart played Armand Duval, Pygmalion, Napoleon, and other challenging roles with Rhea, whom he regarded as "a delightful woman, never a great actress." Yet Madame Rhea had spent a decade as leading lady at the Court Theater in St. Petersburg, Russia, and had developed social skills that served her well. The actress gave parties almost every night after performances, during which Bill met interesting people and heard sophisticated conversation that he found both a treat and an education. In Washington, D.C., he was introduced to General Wade Hampton, the Southern cavalry officer, and enjoyed Hampton's company throughout the engagement there. "I used to walk home with him at night," Hart wrote in his memoirs. "He was an old man with a cork leg."

With difficulty Bill was acquiring a bit of finesse, and women particularly responded favorably to his gentle manner. Quibblers maintained that he spoke too fast in performances and tended to run his lines together. But most reviewers agreed that Bill had talent, cut a dapper figure with his rakish profile and solid physique, and was an intensely serious young man who had the drive necessary to advance his career.

Hart stayed with Madame Rhea through the spring of 1895, playing with her in *The Queen of Sheba*, *La Gioconda*, *Much Ado About Nothing*, *The Lady of Lyons*, and other contemporary favorites. The company played cities around the Great Lakes, went west to the northern plains, and crossed over into Canada for stops in Montreal, Halifax, and St. John. In April 1895, near Manistee, Michigan, the train on which Rhea's company was traveling derailed, and the locomotive turned over, trapping its engineer and fireman in the wreckage. Bill heard their call for help, dashed into the scalding steam that enveloped the two men, and bent steel to free them. The engineer's arm was broken, but he recovered. The fireman died with Bill's overcoat wrapped around him, as a special car backtracked to carry the injured men to Manistee.

During Bill's engagement with Rhea, his father's health began to fail, and Bill persuaded him to go to England for a visit to his boyhood home. They agreed that Bill would go to Paris during his summer break from acting, visit the art galleries there, see as much French theater as possible, and meet Nicholas in Liverpool. The tone of his father's letters from England became so alarming, however, that Bill cut his stay in Paris short. In Liverpool he took Nicholas to a doctor, who examined the ailing man, discovered an enlargement of the spleen, and advised him to go home to his family. Nicholas Hart died in New York on June 20, 1895.

Bill, thirty years old at the time of his father's death, felt keenly the responsibility of taking care of his mother and unmarried sisters, but his means remained limited. Fortunately he had been hired the previous spring as leading man on what would prove Helena Modjeska's farewell tour. By then the Polish-born actress was a legend, and acting opposite the great Modjeska represented an enormous leap forward in Hart's career. He was slated to play Macbeth, Angelo in *Measure for Measure*, the Duke of Malmsbury in a new play by Clyde Fitch, and other roles that would have shown his talent to good advantage.

Modjeska opened her last season at the Garrick Theater in New York, played there for three weeks, then moved to the Montauk Theater in Brooklyn for a week's engagement before going on tour. In Cincinnati the actress suffered a partial paralysis, which affected her side and arm, and the tour had to stop, leaving Hart desolate. His father had been dead only a few weeks, and Madame Modjeska's stricken condition added to his grief and left him with no income.

Toward the end of his life, Nicholas had apologized to his son for being such a financial failure and for leaving his family almost penniless. Bill loved his father, acquired many of his basic values and his love for the West from him, and sympathized with the disappointments he had faced in his life. As a token of his remorse, the sentimental Bill hired an undertaker's wagon, rode with it to West Farms, disinterred his little brother's body, and took Nicholas, Jr.'s remains to Greenwood Cemetery in Brooklyn, where he placed them beside his father's grave.

With the family's financial situation desperate, Bill joined Robert Mantell's acting company for a week in Newark, New Jersey, where he played Iago, but business was so bad that he ended up with no salary. He fared better performing Shakespearean roles opposite an unnamed actress who had recently separated from her wealthy husband. "The lady was not a soiled dove by any means," Bill said. "She was just a party fiend that never seemed to sleep." Wild living and drink caused the woman to die young, but Hart earned a hundred dollars a week while working with her.

Despondent and apprehensive that he might become the failure in life that his father had been, Bill appeared lost, uncertain about what direction to take. He shot pool, bowled, and roamed the streets of New York with his friend William Farnum until the wee hours of the morning. Bill later said that he and Farnum reveled in crazy pranks that should have landed them to jail. "It was anything, anywhere, except go home," he said.

Between engagements Bill coached a young girl who wanted to become an actress, but he went for weeks with no income at all. He played the hero in *The Great Northwest*, a melodrama that rehearsed for four weeks but played only three at the American Theater in New York. The production's budget was so tight that he again received no money.

He next went into William A. Brady's production of *Under the Polar Star*, which was staged by the great producer-director-playwright David Belasco, the lion of Broadway at the turn of the century. The play had an able cast and eight huskies, which Admiral Robert Peary had brought back from the Arctic, to pull a sled onstage. "Hart's acting as the hero is one of the bright spots in the cast," the *Brooklyn Times* reported on January 5, 1897, "but his fitness almost clouds the efforts of Grace Henderson as the heroine and Cuyler Hastings as the villain."

Family responsibilities demanded that Bill earn more money, and he decided that the time had come for him to go on the road as a star. Hired by John Whitely, who had managed both the Prescott-MacLean company and Madame Rhea's troupe, Bill scraped together $250, and Whitely booked a tour for the 1897–98 season. Bill concluded that *The Man in the Iron Mask*, with its dual roles, was an ideal vehicle for him, even though he thought the story was a bit gloomy for popular audiences. He revised the third act of the drama and made a big enough hit of the play that he opened with it in most towns. The tour began in Traverse City, Michigan, then went through the middle western states and down into the Southwest. Hart's repertoire included *Camille* and *The Lady of Lyons*, and while audiences seemed to like what they saw, he made no more than a bare living.

Oklahoma was still Indian Territory when the troupe played the Turner Opera House in Muskogee. Streets in the town were dirt, with board sidewalks on either side of the main thoroughfare. During the engagement in Muskogee, Hart saw the bodies of two men hauled into town and was told that a new marshal was on his way to Oklahoma with orders to round up the notorious Jennings gang. Hart asked around and found that Al Jennings and his brother, Frank, were local gunmen and train robbers. Al was a small man, barely five feet tall, with sandy hair, steel blue eyes, and a craving for adventure that was matched by his keen sense of humor. Eventually Jennings would be sent to the Ohio State Penitentiary.

One morning during his stay in Muskogee, Hart rented a horse and went for a ride through the outlying country. Around eleven o'clock he came upon four rough-looking men camped in some cottonwoods along a creek bank. He asked them directions to the nearest trail back into town. The foursome eyed Hart suspiciously at first but gradually relaxed and asked him to share their grub. Hart in turn invited the men to see his play that night as his guest. "I was very young at the time," the actor told a Hollywood reporter years later, and "very proud of my status as a kid actor, so I talked quite a lot about myself." As the immodest thespian was leaving, the leader of the group confessed that he was the infamous Al Jennings and that the fellows with him were members of his gang. Hart later claimed, "We shook hands and parted on the best of terms."

When Hart came onstage that night at the Turner Opera House, he recognized Jennings and his gang sitting in the front row. A few feet away, in a box decorated with flags and bunting, sat the new marshal who had sworn to arrest the outlaws, totally unaware that the men he sought were in the theater. "I still feel a certain satisfaction that Al got away with it," Hart wrote later. In Hollywood, Jennings and Hart would run into one another again when they were both making movies.

Continuing his first starring tour in Kansas, Bill arrived in Coffeyville, where five years earlier the famed Dalton gang had been shot attempting to rob two banks simultaneously. He acquired a dog there, and they had great times running across the prairie after jackrabbits, which brought back memories of the childhood he increasingly cherished. In Peoria, Illinois, the manager of the hotel where the company stayed would not permit the hound in the rooms, so he was tied in a checkroom downstairs. When he chewed the end off a leather trunk, the hound was shipped back to Kansas, much to Bill's regret.

With the tour making so little money, Whitely abandoned the company in Illinois and advised Hart to do the same. But Bill and the other players decided to continue the tour and fulfill a booking in Youngstown, Ohio. By the time they reached Youngstown, Bill had secured a contract for a week's engagement at the People's Theater on the Bowery in New York, where he had performed earlier in *Under the Polar Star*. The troupe opened the Bowery engagement with *The Man in the Iron Mask*, which attracted major critics and received good notices. Frank Dietz, a prominent theatrical manager, promptly offered to finance Bill on a short spring tour.

Hart closed his first starring season of eight months showing a profit of only $2.60. After returning to New York, he and six other men shared one room in a boardinghouse on Fifteenth Street. Bill's mother and unmarried sisters by then had moved to the outskirts of Asheville, North Carolina, where they lived virtually destitute in two rooms of an old brick house. Bill visited them and found his family in need of proper food and clothing. "I then and there resolved I would

never again try to become a star at such an expense," Hart wrote in
My Life East and West.

He made the rounds of the agents and producers in New York
but found no work until the leading man playing opposite Julia Arthur,
an established actress, committed suicide as Arthur's company was
about to go on tour. Hart was hired to take the actor's place. The
troupe had been in rehearsal for several weeks with a repertoire that
included *As You Like It, Pygmalion and Galatea, Romeo and Juliet,*
and *Ingomar,* so stepping into the dead man's roles was an ordeal for
Hart. The company left for Detroit on a Friday night, had a dress
rehearsal on Sunday evening, and opened in *A Lady of Quality* on
Monday. "How I got through [the performance] I don't know," Hart
said, "but I did." His salary was again one hundred dollars a week,
although he did not have to supply his own wardrobe, which was the
most magnificent the fledgling actor had worn. In *Romeo and Juliet*
alone he had five changes, all heavy silks and fine brocades. For the
first time in his career, Hart had a dresser to help with his costumes.

After playing several weeks on the road, Arthur's troupe went into
New York for a lengthy engagement at Wallack's Theater. Critics
were kind; Hart's Romeo was deemed romantic, youthful, and filled
with fiery impetuosity. Playing the Veronese lover was "such a far cry
from the Western prairies," Bill said, "that somehow I wished my
father could have been there."

On completing his stint with Julia Arthur, roles proved so scarce
that Hart took a temporary job as a yard detective for a railroad. But
soon he got his biggest break yet. In the spring of 1899 he was
engaged by Klaw and Erlanger to play Messala in the original staging
of *Ben Hur.* Based on Lew Wallace's best-selling novel and dramatized
by William Young, the Roman epic called for an elaborate production,
a chariot race, a sea rescue, and an enormous cast. The deterioration
of the friendship between Messala and Ben Hur, Roman and Christian
respectively, is the spine of the drama, and in many respects Messala
is the more complex and interesting of the two roles. Klaw and
Erlanger's company rehearsed under Ben Teal's direction for six weeks
with the author present, but pulling the unwieldy piece together had its
trying moments. Broadway producer Charles Frohman watched one

of the final rehearsals and left the theater saying, "I'm afraid you're up against it. The American public will never stand for Christ and a horse race in the same show."

In the third act of *Ben Hur*, Hart was to drive a team of horses onto the stage among a cluster of dancing girls. On opening night the owner of the horses shaved off his mustache and doubled for the actor, fearing that the team might not behave well and become too much for Hart to handle. The climactic chariot race was created with two horses, a white and a black, side by side on double treadmills, supplemented with a mass of wheels, steel cables, levers, the sound of cracking whips, and a panorama of the Circus Maximus racing past as the two finalists struggled for victory. Ben Hur's and Messala's horses alternated in front of one another until they reached stage center, whereupon Ben Hur's chariot slowly pulled ahead and Messala's collapsed. The sea rescue was achieved by stagehands in the wings shaking pieces of cloth to simulate waves. Audiences left the theater dazzled by the spectacle they had seen.

Ben Hur opened on Broadway on November 29, 1899, and proved a tremendous hit, ensuring the company of a run that lasted until the following May. Reviewers were less enthusiastic about the show than the general public was, and the distinguished critic and theater historian William Winter trashed the cast. "More bad elocution has never, surely, been heard in one performance," Winter wrote in his notice. Still, after the first performance Lew Wallace told Hart, "I want to thank you for giving me the Messala that I drew in my book."

Sculptor Eden Musee made a wax figure of Hart as the Roman aristocrat, and the actor posed for the artist several times. If nothing else, Hart made a muscular Messala and was hired to play the part for a second season, supported by an almost completely new cast. In Boston, Hart's friend William Farnum took the role of Ben Hur, and on at least one occasion Hart played the title role himself. When a friend from Asheville came to see the drama, Hart asked him what he thought of his interpretation of Messala. "Fine! Fine!" the slightly inebriated man replied. "The horses were great!"

Hart's second season with *Ben Hur* ended at the Columbia Theater in Brooklyn, and he went to Asheville to spend the summer with his family. They attended church services at Biltmore, George Vanderbilt's nearby palatial estate, and Bill coached an amateur theater group at the Asheville Opera House to help pay the family's outstanding bills. During his stay, he became almost a father to his baby sister, Lotta. Mary Ellen had assumed the major responsibility of caring for their aging mother and continued to be a companion and comfort to Bill. Hart recalled this brief respite as one of the happiest times in his life. As fall approached, he hated to leave his family, but he had to prepare for another tour. "It seemed so hard again to break the chain," Hart wrote. "Dear little Lotta smiled through her tears until she could not stand it any longer."

The next season Hart was playing John Storm, a minister, in *The Christian* during a matinee in Providence, Rhode Island, when a telegram arrived informing him that Lotta was dying of typhoid fever. He caught a train back to Asheville and arrived to find his youngest sister in delirium, with a temperature of 105 degrees. She died three days later with Bill at her bedside. "My world could never be again the same," Hart wrote, "a part of my life passed from me." The family left Asheville together. Bill placed his mother and Mary Ellen in a boardinghouse in Brooklyn, stayed with them long enough to oversee the burying of his little sister beside their father and brother, and rejoined the company performing *The Christian*.

In February 1902 the troupe was playing a one-night stand at the Grand Opera House in Great Falls, Montana. On the afternoon before the performance, Hart and several other members of the company were invited to meet cowboy artist Charles M. Russell at the Park Hotel in Great Falls. Still in bereavement over Lotta's death, Hart seemed withdrawn and had little to say. Russell later commented on the "feller who doesn't talk none" during the daytime but rendered such eloquent discourse during the evening's performance. Hart saw some of Charlie's paintings in a saloon when the troupe played Helena, and the vitality of the art impressed the actor deeply. "When I look at these mountains and plains out here and then at your pictures which speak as no language can of a whole race that is forever gone," Hart wrote in a letter to Russell, "I feel a great deal."

After he left Montana, Bill sent Charlie two photographs of himself and the hope that their paths would cross again some day. Russell took four months to respond, explaining when he did that writing was no pleasure for him and that he tended to go blank when he took pen in hand. Russell said how much he had enjoyed Bill's play and added, "if you ever drift West again, which I hope you will, and sight the smoke of my camp, come and, as our red brothers say, 'My pipe will be lit for you.'"

The actor knew of the untutored artist's early life as a cowhand and the months he had lived among the Indians. "You have had the greatest college on earth to grow up in—Nature," Hart wrote Russell on his return to New York. "You were cradled in that great west at a time when the air and water and the ground were free gifts to man and no one had the power to portion them out by measure or weight." Bill loved Charlie's paintings and considered him a genius, capable of making the frontier live again on canvas. Both men lamented the passing of the West they had known in their youth, and while Bill Hart was not the homespun personality that Charlie Russell was, their nostalgia for the dying frontier served as an immediate bond. "The range with a boundless view of the naked plains would be the place of all places on earth for me," Bill wrote Charlie, "and if ever in later years it is my fortune to strike a lucky streak and make my little pile, it will be in that west I love so well that I will pitch my tent and end my days."

Russell's wife, Nancy, was far more concerned than Russell about establishing the painter's reputation in the international art world, and she was determined that her husband must travel east and introduce himself to the critics there. For two years Hart urged the couple to come to New York. In 1904 Hart received a card from Russell with a Manhattan postmark saying, "How! I'm in the big camp," and bearing the artist's familiar buffalo skull as the only signature. Hart went to see the timid painter and his resolute wife and accompanied them to the office of the Sunday editor of the *New York Herald*, where they hoped to generate some publicity. Later Hart secured passes on the Long Island Railroad and took the Russells out to a secluded beach so that Charlie could see the ocean for the first time.

"When the great body of water was lashed and tossed by the elements," Bill wrote Nancy years later, "I will never forget the picture [Charlie] made, his body bulging with muscular strength, his leonine head uncovered, his tawny blond hair whipping in the wind, his outstretched hands saluting the waves with the tenderness of a child. He seemed the reincarnation of some giant Norsemen of the early ages."

Bill was living with his mother and sister in a flat on West Thirty-fourth Street during the Russells' initial visit to New York. Whenever Charlie sold a painting during their stay, he and Nancy would stop by the Hart residence to celebrate. Roseanna would cook boiled beef, which she served with horseradish, while Charlie and Bill rejoiced by downing a few fingers of whiskey. The first picture Russell sold brought $300, and he insisted that Nancy buy herself a fur coat with the money.

Russell delighted in male companionship, and Hart was pleased to be available as Russell established contacts with gallery owners and visited artists' studios. Neither of the men were making much money at the time, but they enjoyed swapping yarns and reviving memories of bygone days in the unsettled West. The Russells' hotel was in a rather rough section on Forty-second Street, teeming with hustlers, hoodlums, and other unsavory types. Hart remarked after a visit there that it seemed "like more shots were being fired than had been in the Spanish-American War." Charlie smiled and answered, "Seems like old times."

Hart considered Russell "one of the greatest men that ever pulled on a pair of cowhide boots." They shared a common vision of the vanishing West and felt the need to preserve its image. To both men the westward movement was the nation's creation experience and a constructive guide in determining lasting values. Their depictions of the West had similarities—an everyday reality seen through romantic eyes and lifted to an exalted level. But whereas Russell's work mixed humor and fun with action and devotion, Hart's was often dour, implacably righteous, and melodramatic. Each had a sentimental streak, but Hart added amorous sweetening whereas Russell diluted his sentiment with merriment, audacity, and bliss. Hart's postured heroics were those of the stage, as opposed to Russell's kinetic, almost cinematic approach.

Despite Hart's success in *Ben Hur*, his income from acting remained paltry. The tour with *The Christian* ended in Vancouver during the latter part of March 1902. Hart made the long trip back to New York City by train, sitting in a smoking car with nothing to eat but crackers and cheese. Fortunately he went almost immediately into another play, *The Suburban*, a racing drama that opened at McVicker's Theater in Chicago early in May. He toured with that show for an entire season and closed in it at the Academy of Music in New York. In July 1903 Hart began rehearsals opposite Orrin Johnson in *Hearts Courageous*, a decorative production that found Hart cast as Patrick Henry. He loved playing the part of the American Revolutionary War patriot, which he did with a touch of an Irish brogue. Later, when he was making silent pictures, he wanted to reprise the character. *Hearts Courageous* toured for seven or eight weeks, with engagements in Philadelphia and Chicago, but did so little business that the play closed prematurely.

Hart admired Orrin Johnson, an excellent actor and a generous colleague, who eventually starred in movies. While traveling with *Hearts Courageous*, Hart developed friendships with Frank Stammers, who became a musical comedy director, and Thomas Ince, who a decade later would be responsible for launching Hart's career in Hollywood. The trio spent so much time together that Johnson referred to them as "The Three Musketeers." Ince, who already showed a keen interest in theater management, seemed eager to hear Hart's stories about the West and the Indians he had known as a youth.

When *Hearts Courageous* closed after bookings in New England, Ince, Stammers, and Hart returned to Manhattan and lived together for a time in a small suite in the Barrington Hotel at Broadway and Forty-fourth Street. Ince and Stammers occupied the larger of the two rooms and shared a double bed; Hart slept on a cot in the adjoining room. Although the living accommodations for the threesome cost only $9.50 a week, they were still hard pressed for money.

At a bakery on Eighth Avenue, they bought tin pans of baked beans for a dime and three loaves of stale bread for a nickel and stretched the meal over two or three days. Stammers entertained his suitemates by playing the cello, and Hart related endless tales of experiences he claimed to have had on the prairie. He talked about the deer, the elk, and the bears he had seen, the hills and the woods, the thunder and lightning of summer storms, and the vast snowflakes and biting blasts during winter gales. "I would tell them of a country where there were no spies or newsmongers," he recalled, "only kind-hearted, friendly things."

The idyllic images of Bill's childhood took on added tinges as week after week went by with no job offers. For eight months Bill worked only twenty-two days as an actor. Through his brother-in-law he secured a position with a detective agency, which paid ninety dollars a month. The company assigned Bill an office to himself, and most of his duty was at night. During the day, he looked for acting jobs. He worked a week in a one-act adaptation of *Pagliacci*, which starred Frank Keenan, and took time off from the detective agency to open in *Love's Pilgrimage*, an unmitigated flop. Critic Alan Dale in essence wrote that *Love's Pilgrimage* was the quickest means yet concocted for emptying a theater in the event of fire.

Extra jobs allowed Bill to help make his mother and oldest sister's life a little more comfortable, yet he walked the streets bordering Broadway for months tired and despondent, with little to show for his efforts. He wondered if perhaps he should give up acting, as his father should have given up the dream of becoming an independent mill owner. Bill had been an actor for sixteen years, enjoyed enough success to boost his ego and encourage him to continue, but aside from Messala in *Ben Hur* there were few victories and nothing that earned him a sustained living. Like his father, Bill was a romantic, who embroidered his experiences and relationships beyond what they were. While he often gushed about his "darling little sister" and "dear mother," he showed no lasting desire to relate to his family—or anyone—on prolonged, intimate terms. Hart was a monolith—self-contained, highly emotional, and immersed in a world of private

William S. Hart

fantasies. As a struggling actor he had internalized the words and erudition of Shakespeare and the voice and demeanor of melodrama, incorporating the language and some of the excesses into his public persona. At heart he would remain an unhappy, immature man looking for a way to relive his idealized boyhood.

Projecting a Western Image

William S. Hart got his first chance to create a western character in 1905 playing Cash Hawkins, a ranch foreman, in *The Squaw Man*. Hart was working as a detective when he learned that George Tyler was producing the frontier drama. He went to see Tyler, who told him that the show had already been cast. Then, almost as an after-thought, the theater manager said, "There is a bit in the second act you might play. I'll pay you your salary for the three weeks' tryout." Tyler explained that the character was a cowboy and "a mean skunk," who appeared only in the second act. Bill liked the idea of imper-sonating a bad man who is shot by an Indian woman, and he eagerly accepted the supporting role.

Rehearsals began on *The Squaw Man* in Buffalo, New York, in April. Hart grew discouraged with the show when he discovered that Edwin Milton Royle, the playwright, knew practically nothing about the West. Most of the cast was English and spoke with heavy British accents, and the costumes and props were shoddy and inap-propriate. "The chaps they had furnished for us all to wear were made out of old rugs and doormats that had been lying around the storehouse," Hart said. He was eventually put in charge of ordering proper chaps, quirts, and spurs for the production, which he did by wiring an outfit in Pueblo, Colorado. Hart remembered one English actor saying to him, "I say, old chap, you seem to be a bit of an authority on these uniforms." Ever ready to parade his understand-ing of the West, Hart assured his colleague that his knowledge came from firsthand experience.

After the rehearsal period *The Squaw Man* played for three weeks on the road, during which the production suffered more than its share of mishaps. In London, Ontario, the gun that was supposed to fire offstage to kill Hart's character failed to go off. In a panic the show's star, William Faversham, whispered to Hart, "What will we do?" Hart suggested that they fight, which they did, rolling all over the stage. Finally Hart said to the hero, "Stab me!" Faversham did what he was told, even though he had no knife.

During a summer interlude before *The Squaw Man* opened in Manhattan, Hart again worked for the detective agency. He claimed that he was nearly manhandled when he stumbled onto a group of robbers the agency had been trying to snare for two years. But Hart's view of life seems to have become increasingly melodramatic, and by the time he wrote his autobiography, his mind was filled with distortion.

It was during the run of *The Squaw Man* that Hart's early association with the West was first publicized in newspaper articles. Before the show opened in New York, the *New York Morning Telegraph* announced that William S. Hart would play a cowpuncher in an upcoming production. "Considering that for a number of years he roamed the plains in that capacity," the report continued, "a few rehearsals should suffice for him." Until 1905 the press did not seem to be aware of the actor's western background. In interviews he had simply stated that he had been reared in New York and was trained as an actor. Playing Cash Hawkins gave him the opportunity he needed to create a more appealing image and energize fantasies he had savored since adolescence.

The Squaw Man opened at Wallack's Theater in Manhattan on October 23, 1905. Hart maintained that the drama was "the first presentation of a real American cowboy that Broadway had ever seen." Three years earlier Owen Wister's best-selling novel *The Virginian* had made an impact on the literary scene by glorifying the cowboy and defining the code of the West for intelligent readers, and the American public, enchanted at the moment with Theodore Roosevelt, then president and a self-styled outdoorsman, was ready for enactments of life on the recent frontier. Audiences greeted *The*

Squaw Man with enthusiasm, and critics singled Hart out for kudos. "W. S. Hart plays the part of Cash Hawkins with power and conviction," *The Stage* reported on November 4, 1905. Bill quickly grasped that he had found the vehicle he needed to propel him to fame.

On *The Squaw Man*'s opening night in New York, Buffalo Bill Cody, by then the dominant symbol of the untamed West in the popular mind, sat in a box at Wallack's Theater. When the curtain fell, Cody asked permission to meet the show's actors. He particularly wanted to talk with the fellow who had played Cash Hawkins. "Who'd you ride for?" Cody asked Hart as they shook hands. Hart answered that he hadn't ridden for anyone. "But I knew the West," the actor said. "I've ridden all over it with my father, Nick Hart." Cody supposedly beamed and exclaimed, "My God, are you little Willie?"

Whether or not Buffalo Bill had actually met Nicholas Hart and his young son on the frontier is questionable. But Cody's stamp of approval added authenticity for future fans to Bill Hart's title as a true man of the West. Through dime novels and his perennial Wild West shows, Buffalo Bill had become a signature for westward expansion, as well as an emblem of national strength and high moral character, qualities that William S. Hart tried to absorb into his own public image.

Hart's passion for the West probably helped him to make the role of Cash Hawkins a vivid characterization, but his romantic concept of the frontier wedded comfortably with contemporary melodrama. The West that Hart saw as a boy was primarily the agricultural frontier and had little to do with ranches, cowboys, or cattle drives. Still, *The Squaw Man* and Hart's portrayal in the show were successful enough that the play ran in New York and on the road until May 1907. The production made money, and Hart's villainous character led to a string of western roles that would lift the struggling actor toward a bigger career. "Many persons who were interested in my work marveled at the realism of the interpretations," Hart wrote in the foreword to *Pinto Ben*. "Their enthusiasm persuaded me that the entire American public loved the West and its traditions when presented with truthfulness."

In May 1906, while playing an engagement at the opera house in Troy, New York, William Faversham was taken ill, and Hart appeared in *The Squaw Man*'s title role. Yet Bill preferred the color and multiple shadings of the more villainous part, for Cash Hawkins, like Messala, was a character an actor could "sink his spurs" into. "Of all the Western plays I have ever known to be produced on the stage," Hart said, "*The Squaw Man* is my first and only love. It stands supreme in my estimation."

Pioneer moviemaker Cecil B. DeMille would film *The Squaw Man* three times, twice as a silent picture (1913 and 1918) and once with sound (1931). While the story contained action and sentimentality, it also portrayed freedom and redemption in a frontier setting without the excesses of the more sensationalized pulp thrillers. On the stage Hart contributed to making an essentially melodramatic plot convincing, and the play brought him attention from unexpected sources. W. B. "Bat" Masterson, the famous western lawman who was living a sedate life in New York City as a sportswriter at the time, wrote Hart thanking him for a photograph the actor had sent him. "Your portrayal of Cash Hawkins, the cowboy desperado, is exceptionally good," Masterson said, "giving as you do to the part the proper atmosphere in every detail."

Bill had learned the value of self-promotion. He recognized that to advance his career he must become more of a social climber. "Managers have very large ears and are very prone to listen to society," he said. "It means swell first-night audiences." Though he was ambitious, Bill was seldom comfortable in social gatherings, largely because of his lack of education. "Every time I was boosted up a rung on the social ladder," he said, "I slipped back two."

Working with Hart in the company of *The Squaw Man* was Giulia Strakosch, daughter of the distinguished grand opera impresario. Giulia was well placed socially and was a close friend of actress Ethel Barrymore. Through Giulia, Bill was invited to a number of parties where he met important people, and Giulia had her brother accompany the unworldly actor to buy two suits that would be appropriate for him to wear on formal occasions. Still, Hart did not fare well when he was invited to a soiree in a mansion on Seventeenth Street, where many of New York's rich and famous were gathered. "I wound up in the butler's pantry mixing punch and opening champagne for the servants," he said, "my only consolation being that working diligently beside me was Jack Barrymore," Ethel Barrymore's matinee-idol brother.

Hart showed up for another gala event in what he thought was proper attire only to be told by his host that the affair was a costume ball and he had been expected to come wearing his cowboy outfit. The host dispatched a manservant to Wallack's Theater to pick up the costume Hart wore as Cash Hawkins, and the actor changed clothes before joining the party. After several drinks Hart responded to requests for a demonstration of his marksmanship by firing a pistol into the ballroom's hand-painted ceiling. His hostess for the evening later wrote him that he had been the life of the party. The gracious lady even said that she didn't mind the damage he had wrought to her ceiling, although she pointed out that it was going to be difficult to find the Dutch artist who had painted the ceiling to make the necessary repairs.

For the first time in his life Hart had a few hundred dollars in the bank. In the summer of 1906 he rented quarters for his mother, Mary Ellen, and himself at the beach on Long Island, but the day before they were to leave for their vacation, Roseanna slipped and fell, breaking her hip and thigh. Hospital bills depleted Bill's savings, so that when time came for him to tour with *The Squaw Man* in the fall, he had to pawn his watch to buy a train ticket to join the cast where rehearsals were to begin. Meanwhile Mary Ellen and Roseanna settled into a comfortable boardinghouse on Classon Avenue in Brooklyn.

The Squaw Man continued to win accolades from critics on the road and do a profitable business. When Bill returned to New York with $900 in cash, he decided that the time had come to buy a home for himself and his mother and sister. He paid $800 down on an $1,800 house in Westport, Connecticut, overhauled the place, and the family moved in. "For the first time in my life I could sit under a tree on my own property," Bill said.

Hart's prospects for the immediate future looked good: he was engaged to take over the title role in a dramatization of Owen Wister's

immensely popular *The Virginian* the following season, at a salary of
$125 a week. The role had originally been played by Dustin Farnum,
but *The Virginian* did much to solidify Hart's reputation as a Western
star. He opened in the show at the Broadway Theater in New York
on September 9, 1907. The *New York Morning Telegraph* maintained
that Hart demonstrated "what few actors can boast of, the gift of
characterization."

Despite its success, Bill felt that there were many things in *The Virginian* that did not ring true. "It is a beautiful story and a beautiful
play," he said, "a monument to the fact that a truly great writer can
make the moon look like green cheese and get away with it." Although
he loved the part, Bill thought the character of the Virginian lacked
authenticity. A real westerner, he maintained, would have refused to
hunt down his friend Steve, who was accused of rustling cattle. If the
Virginian had led a posse to Steve, he would have come to his friend's
defense once they had found him and, according to Bill, would have
said, "Well, gentlemen, I have done my duty and brought you here,
but if you hang him, you've got to hang me, too!" Bill insisted that
friendship was more important in the West than the illicit branding of
cattle. Real ranchers would not have expected the Virginian to lead
them to Steve and would have respected the cowboy's refusal to
participate in hanging his friend once he was caught. "There is an old
adage in the cattle country," Bill said. "'Never set a cow-puncher to
catch a cow-puncher.'"

Hart's reading of the code of the West is arguable, and he grew
more unqualified in his pronouncements on western ways as his connection with the frontier became more public. "The truth of the West
meant more to me than a job and always will," Hart said. He lost
Owen Wister's friendship when he brazenly pointed out to the
Philadelphia writer the flaws in his classic novel. Hart admitted that
Wister's work, which had been reprinted fifteen times within a year
of its initial publication, was "human, simple, and delightful," but he
stated categorically that there was much about the West that Wister
did not know.

Authentic portrait or not, *The Virginian* made money wherever it
played, and Hart was engaged for a second season in the title role,

with his salary increased to $150 a week. He tried to make the part as realistic as possible by wearing no makeup and correct garb. "I felt that I could drag on a suit of old clothes and roll around in the dirt just before going on the stage," he said, "and I would have the best makeup possible."

While Hart was playing in *The Virginian* at McVicker's Theater in Chicago, the Miller Brothers' 101 Ranch Show was performing at the Coliseum there. Seeing a chance for a story, the local press began badgering Hart to prove his worth as a cowboy by riding one of the 101 Ranch's horses in their "Real Wild West Show." Since Hart had not been on a horse in years, he declined and tried to make a joke of the offer, but the press would not be put off so easily. "Something had to be done," Hart said. "I knew if I tried to bluff it through, I'd draw the meanest twister in the show."

Bill told the newspapermen to meet him in his dressing room at the theater, where he made himself up as an Indian in their presence. He then went to the Coliseum, greeted the Sioux Indians who worked in the 101 Ranch Show, talked to them in their language, and paraded with the Indians before the show began. It was a cold, windy day, and although he was chilled to the bone, Bill rode bareback and did stunts in the arena that afternoon. The *Chicago Journal* had announced a prize of fifty dollars to the first person who could identify the white man who was riding among the show's sixty Indians. A young boy in the crowd detected that Hart's eyes were blue and won the fifty-dollar prize.

When *The Virginian* played the Coulter Opera House in Aurora, Hart took the show's attractive leading lady out to see the mill where his father had once worked, and John Scheets, who had known Hart as a boy, showed them around. "William Hart was a fine young man, a scholar, and a gentleman," Scheets recalled. "He was a wonderful and interesting talker, with a beautiful voice. Somehow I have always thought of him as a model of what I would like to have been—not an actor, but a man of his presence, culture, and mastery of the English language."

In February 1909 the company performed Wister's frontier drama in Great Falls, Montana, and Charlie and Nancy Russell were at the station to meet Bill's train. The Russells invited Hart and his leading lady to their home for dinner, and afterward Charlie presented the actor with a painting of Hart in western attire riding a horse through sagebrush. "It is one of my most prized possessions," said Hart. He later used the portrait as the frontispiece in his autobiography.

While Bill was on tour with *The Virginian,* his mother and Mary Ellen enjoyed the security of living in their own home at last. Roseanna spent hours sitting on the porch in Connecticut, looking down a hillside, and on the rare occasions when Bill was there, he traipsed over the countryside with his bulldog, Mack. During the winter of 1909, Roseanna became seriously ill and had to be taken to Stamford for an operation. Mary Ellen made daily trips by trolley to visit her mother, then nursed her through a long convalescence at home. Bill returned to Westport the next summer to find his sister exhausted.

After four years of success in *The Squaw Man* and *The Virginian,* Hart had begun to accept his own professional ability. Yet he returned to New York in the fall of 1909 to find there was no work. He made the rounds of the theatrical agencies, but no one offered him a job. "Nothing had changed," Hart said. "I had merely been asleep for four years." His pride was hurt, and he considered switching to another occupation. "I would have signed a twenty-five-dollar a week contract," he said, "to saw wood, teach acting, hoe potatoes, or any steady, honest employment."

Despondent and ready to quit his profession, Bill received a call from Klaw and Erlanger's office inviting him to take over another western part. The producers had ignored Hart when they were first casting the role of gambler–bad man Dan Stark in Rex Beach's melodrama *The Barrier,* and when the actor they had selected was let go, the managers slighted Bill again by giving the part to another performer who knew nothing about the West. After rehearsals had started the second actor cast as Dan Stark refused to continue in the part, leaving the management in a quandary. In desperation Klaw and Erlanger turned to Bill, who performed the role for an entire season.

The company played a week of one-night stands on its way to Chicago, where *The Barrier* opened at McVicker's Theater in October 1909 to enthusiastic reviews. The *Chicago Daily News* reported:

"Mr. Hart, smooth as ivory, clear cut, dominant, instantly brings sensational elements into the scenes when in the familiar but welcome black and white of the cool Western gambler, he glides into the plot."

During the engagement at McVicker's, Bill received a telegram from Mary Ellen informing him that their mother had suffered an attack and was not expected to live. Mary Ellen urged her brother to come home immediately. The season had just opened, however, and Klaw and Erlanger had not had time to hire understudies. If Bill left the cast, *The Barrier* would have to close, and the chances of its reopening would be slim. Hart decided not to go to Connecticut, yet he was haunted for the rest of his life that he was not at his mother's side when she died. He felt forever guilty that he had left Mamie with the burden of making the funeral arrangements. "At the hour when my mother was being placed in her last home," Hart wrote, "I went to an empty church on the North Side [of Chicago] and said my prayers."

The Barrier played at McVicker's Theater for several weeks. The drama revolved around eight characters, six of which were starring roles. The company was congenial and spent much of its time backstage in harmless kidding. One payday toward the end of the Chicago run, three of the actors in the cast planned to attend a party after the show and asked Bill to take their salary envelopes back to their hotel for safekeeping. Since there had been a number of recent holdups in the city, one of the men took a pistol from his trunk, loaded it, and urged Bill to take the weapon for protection. "I had never packed a gun before," Hart said, but he took the pistol, thinking of the large amount of money that had been placed in his care.

The shortest route back to the hotel where the troupe was staying was over the Rush Street bridge. A short distance from the bridge there was a dark place with several blind alleyways leading off of it. As Hart approached the spot, a large man with a cap pulled over his eyes stepped out of the shadows. Convinced that the fellow meant to rob him, Hart jammed the borrowed gun into the man's ribs, marched him across the bridge, and then ordered him to be on his way. The would-be robber did as he was told, pausing long enough to ask Hart where he had gotten the gun. One suspects that the melodramatic

Hart had begun to internalize the six-gun-toting image he was portraying on the stage.

The Barrier opened at the New Amsterdam Theater in New York on January 10, 1910, again to favorable reviews. Hart was even singled out for a solo curtain call. But the plaudit that meant most to him came from former gunfighter Bat Masterson, who wrote in the *New York Morning Telegraph*: "The part of Dan Stark by William S. Hart seems to have been made to order for that clever impersonator of Western characters. Anyone familiar with the character of the cool, calculating, and daring desperado, whose presence was a part of frontier life a generation ago, will instantly recognize in Mr. Hart a true type of that reckless nomad who flourished on the border when the six-shooter was the final arbiter of all disputes between man and man. Mr. Hart looks the part, dresses the part, and acts as if he were the real Dan Stark and had stepped out of the book upon the stage."

Later Hart met the old lawman and came to revere him as an emblem of the bygone West. "I play the hero that Bat Masterson inspired," Hart later told Hollywood gossip columnist Louella Parsons. "More than any other man I have ever met I admire and respect him." Masterson's legacy as sheriff of Dodge City epitomized the autonomy, the gallantry, and the color that Hart treasured as part of the vanishing frontier. Hart's brief association with Masterson, like his earlier brushes with Al Jennings and Buffalo Bill Cody and his friendship with Charlie Russell, served to validate for him the romantic vision he held of the unsettled West.

Shortly after *The Barrier* closed, Taylor Granville, an actor Bill had once worked with, came to him with a problem. Granville had tried out a vaudeville act, which he called "The Hold-Up," but it had failed. The distressed performer had the scenery he needed and two appropriate railroad effects for the sketch, yet none of the theater managers would book the act. Bill agreed to rewrite the material and gladly assumed the starring role of Lonesome Joe Brandt. By then Bill had devised a way of working the hammer of a gun with his thumb that sounded menacing to audiences. When he and Granville tried out the revised act in Brooklyn, they found they had a hit. In late April 1910, "The Hold-Up" was booked into the American Theater in New York, where it drew top critics and approving notices. "Mr. Hart has long been famous for the way of depicting the rough-and-ready Westerner handy with his shooting-irons," the *Morning Telegraph* reported on May 2. The act played a three-week run in Chicago, whereupon Hart and Granville quarreled. Hart ended up buying the act for seventy-five dollars.

During the summer of 1910, Bill and Mary Ellen lived alone in the small white house in Westport. Bill devoted most of his vacation to building an addition onto their home and romping with his dog over the neighboring hills. When the time came for him to leave Connecticut in the fall, he took his sister and Mack, the bulldog, with him to New York, and the three of them crowded into a small apartment.

Hart was hired at the beginning of the 1910–11 season by the distinguished producer Charles Frohman to play Sherlock Holmes in *The Speckled Band*, a melodrama by Sir Arthur Conan Doyle that had been successful in London the year before. Hart rehearsed with the company for one week and then quit, sensing that the show was headed for disaster. Sure enough, *The Speckled Band* closed in Boston and never opened in New York.

Hart was next offered a part in *These Are My People*, a sequel to *The Squaw Man*. The show had been a failure on the road, but the producer, George Tyler, thought he could save it by getting together members of the old *Squaw Man* cast. He was wrong. The reassembled company closed after a week on the road, then returned to New York and rehearsed *The Squaw Man* for two days. The revival of the popular frontier drama opened at the Broadway Theater on New Year's Day 1911 and proved successful enough to run for nearly four weeks.

Bill's salary had stayed at $150 a week for three years, but he was unemployed for two months during the winter of 1911. He finally got a part in a revamped show called *The Quality of Mercy*, which played on the road for about ten weeks. The company traveled as far west as Minneapolis but closed in Chicago.

Hart survived that summer with no engagements but made daily trips from Westport into New York by train to check with the agencies about plays for the coming season. He learned that Klaw and

Erlanger were producing *The Trail of the Lonesome Pine* and that his friend Fred Watson, with whom he had acted in *The Squaw Man*, had been cast in the show as Devil Judd Tolliver, a vengeful Blue Ridge Mountain patriarch. When Watson got sick and died before the play opened, Hart was hired to play the role.

The Trail of the Lonesome Pine tried out in Boston for the month of January 1912, then opened at the New Amsterdam Theater in New York. The story, based on John Fox's novel, was dramatized by Eugene Walters, whose wife played in the production opposite Hart. "Devil Judd Tolliver was one of those rugged, gun-fighting mountaineers that an actor could not go wrong in," Hart said. He scored another hit and performed in the show in New York and on the road for two years.

When performing on Broadway, Bill kept Mary Ellen and his bulldog with him. Finding quarters in Manhattan that would take a fifty-pound dog was not easy, and after trying various boardinghouses, Hart and his sister ended up staying at the Remington on West Forty-sixth Street. Walking Mack on icy streets, with the dog tugging on his leash, offered another challenge. Mary Ellen was Bill's only family, aside from his married sister, and the two became codependent. Bill always referred to Mary Ellen as his "loyal sister," yet he came to resent her possessive attitude toward him. Hart was nearing fifty years of age, and there had been no mention of any serious romantic attachment. In every respect but the physical, Mamie had become more wife than sister to her peripatetic brother, and she was not about to surrender her turf. Bill felt responsible for his spinster sister, was lonely without her, yet quickly grew claustrophobic from her persistent smothering and the guilt she burdened him with.

On hiatus from *The Trail of the Lonesome Pine* in the summer of 1912, Hart performed a new vaudeville act called "Moonshine," written by Arthur Hopkins. Hart played Luke Hazy, another mountaineer, and introduced the sketch at the Alhambra Theater in New York. Critics found the act a disappointment. "What little action blazes up toward the end is dull and commonplace," *Variety* maintained. "The dialogue is rather long and drawn out and is far from entertaining." Bill himself liked the part but agreed that the piece "lacked the snap or gunpowder that is necessary to put over a dramatic act in vaudeville." He abandoned the sketch after playing it for one week and rejoined the cast of *The Trail of the Lonesome Pine* in Chicago.

Mary Ellen traveled with Bill during most of the ensuing tour. The company performed in Indianapolis and Cincinnati and went on to one-night stands in Dayton and Springfield, Ohio. In Ohio it rained so hard for a week that the train tracks in Dayton were two feet underwater. "We just did get out," Hart recalled of the 1913 flood. In Springfield the company went onstage during a deluge, with only a few drenched people in the audience, and the players were marooned in the city for ten days. "The town was under martial law with soldiers patrolling the streets night and day," Hart recalled. "Depots were established to take care of all refugees who managed to get in from the surrounding country." When the actors finally were able to leave Springfield, they traveled to Toledo by train, passing damaged bridges, railroad cars in rivers, and track twisted beyond use. "We would take an hour to make a mile," Hart said, so that it took the troupe eighteen hours to reach Toledo.

In Cleveland, Bill saw his first Western movie and was aghast at its glaring inaccuracies. He later called the film "a debauchery of trash" and said that the sheriff in the movie looked like a "cross between a Wisconsin woodchopper and a Gloucester fisherman." Horrified though he was at the misrepresentations, Bill immediately recognized the potential of motion pictures and the possibility of using movies to re-create the old West in a truthful fashion.

Although stage people generally despised "the flickers," nickelodeons had been siphoning off live theater's audience for nearly a decade, which eliminated scores of the old traveling stock companies. Western movies had soared to popularity after *The Great Train Robbery*, a one-reel horse opera shot in New Jersey for the Edison Company, scored a monumental success in 1903. Broncho Billy Anderson, who admittedly knew nothing about the West, appeared in the film and soon became motion pictures' first cowboy star. Anderson had no ranch or rodeo background and could barely ride a horse when he began his film career. But he was ambitious and approached the task of becoming a Western picture star with determination. Within five years after the release of *The Great Train Robbery,* the Western field, consisting mostly of one- and two-reelers, had become so lucrative that actual late frontier figures were attracted to the movie business. Al Jennings, fresh out of jail for his misdeeds as an outlaw in Oklahoma and Kansas, starred in *The Bank Robbery,* a Western directed in 1908 by William Tilghman, a former buffalo hunter, rancher, and lawman. In 1912 Emmett Dalton, after serving fourteen years of a life sentence for his involvement in the infamous Coffeyville raid and similar exploits, produced and starred in *The Last Stand of the Dalton Boys,* which Dalton remade six years later with John Tackett, who ironically was the photographer who took the grisly picture of the bullet-ridden bodies of Grat, Bob, and Broadwell Dalton propped up in an alley just hours after the Coffeyville shoot-out. But most Westerns before William S. Hart began making films in 1914 and John Ford teamed with actor Harry Carey to launch the Cheyenne Harry series in 1917 were rubbish.

Sickened yet fascinated by his introduction to Western movies, Hart sensed that his moment had come. "I had been waiting for years for the right thing," he said, "and now the right thing had come. I was a part of the West. . . . [I]t was in my blood. The very love I bore it made me know its ways." Hart resolved to find a way to make realistic Western pictures. "Hundreds of ideas seemed to rush in from every direction," he said.

For the remainder of the tour with *The Trail of the Lonesome Pine,* Hart saw as many Westerns as he could. As he studied them, plots began to take shape in his imagination. In Westport and New York he saw more Westerns during the summer of 1913. Many of his actor friends in the Lambs Club were working in Western films that were being shot at the time over in New Jersey. Bill felt that he, far more than any of his peers, was ideally suited for such parts. "I was considered the outstanding portrayer of Western roles on the American stage," he said. "It was the big opportunity that a most high Power, chance, or fixed law had schooled me for." At last Hart glimpsed his destiny, what he had spent years working toward. "And I would go through hell on three pints of water before I would acknowledge defeat," he vowed.

In the fall of 1913 Bill went back on the road with *The Trail of the Lonesome Pine*. His salary had been raised to $175 a week, but he knew that he was biding his time. The company was scheduled to go to California, and during his summer layoff, Bill had met actors who were headed for the West Coast to work in Western pictures. When the *Lonesome Pine* troupe reached San Francisco, Bill learned that all of the major film studios had moved to Los Angeles. The two principal companies making Westerns were Universal, in the San Fernando Valley, and the New York Motion Picture Company, located on the Pacific coast near Santa Monica. The latter had a contract with the 101 Ranch Show for horses, cattle, cowboys, Indians, wagons, gear, and equipment that the movie company needed to make Western films. Bill had ridden with the Indians in the 101 Ranch Show in Chicago and knew that the 101's spread in Oklahoma was owned by the Miller Brothers.

Fortunately for Hart, *The Trail of the Lonesome Pine* had been booked for an engagement in Los Angeles. The company had no sooner arrived in the budding movie capital than Hart raced to a telephone and called the New York Motion Picture Company. He asked to speak with Joe Miller. "I am an actor," he said, "and I want to see about making some Western pictures." Hart was informed that Miller only owned the company's stock and its ranch near Marland, Oklahoma. "If you want to see about acting," a voice on the telephone told him, "call up Thomas H. Ince. He is manager of the picture company."

Ince was Bill's old friend, fellow actor, and roommate from his days playing in *Hearts Courageous*. By 1913 Ince had become a leading producer and director in Hollywood and had developed into a shrewd businessman. Hart left word for Ince to call him as soon as possible. The next day Ince contacted Bill and took him out to Inceville, near where present Sunset Boulevard runs into Pacific Coast Highway. The hills and canyons around Inceville served as the background for the New York Motion Picture Company's Western movies. "I was enraptured and told [Tom] so," Hart wrote in *My Life*

East and West. "The very primitiveness of the whole life out there, the cowboys and the Indians, staggered me. I loved it. They had everything to make Western pictures. The West was right there!"

Yet when Bill told Ince of his plans for making Western films, his friend offered no encouragement. The public had been flooded with Westerns and had grown tired of them. Since Westerns could be filmed outdoors, they were cheap to produce, and every company in the business had been cranking them out at a frenzied pace. "You simply cannot sell a Western picture at any price," Ince told Hart. "They are a drug on the market."

Bill replied that the Westerns he wanted to make would not be the burlesque misrepresentations he had seen in nickelodeons. He intended to film the West as it really was. "I'm an actor," said Hart, "but I know the West." Ince explained that he had recently made *Custer's Last Fight*, which was an exciting movie with lots of horsemen and Indians and thrilling action, but the picture had not sold. "Bill, it's a damn shame," Ince said, "but you're too late."

As Hart and Ince walked around the film company's camp, Hart learned that the contract the owners had with the 101 Ranch Show still had another year to run. "Let me make some Western pictures and use these people," the determined stage actor said. "It just can't be done," Ince insisted. Then as Hart was about to leave Inceville, he began speaking in Sioux to some of the Indians in the camp, and Ince was astounded at the response. Perhaps his old friend really did know the West. "Bill," he said, "if you want to come out next spring and take a chance, I'll give you seventy-five dollars a week to cover your expenses and direct you in a picture myself."

Hart was so ecstatic that he stayed on to talk about the kind of pictures he envisioned making. He was so late getting to the theater that evening that the manager had to hold the curtain for him. Before leaving California, he assured Ince that he would be back as soon as the tour of *The Trail of the Lonesome Pine* finished.

Bill remained with the play until spring. He was offered a leading role in Eugene Walters's *The Woman* for the fall, but he turned it down. Walters twice raised the fee he was willing to pay the actor, but Hart held firm. "I was determined to go into pictures," he said.

Abraham Erlanger and other members of the New York theater establishment thought Hart was crazy to refuse a prestigious stage offer in favor of the despised "flickers," yet Hart had his mind set. Soon after *The Trail of the Lonesome Pine* closed at the Grand Opera House in New York, Hart bought a train ticket to Los Angeles and left Mary Ellen and Mack in Westport. He would never return to the professional stage.

Hart was forty-nine years old when he began his movie career. He had trained in the theater for a quarter of a century and had learned a great deal about dramatic situations. What he knew about being a cowboy he had learned on the stage, not on the open range. But Hart had absorbed the mystique of the old West, revered and embellished the experiences he remembered from his boyhood, and stubbornly determined to preserve the legacy of the late frontier on film.

Convinced, as historian Frederick Jackson Turner was, that the westward movement had shaped the American character, Hart wanted to project images of the vanishing West that would generate ethical attitudes and stimulate a communal identity. "My continued success in Western roles on the stage revealed to me that what the public desired most of motion pictures of the West was consistent realism," he wrote in his foreword to *Pinto Ben*. "Of this fact I was so thoroughly convinced that I was ready to sacrifice my standing on the legitimate stage, purchased by long years of toil and hard knocks, to gamble with fate."

Hollywood became Hart's resuscitated West, as it was for many of the working cowboys who drifted into Los Angeles seeking jobs as wranglers, doubles, and stuntmen after the unfenced range was no more. In movies William S. Hart would earn distinction, material comfort, and for a time the independence to make the kind of product he wanted. His sad-faced image, with protruding jaw and beaklike nose, would be seen on the screen for a mere decade, yet its mark would remain indelible around the world. Although Hart most often played a reformed bad man, a generation of moviegoers viewed him as a champion of virtue and independence. His became an endearing screen personality that reminded audiences of their fathers or grandfathers, a stalwart force that embodied courage, honesty, and ultimate justice. For William S. Hart, making movies meant more than the creation and marketing of popular entertainment. His Westerns were monuments to the recent West, to his own childhood, and—in his words—captured the "very essence of national life."

Inceville Cowboy

Thomas Ince had come to California early in November 1911, after a year of moviemaking in New York and Cuba. When he entered the motion picture industry, Ince said, "[t]here were no accepted standards, no patterns on which to build, no organized business methods or efficiency." Like most contemporaries from the theater, Ince was disdainful of films at first, but when acting jobs on the stage proved scarce, he turned to the flickers, as many unemployed performers did. Ince acted in one picture at the Imp studio in New York, where he earned five dollars a day, then moved to Biograph for assignments that earned him more money. He returned to Imp when the company promised him the next director's post that became vacant. Ince wrote and directed his first movie for Imp but moved to the West Coast when the New York Motion Picture Company hired him to make Westerns.

A short, stocky man with a large head, Ince was a human dynamo, full of creative ideas. He spent long nights laboring over scenarios with writers, whipping them into shape, filling them with suggestions for action, and constructing plots that had human interest and dramatic punch. Although an excellent showman and a gifted director, Ince soon preferred to supervise pictures as an executive producer. He introduced business efficiency into the infant movie industry, streamlined production methods, and exercised control over his pictures from scriptwriting through the final editing process. By 1912 Ince's status among Hollywood producers was without peer, and he had been labeled "the Belasco of the moving picture business."

The New York Motion Picture Company, for which Ince worked during his early years in Los Angeles, was owned by Adam Kessell and Charles O. Baumann. The company built a laboratory in New York for processing its films, made pictures in California, and released them through Mutual Film Exchanges. Thomas Ince became the company's mastermind in charge of production, and, like the later studio moguls, he developed a keen sense of what the public wanted in entertainment.

When Ince began making movies, the American frontier was recent history, within memory of most adults. Moving pictures seemed an ideal way to capture America's unique heritage and give younger generations exciting images of the risks and challenges their ancestors had confronted during the country's pursuit of manifest destiny. But the rash of Westerns marketed in the decade after *The Great Train Robbery*'s success soon began to follow hackneyed formulas. What in 1903 had seemed thrilling entertainment by 1914 had worn on the public's patience. Ince had had success with such two-reelers as *War on the Plains* (1912), and cowboy pictures were still in demand in Europe, but the domestic market appeared to be saturated. As Ince himself said, "The cowboys rode uphill on Tuesday, and downhill on Thursday," and discerning audiences had grown bored with such antics.

Ince knew that scenery and credible landscapes were vital to the continuing popularity of Westerns. Fortunately the New York Motion Picture Company had leased a spread of eighteen thousand acres in California's Santa Monica Mountains, which became Inceville in 1911. Originally the land had been part of a Spanish ranch that stretched from Santa Monica to Malibu and contained vineyards and orange and banana groves. But the ranch's canyons and mountains provided ideal backgrounds for making Western movies, and the secluded sanctuary, with only one entrance at the mouth of Santa Ynez Canyon, offered protection from the Patents Company that was causing trouble for independent picture makers. The entrance to the canyon could be guarded, so that workers were assured of not being disrupted or becoming caught up in the patents war that resulted from Edison's declared monopoly on motion picture equipment.

Inceville started with one simple glass-roofed stage, but the facilities quickly expanded to include a town of adobe buildings, log cabins, and sod and clapboard houses. Practically all of the filming, even interiors, was done outdoors. Sets consisted of a few pieces of antiquated furniture and a backdrop. Interior scenes might have two, possibly three, side walls, but in many cases there was just one. No ceilings were used in filming, and tablecloths, wall hangings, and women's dresses in rooms supposedly with the windows closed often fluttered as gusts of wind blew in from the oceanfront.

Out back in the scrub country, conditions were truly primitive. Production was sometimes interrupted by storms and fog from the sea, and brush fires and rattlesnakes were seasonal dangers. In time there were standing sets at Inceville, a commissary for serving lunches, stables and sheds, and an office for Ince. The tents that had originally served as dressing rooms for actors were eventually replaced by a row of barrackslike structures. For years drinking water had to be hauled in, and insects and vermin were constant nuisances.

Actors living in Los Angeles went by automobile, trolley, or bus to a little railroad in Santa Monica, which took them out to the Inceville camp. From there they got on a horse and rode into the hills for the day's work. Getting into makeup and costume required arriving at the camp early, usually no later than seven o'clock in the morning for women, and filming continued until eight o'clock at night during the summer. "Then we got on our horses and rode back to the streetcar," actress Ann Little remembered.

By the time William S. Hart reached California, more than three hundred people worked at Inceville, and the company had a weekly payroll of $10,000. Many of the cowboys hired to perform there came from working ranches and brought with them the attitudes of the dying Cattle Kingdom. They worked hard, welcomed opportunities to demonstrate their courage and skill, and enjoyed the camaraderie of their own kind. Experienced cowboys were expected to train new arrivals, and if agents of the Patents Company were rumored to be in the area, armed sentries, recruited from among the wranglers and stuntmen, were sent out to patrol. When not needed for filming, cowboys practiced roping, shooting, or riding bucking bulls and horses.

The Indians used in the Inceville Westerns put up their tepees back in the hills amid the sage and yucca. Most of the Indians there were Sioux, brought out from a reservation in South Dakota and still wards of the federal government. They had been loaned by the government to the 101 Ranch Show, which in turn leased their services to the New York Motion Picture Company. "They always had one chief with them," Little recalled, and "they were there a couple of years. They'd send twenty-five of them back and bring twenty-five more out." Although Ince's films were generally deferential to the Native American, there is little question that the Sioux working in early Western pictures were exploited. Life at Inceville was scarcely better than what the Indians had experienced on the reservation, and they were encouraged to stay within the limits of the camp. Still, the movie Indians found ways of leaving the compound to prowl the streets of Santa Monica or Venice, a neighboring resort community, without supervision.

Except for the Indians, a democratic spirit reigned at Inceville. Star-like behavior in Hollywood was still in the future. "We were all one," Little said. "The director didn't mean any more than the cowboy." Actors put on their own makeup and did their share of the drudgery. Most performers had some skill with a horse, did all but the most difficult stunts, and got used to waiting in the sun for hours while workers prepared the next setup. "We depended upon the daylight," Little said. "We had those big silver screens with the sun shining on them thrown up into our faces to get light." A man named Gellow, who had been a cook for the 101 Ranch, prepared noontime meals that were hardy enough to satisfy a field hand. "We would come in from location, hungry and tired," actress Enid Markey said, "and he would produce fried ham, fried eggs, steaming pots of coffee and thick cream."

The aim at Inceville was to give Western pictures a look of reality. Ince turned out compact, well-plotted movies, produced with assembly-line proficiency. Like Hart, Ince wanted to re-create life in the untamed West accurately on the screen, and he became convinced that Hart had something special to bring to the craft. Yet Ince was unwilling to surrender much control over productions and watched over the early Hart films in a supervisory capacity.

When Bill returned to Los Angeles in the spring of 1914, Ince put him on salary immediately, although the actor's weekly fee dropped from the $175 he had been earning in the theater to a mere $75. Hart oriented himself to filmmaking by wandering about the camp, watching how technicians in movies worked. He later claimed that the cowboys at Inceville mistook him for a new ranch hand and couldn't believe that he was a New York actor, but in truth Hart mystified most of them. "The cowboys didn't take to him," said Diana Serra Cary, daughter of Jack Montgomery, a veteran wrangler in silent pictures. "They said he always wore those great big hats and a bandanna as big as a Harvey House half tablecloth. He didn't look like a working cowboy at all."

Having reinvented himself when he began playing western characters on the stage, Hart was prepared to expand that image in Hollywood. He appeared at Inceville in cowboy getup and each morning asked for a horse to ride into the hills. Every day the cowboys in charge of the stable gave him a horse that was a little more spirited than the one before. "One morning they gave me a stubborn, wild little buckskin," Bill recalled. About two miles away from the camp the buckskin grew rambunctious and started to buck. Hart managed to calm the mount and returned to the stables still in the saddle. But he realized that the cowboys gathered there were watching and enjoying his discomfort.

The only person who offered Hart real encouragement during his first weeks at Inceville was Broncho Billy Anderson, hero of the early Western one-reelers. Anderson thought Hart had the right personality for Western movies. "I'm quite sure that you'd create a character that would be loved, and people would want more and more of you," Broncho Billy told the newly arrived stage actor. But Ince seemed satisfied that there was only slight demand for Western pictures and showed little willingness to invest much of the company's money in trying to revive their popularity.

Finally, as Hart's cash reserve dwindled, Ince authorized the making of *His Hour of Manhood*, a two-reeler, with Hart assigned to play Pete Larson, a brute who mistreats his wife, engages in foul play, and is hunted down by a posse and killed. Thomas Chatterton played the

picture's hero and also directed, although it was his first time working behind the camera. Clara Williams, a good actress but no beauty,
was the leading lady, and the film's budget came to less than $8,000.
Not used to motion picture technology, Bill was uncomfortable making the movie, which began shooting on May 13, 1914, and ended
twelve days later. "I did as I was told," he said, "but I felt terrible, and
when I saw the rushes on the screen, I knew I was terrible."

Critical reaction was equally negative. *His Hour of Manhood*'s
story was melodramatic and not particularly interesting. "This two-
reel picture may please those who mainly view but do not analyze,"
Moving Picture World said. "It is hardly logical in its plot." The movie
followed familiar themes and offered little or none of the "consistent
realism" that Bill wanted to introduce into Western films.

The same day that Hart finished *His Hour of Manhood*, he started
work on *Jim Cameron's Wife*, another two-reeler directed by Thomas
Chatterton. Ince had a hand in writing the scenario, and Clara Williams
again played the leading lady. This time Hart played Andy Stiles, the
leader of an outlaw gang and Hart's first good bad guy. Stiles reveals
his basic decency when he allows the impoverished Mrs. Cameron to
capture him and receive the $500 reward offered for his arrest.

Bill saw the rushes of his second movie and was again "heartsick."
Moving Picture World was kinder to *Jim Cameron's Wife* than it had
been to Hart's first film: "In the picture there is plenty of fast riding,
shooting off of pistols, a stage holdup and other things that are liked
by the more elemental spectators. A fair rather than a noteworthy
offering. The photography is clear and the characters are played
pleasingly."

Still, Bill was not satisfied with the way things were starting off for
him at Inceville. When Thomas Ince suggested a similar assignment
as a follow-up, Bill revolted. "I felt too much hurt to talk, so I wrote
Tom a letter," the disappointed actor said. "I refused to do the new
picture and told him that I was not doing what I came out to do,
and that unless he could do as he had promised I was going home."
Bill wanted to make a feature film, a longer and authentic Western,
not another two-reeler in which "the true West was sacrificed on the
altar of sensationalism."

Ince remembered a short movie he had made three years earlier called *Getting His Man* and thought perhaps the plot was engaging enough to be expanded. Bill asked Ince to tell him the story. "I like it," the actor said when Ince finished his narrative. "Let me have it and give me three days. I think I can build it up." Five days later Bill gave the story back to Ince doubled in length. The producer then turned the treatment over to C. Gardner Sullivan, Inceville's best screenwriter and later a film executive. What resulted was a five-reel Western called *The Bargain*, directed by Reginald Barker, a young Scotsman whose work Hart liked. Once more the homespun Clara Williams was the leading lady.

Shooting on *The Bargain* began on June 11, 1914, and continued until August 5. Hart talked Ince into allowing Barker to take a small crew to the Grand Canyon to film some scenes, which added grandeur to the picture. "What a glorious trip it was!" Hart recalled. "I wore spurs and rode a horse at a full gallop on the worst turns of the narrow Hermit Creek Trail, on the brink of a straight drop of thousands of feet." The unit camped for several days beside the Colorado River, and the heat at the bottom of the canyon was so fierce that the actors' makeup melted in its containers. But the location work resulted in fairly dazzling footage by 1914 standards. Hart estimated that the trip to Arizona cost the New York Motion Picture Company about $600, but the sequences shot there gave *The Bargain* a look of importance.

When the crew returned to Inceville, Barker photographed scenes to match the location work in nearby Topanga Canyon. The moviemakers reached the area by traveling over a narrow dirt road, full of washouts, but the rustic country outside Malibu corresponded well with the opening views of the Grand Canyon. Hart is seen racing on horseback along a steep ridge, against the sky, then horse and rider tumble down a hillside, creating a stunning effect. Bill rode five horses in the movie, but his principal mount was a coal black steed named Midnight. The horse "was nervous and had broken a director's arm and an actor's leg," Hart said. But Hart handled the animal with no trouble.

Although Hart's acting was too inflated to satisfy current tastes, *The Bargain* is classic William S. Hart. The opening title rings with the actor's personal sentiments: "The West! The Land of Vast Golden Silences Where God Sits Enthroned on the Purple Peaks and Man Stands Face to Face With His Soul." Hart is first seen in western garb rolling a cigarette. In the picture he plays Jim Stokes, the "Two-Gun Man," a bandit ready to shoot the first man who makes a hostile move. Hart looks imposing, younger than his years, with eyes of steel peering through heavy makeup. After a stagecoach robbery, Stokes falls in love with a virtuous woman, marries her, and vows to reform. Captured by a paunchy sheriff who proceeds to gamble away the money Hart's character had recently stolen, the reformed outlaw bargains for his freedom to commit one last crime—stealing back the pilfered money from a gambling den and righting the sheriff's wrong. As Stokes returns to his captor with the stolen money in hand, a bit of humor is inserted when Hart's good bad guy tells the law officer, "There May Be a Little More Than You Lost But I Was in a Hurry!" Thankful to be vindicated, the sheriff frees Stokes to fetch his wife and cross the border into Mexico. Such became the formula for the actor's Western plots, and his movies were popular in large measure because of their moral lessons and the implication that in nature man's rejuvenation is possible.

In addition to its appealing landscapes, *The Bargain* contains the dusty, gritty look of the old West. Its massive saloon is unadorned, and a prospector's cabin is appropriately crude. Many of the extras used as atmosphere sport handlebar mustaches or beards. Although the movie suggests impending danger, it moves at a gentle pace that appealed to post-Victorian audiences.

Barker and Hart worked well together, and Hart found making *The Bargain* "an exquisite pleasure." Ince agreed that the completed picture had the earmarks of success, probably too big a hit to be released through Mutual. Instead, Ince sold the distribution rights to the movie for three years to Famous Players–Lasky, the forerunner of Paramount, where film pioneer Adolph Zukor was forging the first of Hollywood's giant amalgamations that would integrate production, distribution, and exhibition. Already a powerhouse, Famous Players could book *The Bargain* into premium theaters, many of which the studio either owned or controlled. Overnight Hart's third Western created a sensation. The *New York Dramatic Mirror* judged the movie "a model of what can be accomplished in a popular field of photoplay work. The exteriors . . . offer a sequence of glorious views in which the rugged wilderness of a virgin country predominates." Some reviewers labeled *The Bargain* a spectacle, and many commented on its spacious saloon and believable sets. *Variety* called the movie "one of the best feature-length Westerns ever shown." Yet Stephan Bush, writing for *Moving Picture World*, considered *The Bargain* "a reckless attempt to revive a style of motion picture which we had hoped was a thing of the past. . . . There can be no doubt whatever that a picture of this kind has a bad influence on youthful minds."

By present standards *The Bargain* is filled with lurid drama and hammy histrionics. Leading players are introduced and take a bow in evening dress, then appear in costume. Hart's austerity in tense moments takes on granitic proportions, with more eye rolling and heavy breathing than reflective acting. And the titles express sentiments that now seem ridiculous. "No Star Is Lost We Ever Once Have Seen," the final epitaph reads: "We Always May Be What We Might Have Been." But for its day, *The Bargain* was a bold attempt to inject vitality and truth into the ebbing screen Western.

The film's strengths convinced Ince to put Hart under a short-term contract, both as actor and as director, at $125 a week. Although Ince himself was given directorial credit in *The Bargain*'s opening titles, he had operated solely in a supervisory capacity. If the company's Westerns had any chance to flourish, the producer needed someone with the interest and flair to devise ways of making them seem original and genuine. C. Gardner Sullivan understood the mechanics of screenwriting and was the highest-paid scenario writer in Hollywood at the time, but Hart was the one who made suggestions that strengthened Sullivan's scripts and increased their flavor.

The day after *The Bargain* wrapped, Hart began shooting *On the Night Stage*, again with a screenplay by Sullivan and directed by Reginald Barker. Another five-reeler, the picture had a twenty-eight-day production schedule and followed the blueprint Hart would use in future movies. Released through Mutual, *On the Night Stage* was the kind of film Bill wanted to make. It was "full of the life of my boyhood," he said, "reproducing days that were dear to me." In the picture Hart plays another bandit who holds up stagecoaches, slugs down whiskey, treats women in a rough manner, but is redeemed before the final reel. At the end Hart's good bad guy is pictured alone, looking sad and hugging the neck of his horse. "I Ain't Got Nobody But You, Midnight," he says. "Nobody At All."

On the Night Stage makes less use of landscapes than *The Bargain* and lacks its predecessor's epic sweep. The movie's plot, like those of all of Hart's early films, is rooted in nineteenth-century melodrama, and Hart appears more horse-faced than he did in his previous feature. At times he seems laughable, decked out in chaps of Angora goatskin, an enormous bandanna, and leather cuffs on his forearms. Hart acts with the ferocity of Arnold Schwarzenegger and almost matches the later bodybuilder's set jaw.

Yet critics in 1915 found the new cowboy star's performance riveting. "Mr. Hart's is a face that photographs to a nicety," the *New York Dramatic Mirror* reported. "Small wonder, then, that he should be able to monopolize the action, for one follows his movements with the fascination that a snake has upon his feathered prey. . . . It is a picture in which the character will persist after the story is forgotten." The reviewer agreed that the West of boundless prairies had been effectively represented in *On the Night Stage* and that the picture's atmosphere proved that the New York Motion Picture Company was master of the Western genre.

Despite two strong contenders, Ince was still not persuaded that Westerns had been restored to lasting popularity. Hart was pleased with his two features and had already learned a great deal about filmmaking technique, but he was by no means certain that he had earned a permanent place in the industry. He returned to New York in September 1914, before either *The Bargain* or *On the Night Stage* had been released, unsure of his future, too strapped for funds to afford more than a second-class train ticket.

When he reached Westport, Mary Ellen and his dog were waiting for him at the gate. Fearing that he had failed in Hollywood, Bill tried to make his experiences in California sound as upbeat as possible. "I was like a boy going through a churchyard, whistling to keep his courage up," Hart said, but he sensed that his employers at the New York Motion Picture Company were ready to terminate their agreement with him. He took the train into Manhattan several times a week from Connecticut to look for jobs, visiting the same offices he had for years, yet he found no work. "An actor seeking employment is as popular with the derby-hatted managerial gentry as a ruptured barnacle," he said.

Then came a telegram from Ince offering him a role in another two-reeler and the chance to direct the picture. Bill decided to close the house in Westport and take Mary Ellen and his bulldog with him to California. Money was still short, so he and his sister ate sandwiches and drank milk whenever the train stopped long enough at stations for meals. Bill took advantage of those occasions to walk Mack, who was riding in a box in the baggage car. Soon after arriving in Los Angeles, Hart rented a modest house in the hills near Inceville so that he could be close to his work.

The first picture Hart directed was *The Passing of Two-Gun Hicks*. Bill asked Ince to let Clifford Smith, already a veteran in the business, work as his assistant director, and the two men remained a team on many later projects. Although Two-Gun Hicks is a gunfighter, he is more hero than villain and willingly gives up the woman he loves rather than threaten her marriage to a drunkard she apparently loves. "When I want a woman, I take her," Hicks says, "but I don't care to have 'em hanging round."

Hart thought the plot of the two-reeler was "about the best story [he] ever screened," and he saw himself as the same kind of sacrificing, misunderstood man as the character he portrayed. Still a confirmed bachelor, Hart loved animals but seemed to have little need for women other than his sister. Idealistic, puritanical, self-righteous, and distrustful of people, he appeared content with his celibate life and had trouble relating to male acquaintances on anything more than a casual or business level. He was happiest when camped out in the hills with his production company, re-creating memories from his childhood. "I was surrounded by no greedy grafters, no gelatin-spined, flatulent, slimy creatures," he said of his months at Inceville, "just dogs, horses, sheep, goats, bulls, mules, burros, and white men and red men that were accustomed to living among such things."

When *The Passing of Two-Gun Hicks* was released in December 1914, *Moving Picture World* said: "Rarely does a photoplay carry with it the strong quality of interest that is found in this two-reel number by Ince and Sullivan. William S. Hart makes a compelling figure. . . . It is the best type of Western drama, finely pictured and convincing. The climax, which is really no climax at all, shows Hicks riding away in the dusk 'for her sake.'"

Working in tandem with Cliff Smith, Hart directed himself in five more two-reelers before the year was out: *In the Sage Brush Country, The Scourge of the Desert, Mr. "Silent" Haskins, The Sheriff's Streak of Yellow,* and *The Grudge.* Hart plays a bandit with a noble side in three of the pictures, and all but *The Scourge of the Desert* and *The Sheriff's Streak of Yellow* had screenplays by Gardner Sullivan. Hart later said that the New York Motion Picture Company would sometimes pay fifteen or twenty dollars for a story, written on a few pages in longhand, and turn the pages over to him and expect him to make a picture from them. All of the early movies he directed at Inceville were made for around a thousand dollars, and most critics found them appealing entertainment with rousing action and effective photography.

Hart had worked steadily since his return to California with Mary Ellen, but on Christmas Day, 1914, he took advantage of time off to find a furnished bungalow for his sister and himself near downtown Los Angeles. Their principal requirement was an enclosed yard for Mack. Hart found a place at 534 Figueroa Street, twenty-five miles from Inceville but inexpensive enough to meet a beginning movie actor's budget.

"There were no restaurants in Hollywood," Hart remembered. "Not even a lunch-stand where one could buy a sandwich." He discovered a cafe on Sixth Street where he could eat breakfast every morning before taking a bus out to the camp. He had to get up at five o'clock to be at work by eight, and he seldom got home before seven or seven-thirty at night. After taking Mack for a walk, he and Mary Ellen usually ate dinner at the Hoffman Cafe on Spring Street and sometimes took in a movie at the Lyceum Theater, a few doors away. "When we reached home I would go over the story for the next day's work," Bill said. "For three years I worked sixteen hours a day and worried eight."

By the end of May 1915, Hart had directed and starred in twelve more pictures, all but one of them two-reelers. His reputation with the public became established soon after the release of *The Bargain* and *On the Night Stage*, and Ince allotted Hart considerably more freedom to make his own kind of movies. The New York Motion Picture Company's arrangement with the 101 Ranch Show had ended in November 1914, but Hart was given his own cameraman and crew to film Westerns and the star resented any interference.

"I had to teach the picture people what the West was," Hart said shortly before his death. "Nobody in Hollywood knew how cowboys acted." Former ranch hands at Inceville found Bill's claims to knowledge of the old West amusing. Some of the cowboys who worked with him maintained that he did not ride well and was actually afraid of horses. The opinionated star had experienced little of the life that former ranch hands had, and his concept of western attire made better theater than practical dress for working cowboys. Picture people soon found Hart difficult to deal with, and his pompous, sanctimonious attitude irked most of them. "I didn't get along well with Bill Hart," said film editor Irvin Willat, who later became a silent movie director. "I supervised the cutting of one or two of his pictures. He was a bit of a ham, but a tremendous asset. I never considered him a great actor. He belonged on Fourteenth Street in New York and not in the New York Motion Picture Company in Los Angeles."

Once Hart had demonstrated his appeal at the box office, Ince was willing to let the star have his way in most matters and freed Gardner Sullivan to write stories that supported the heroic persona the actor wanted to project on the screen. Ince himself lent a supervisory hand whenever time permitted. As the cowboy star's image grew, tension developed between him and Ince, since neither was generous about sharing credit. Hart later claimed that Ince took advantage of him, but that was after the actor's defiant face had become familiar to movie audiences around the world.

On January 6, 1915, Hart began shooting *The Roughneck*, the first of the twelve films he would make for the New York Motion Picture Company between January and May of that year. Hart plays a mine superintendent in the picture, but his character is in the East throughout most of the story trying to straighten out his wealthy employer's will. The production marked a change of pace from the good bad guys Hart liked to play, but the day after *The Roughneck* wrapped, the actor-director went back before the camera in the more familiar role of a good-natured miner turned temporarily bad in *The Taking of Luke McVane*.

Hart's sentimentality was becoming more evident in his work, although he preferred to see his movies as affirmations of "treasured American values." In *The Taking of Luke McVane*, the cowboy star rode a pinto horse named Fritz for the first time. "He weighed only one thousand pounds," the actor said of the horse, "but his power and endurance were remarkable." Fritz would be Hart's favorite horse and was as well known to Hart's audiences as Champion and Trigger were to Gene Autry and Roy Rogers fans. Originally the property of the 101 Ranch Show, Fritz had been ridden by several of the movie people, including Ann Little. Hart eventually bought the pinto, rode him in pictures for years, and kept him at his ranch until the horse died at an advanced age.

In the early months of 1915, when he was turning out a two-reeler every ten to fifteen days, Hart was ecstatic, doing work he loved and trying his best to blend sentiment and realism into poetic cinema. *The Man from Nowhere* was followed by *"Bad Buck" of Santa Ynez*, the latter presenting Hart in his familiar good bad man role. The settings of the early Westerns Hart directed are appropriately desiccated and drab, and the shack towns, with their false-front stores and muddy, wagon-rutted streets, are commendably authentic. But the documentary-like quality that film scholars find in Hart's movies is most apparent pictorially and yields to melodrama in plots and character relationships. What William S. Hart gave audiences was a mythic frontier, less full of hokum than most of the Westerns that came before and immediately after his, with the notable exception of John Ford's films with Harry Carey. Hart's reality is laced with nostalgia and moral passion and extols a genteel yet manly Anglo-Saxon heritage that was compatible with prevailing attitudes as the United States tried to remain neutral in the early years of World War I. For later viewers, Hart's pictures reek of racism, sexism, and macho swagger. His heroines are mostly passive and in need of strong male protectors. The actor's love of the old West became his personal antidote for the present, which he regarded as full of liars, swindlers, newsmongers, and obstacles to individual freedom.

The Darkening Trail, the only four-reeler Bill made during the early part of 1915 and his debut directing a longer film, was pure melodrama. Beginning with a modern setting and then shifting to Alaska, the movie depicts an utter cad, two wronged women, and an avenger played by Hart. In March the actor returned to making two-reel Westerns with *The Conversion of Frosty Blake.* In that one Hart played a minister who goes West for his health but resolves to save the sinners in the mining camp where he settles. *Tools of Providence* came next, followed by *Cash Parrish's Pal* and *The Ruse.* The latter is a tightly constructed film and contains some fast action in its final scenes. Shot in Edendale, north of Los Angeles, *The Ruse* cost $1,863 and shows that Hart had learned much about effective camera placement and how to build a story to a stirring climax.

Pinto Ben, which started shooting on April 21, cast Fritz in the title role. Based on a poem by Hart, which was first published in the *New York Morning Telegraph* and reprinted many times afterward, the story is a requiem to a cow pony who sacrifices himself to save his rider from a trampling herd. *Pinto Ben* includes some interesting scenes of a cattle range during a roundup and ends with the head of the dying pony, his legs broken, resting in Hart's lap. Later Bill said, "The little horse stole the picture from me."

Keno Bates, Liar and *A Knight of the Trails,* both filmed in May 1915, ended Hart's work for the New York Motion Picture Company. By the time Ince and the cowboy star left the company, Hart's reputation with the public and most critics was secure. "Bill Hart represents that rare combination of lion and lamb," the *Movie Magazine* reported in 1915. "In the melee he is the lion; after it, the lamb." Most reviewers conceded that the actor-director brought a unique quality to Western films. Men and particularly young boys loved his movies. Hart learned how truly popular he was when he attended an exhibitors' convention in San Francisco in July 1915 and drew more attention than most of his celebrated colleagues at the affair.

In Hollywood the reaction to Hart as a person was mixed. For Ann Little, a tireless silent movie actress of American Indian descent, Bill Hart was a typical westerner. "He had a sense of integrity [and] forthrightness," said Little. "With him everything was on the up and up. He was the man least like an actor I ever knew." Gertrude Gordon, writing for *Motion Picture Magazine* in 1916, said that talking to Hart for an hour was "like turning the pages of a Bret Harte story or leafing through a series of Frederic Remington pictures." Others found the actor stuffy, mannered, and constantly "on." Frances Marion, one of Hollywood's most respected scenario writers, thought Hart "looked so much like a horse you were sure he whinnied instead of talked."

In truth Bill Hart was such a loner that few people, even supposedly close friends, got to know him intimately. A formal person, courtly in the presence of women, Hart exhibited a strong sense of honor and much the same inscrutable expression that he wore in his movies. He seemed businesslike, assured in his work, yet consistently guarded. Statements of emotion gushed from the actor with such force that they sounded affected, even when he was voicing his most heartfelt sentiments, as if he were reciting lines from an old melodrama.

An advertisement in *Image* around 1915 referred to Hart as "The Face of a Thousand Emotions," but his acting was far from multidimensional. He continued to rely on classic postures he had learned on the stage. Hart was best at showing dark emotions, such as hatred, fury, or melancholy, and was least convincing when suggesting joy, tenderness, or personal grief. The same was true in his personal life.

In his memoirs the star bragged about his acceptance at Inceville and the respect he commanded from cohorts there. "All the actors and actresses in camp liked to work in my pictures," he said. "When working with other directors, they would often spend their spare time on our set." But it is more likely that Hart was an anomaly to the picture people, especially to the cowboys who drifted into Hollywood with ranching experience. When they heard Hart dilate on being "part of the West" and how the West was in his blood, many of the former ranch hands chortled behind the actor's back. Hollywood columnist Adela Rogers St. Johns insisted that William S. Hart never failed to use a double in risky action, was "scared to death of horses," and "just never was the Real Thing."

Yet Hart succeeded in molding a more honest western hero than what had appeared in dime novels, the Wild West shows, and on the screens of countless nickelodeons. His were the first of the so-called adult Westerns. Within a year and a half after making his motion picture debut, Hart's squint-eyed look and crouching pose behind drawn six-shooters had become familiar to most American movie fans and would soon be known throughout the world. Although he strove for verisimilitude in his Westerns, Hart's view of the frontier was filtered through reverential eyes and his selective memory of the upper Midwest. From the lore of the frontier he fashioned colorful examples of the western bad men for the silent screen, imbued them with a moral conscience that suited the times, flavored them with his austere personality, and gave an eager public reflections of a heroic past that thickened into the nation's creation saga.

Making Movies for Triangle

Late in the spring of 1915 Thomas Ince joined forces with Harry Aitken, the energetic promoter of Mutual, Mack Sennett, who in 1912 began Keystone Film Company, maker of the Keystone Cop comedies, and D. W. Griffith, the ingenious director of the recently released epic *The Birth of a Nation*, to form Triangle Film Corporation. The new company absorbed the New York Motion Picture Company, Keystone, and Reliance-Majestic and was expressly geared to manufacture and distribute feature-length films. The Knickerbocker Theater, one of Manhattan's principal movie houses, was leased and refurbished to serve as Triangle's showcase theater. A carriage entrance to accommodate wealthy patrons was added to the theater, and the admission charge was boosted to two dollars.

By 1915 actors from Broadway were pouring into Hollywood to work in films, attracted by the unprecedented wages movie companies were offering. Douglas Fairbanks, Mary Pickford, Lillian Gish, Eddie Foy, Dustin Farnum, Orrin Johnson, Billie Burke, Joe Weber, Lew Fields, and DeWolf Hopper were but a few of the newcomers to motion pictures from the New York stage. "It rained stars like hailstones," William S. Hart remembered, "and like hailstones, they melted under the California sun." Yet a few of them survived to become screen legends.

Hart, still working under the original contract he had negotiated with Ince, would make seventeen pictures for Triangle, all of them five-reel features. His salary, as both actor and director, stayed at $125 a week, and the trivial sum soon became a source of prolonged bickering between the former friends. Hart knew that DeWolf Hopper was receiving $1,800 a week just for acting and that Douglas Fairbanks was drawing $2,200. Even when Ince doubled Hart's fee to $250 a week, it was small compensation for an emerging star with a substantial box office draw.

The cowboy actor's first movie for Triangle, made between May 27 and July 2, 1915, was *The Disciple*, which had a budget of $8,300. Hart played a tough frontier preacher in the picture, one who splits with God when his wife runs off with the local saloon keeper. *The Disciple*, filmed at Inceville, was Hart's most complex story to date—full of flawed characters, rich in atmosphere, and adroitly photographed by Joseph August, Hart's chief cameraman for the next six years and later John Ford's cinematographer on *The Informer* and *They Were Expendable*. Hart's minister in *The Disciple* is also a loving father, a forgiving husband, and a man of action. Despite his powerful stares, the star's acting is more restrained than previously, and the film contains poignant moments and dramatic tension. The preacher's reaching out to God at the end and his vision of Christ's crucifixion as he contemplates killing his wife's seducer reveal the movie's debt to melodrama, although much of it, including some excellent storm scenes, was intelligently directed by Hart. The director's eye for detail—for instance, having pigs wander through the main street of the western town—gave the film color and merit. "*The Disciple* is a strong, stirring exposition of primitive human emotions," the *New York Dramatic Mirror* reported when the movie opened in October, "and though it is only another drama written along the lines of the eternal triangle, still this much used theme seems to acquire new strength when given the rough setting of the great uncouth West."

Hart delighted in working exclusively on features with augmented budgets under the Triangle banner. The day after he finished *The Disciple* he began filming *Between Men*, which had a two-month shooting schedule and a budget of more than $19,000. House Peters took the part of the heavy in the picture, and toward the end he and Bill were to tangle in a ferocious fight. Just before the camera was to roll, House refused to do the fight, fearing that he might wind up with a bloody nose or a black eye. "I told him that I had been in about eighty fights on that lot and had never been hurt," Hart said, but the reluctant Peters held firm. Hart, who was also directing, pointed out that they had to do the fight or the movie's plot was ruined. Peters finally agreed to a furniture fight, in which the actors threw things at one another, smashed chairs, and pulled down draperies but never struck a blow or touched one another except in the final clinch. Cameraman Joe August managed to get the necessary action, but the cowboys in the camp, who loved watching a good fight, walked away from the set disgusted that they had been cheated out of seeing a brawl. The script called for Hart's character to win the fight until the villain picked up a bronze vase and smashed it over the hero's head. The prop was supposed to be made of wax, but the vase turned out to be cement. When Peters brought it down on Hart's noggin, he nearly knocked him out. A doctor was called, and several stitches had to be taken in the top of Hart's head.

When *Between Men* was released, the *New York Dramatic Mirror* said the picture "was most elaborately staged, containing some of the best interior photography that has been shown on the screen." Hart's acting had become quieter, and he seemed to have learned that effective movie acting comes mainly from the eyes and subtle changes in expression.

Hart also seemed to be getting a better grasp on directing. *Hell's Hinges*, which he began on September 4, 1915, demonstrates an able handling of crowds, and the burning of a western town, achieved mostly with smoke pots, is superbly executed. *Hell's Hinges* is a William S. Hart classic that holds up despite the evangelistic fervor of such titles as "One Who Is Evil, Looking for the First Time on That Which Is Good."

In the cast of *Hell's Hinges*, as fifteen-dollar-a-week extras, were two future stars of the silent screen, John Gilbert and Jean Hersholt. Actors with no strong marquee value made between thirty and forty dollars a week at Triangle, and ordinary cowboys working at Inceville earned five dollars a week plus board, although top hands received six or eight dollars and their foreman as much as ten.

In *Hell's Hinges*, as in several of Hart's movies, there are strong displays of brother-sister love, which perhaps reflect his symbiotic relationship with Mary Ellen. Night after night his sister accompanied him to Hoffman's Cafe, where they sat at a round table and dined with a group of film people that included Mack Sennett, George Siegmann (a white actor who played the black politician in *The Birth of a Nation*), and Mrs. Talmadge and her actress daughters, Norma, Constance, and Natalie. The friends talked movies, gossiped, and occasionally quibbled. Tall, blond Mary Ellen had done some writing, had published short stories, and took care of her brother's mail, but on social occasions she was content at Bill's side.

Reviewers had begun suggesting that Hart had allowed himself to be trapped in a predictable role that was becoming a bore. *Moving Picture World*, on February 19, 1916, warned that the actor was failing to win a large percentage of eastern movie audiences by his persistent repetition of the "western badman reformed through the sweet and humanizing influence of a pure-minded girl." The critic seemed confident that Hart was a good enough actor to explore other parts and advised him to expand his popularity by demonstrating a fuller range of his skill.

For *The Aryan*, which went before Triangle's cameras in November 1915, Gardner Sullivan created a central character for Hart that was "hard-as-flint." Hart felt that there was no motive for the man's hardness and argued that the part should be softened when the tough guy confronted the innocence of a little girl. Through the years Hart expressed ambivalent feelings about the picture. In his autobiography he referred to *The Aryan* as "a gripping story" and "one of the best Westerns ever made." Yet later, in his retirement years, he claimed that Steve Denton, his role in *The Aryan*, was the most disagreeable part he ever played. "It was hard for me to really feel it," the actor said. "It is difficult to put all one's decent instincts aside and live and think as such a despicable character must have done." Denton was, in Hart's words, "a white man who, forswearing his race, makes outlaw Mexicans his comrades and allows white women to be attacked by them." Hart said that he had to imagine all the terrible wrongs he had ever experienced to make the character believable.

Mexicans repeatedly came off as nefarious in Hart's movies. Recent border skirmishes, the search for Pancho Villa by American troops in Mexico, racist attitudes in California and the Southwest, and the basic Aryanism of screenwriter Gardner Sullivan combined to produce portraits of Mexicans as deceitful, untrustworthy, lustful, and vicious. White villains were sometimes described in Sullivan's titles as having the "oily craftiness of a Mexican," and renegades who sold out Anglo-Saxon interests to Mexicans were viewed as particularly contemptible.

The Triangle Film Corporation had purchased a large tract of land in Culver City and begun construction on a new studio there, which would later become the David O. Selznick Studio. By late 1915 the flooring for Triangle's first stage at the new location had been laid, and Hart sometimes used those facilities when shooting interiors. Inceville, which continued to be a back lot until 1922, eventually became known as Hartville, since most of Triangle's production activity had been transferred to Culver City by then, leaving the camp on the coast to be used mostly for filming Westerns.

In an effort to diversify his roles, Hart began filming *The Primal Lure* early in December 1915. Set in Canada, the picture had Bill playing a Scottish manager of Fort LuCerne, an outpost of the Hudson Bay Company. The production crew spent Christmas that year at Felton, California, where the company shot the trapper story among the giant redwoods. When the movie was released, critics admired the scenic locations, but most found its story ineffective. Diehard fans complained that the picture was a disappointment and urged Bill to stick with his customary good bad guy roles.

When Hart returned to Inceville in January, Ince asked him to undertake the making of two stories simultaneously: *The Apostle of Vengeance* and *The Captive God*. Bill would star in both but direct only the first. In *The Apostle of Vengeance* he was cast as a mountaineer clergyman, whereas in *The Captive God* he played an Aztec chieftain. Bill claimed that his costume in the latter consisted of "half a pint of Bole Armenia Mixture and two feathers." Since the weather that winter was some of the coldest southern California had experienced, all of the actors in the Aztec epic nearly froze. The crew went to San Diego to photograph the Indian cliff dwellings at the Exposition grounds there, and since the railroad between Los Angeles and San Diego had washed out, they had to travel down the coast on an ocean steamer.

With a budget of $50,000, *The Captive God* required weeks of research and months of preparation to re-create Aztec carvings, temples, and villages as accurately as possible. Triangle's pressbook for the movie proposed that exhibitors promote the film by creating eye-catching displays. "It will not be hard to obtain a figure of an Indian god," the pressbook told theater operators. "Anything of the ugly, prehistoric type will do, and it will be a big hit in the lobby." With Hart's popularity soaring and exhibitors becoming more savvy about mass marketing, both *The Captive God* and *The Apostle of Vengeance* were box office successes.

In *The Dawn Maker*, shot in April 1916, Bill tried another change of pace by playing an idealistic half-breed Indian, in love with a white girl and determined to build schools for the children of his tribe. Hart wore a long black wig for the part and welcomed a chance to give a sympathetic portrayal of a people close to his heart. He was still earning a mere $250 a week, but he was happy making movies that encapsulated his deeply felt beliefs. "When I thought of my freedom," he said, "and looked at those hills of throbbing hearts, full of the life of my boyhood, I was content, even if I failed to go higher. . . . I had looked and dreamed honestly. If this mimic world of toil where I was earning a living and reproducing days that were dear to me was to be the top of my mountain, I was content."

Although Hart generally disliked doing tricks and stunts in his pictures and claimed that such antics usually looked artificial, he gloried in finding new ways to demonstrate Fritz's ability. The star was forever fearful that Fritz might get hurt, but he was delighted when he discovered that Fritz could jump through a window with no more than a slight cut on the nose and no injury to the rider. Bill endowed the pinto with almost human characteristics and talked about him as if he were a costar.

Increasingly Hart's primary affection was directed toward animals. When Mack died, Bill took the bulldog to Inceville and buried him in an oak box on a mountaintop overlooking the sea. Mack was quickly replaced by an English bulldog named Congo. Yet seven years later, Bill dug up Mack's remains and transferred them to his ranch outside Newhall, north of Los Angeles.

Despite sporadic blasts from eastern critics, Western movies regained their popular appeal in the years immediately before World War I and held the public's interest for decades afterward, particularly in the small towns and rural areas of the South, Midwest, and West. Westerns offered model subject matter for silent pictures, since they were action-packed, picturesque, and depicted the values that provincial communities, laboring classes, and rugged individualists admired. Hart's Westerns imagined an East full of greed, manipulation, social maladjustment, and humiliation, whereas the West was portrayed as a nirvana, a place conducive to moral and spiritual growth.

Despite Hart's forays into other genres, Westerns would remain his principal venue. On April 29, 1916, he began work on *The Return of Draw Egan*, in which he played the head of an outlaw band who ends up sheriff of Yellow Dog, a town where the bad element has taken control. Egan, under an assumed name, cleans up the town and falls in love with a chaste young woman—the "kind of a girl he had heard of but never believed to exist," according to a title. Fifty-one at the time, Hart looked twice the age of Margery Wilson, his leading lady, and appeared more comfortable giving her a gentle caress rather than anything resembling a passionate kiss. But *The Return of Draw Egan* is consummate William S. Hart, highlighted by exciting shots of fast riding through canyons and over mountains as the posse pursues the bandits, lively saloon scenes with dancing and brawling, and Hart's towering presence.

Draw Egan opened at the Rialto Theater in New York on October 1, 1916, to favorable reviews. The picture was "better than most films of its type," the *New York Times* reported, "because it tells a reasonable story. . . . Hart does this Bret Harte sort of thing so well that he must begin to fear he will spend the rest of his life in chaps and a saddle. He can draw a gun with the best road agents of fiction now, can roll a cigarette with one hand and strike a match on his nails with the nonchalance of Will Rogers."

The cowboy star had received tempting offers from other movie companies, but he remained loyal to Thomas Ince. Robert Kane, representing Paralta Pictures, proposed a contract that would have paid Hart $5,000 a week, with a Stutz car as a bonus, and Joseph M. Schenck, later head of Twentieth Century-Fox, made the actor a lucrative offer. Yet Hart turned them both down. "I did not want to change," he said. "The camp was home; . . . it was a sort of little kingdom to me."

Bill did point out to Ince the injustice of his making only $250 a week when other performers of equal or less reputation were earning far more. Ince appeared hurt when Bill voiced concern over money matters and assured his friend that Triangle would increase his salary as soon as the company could afford it. "I was working sixteen to eighteen hours every day," Hart said. "In addition, once we worked seven straight Sundays. My food was grabbed and gulped, not eaten. All my life I have needed eight hours sleep and could do nicely with ten. I averaged six."

The strain between Ince and Hart quickly deepened. Hart felt slighted when Ince returned from a trip to New York and failed to come out to Inceville for a talk about his qualms regarding salary. After waiting a couple of weeks, Hart went to Culver City to shoot interior scenes, and Ince visited the set. The producer apologized for the delay in their discussion of money and promised that Hart's salary would be raised to $1,000 a week, yet he dated the contract ahead three or four weeks. The actor was grateful for the increase, yet still felt demeaned and exploited.

Hart made five more pictures before the end of 1916: *The Patriot*, a story of American troops on the Rio Grande, inspired by the current crisis with Mexico and shot on the border near Mexicali; *The Devil's Double*, in which Hart played another bad man, with scenes shot in the Mojave Desert; *Truthful Tulliver*, which had Hart cast as a western newspaperman; *The Gunfighter*, with Hart again playing the leader of a band of outlaws; and *The Square Deal Man*, which found the star as the owner of a western gambling den but switching to ranching in an effort to free himself from a disreputable life. Although Hart's formula was wearing thin with some critics, almost all agreed that his films afforded mass audiences the kind of entertainment they wanted. "No actor before the screen has been able to give as sincere and true a touch to the Westerner as Hart," the *New York Press* said in 1916. "He rides in a manner indigenous to the soil, he shoots with the real knack, and he acts with that sense of artistry that hides the action."

By 1916 the Hollywood publicity machinery described Hart as a legitimate son of the West. "Now he is portraying roles in which he simply lives the ideas he has had for years, working out his own characterizations of Western men," Gertrude Gordon wrote in *Motion Picture Magazine*. "His eyes have a trick of suddenly narrowing as he talks, a typical Western characteristic, gained from long days of looking over the vast reaches of prairie in his beloved, open range country." Some wags claimed that Hart had lived for a number of years during his youth among the Sioux. His encounter with Al Jennings and his friendship with Charles M. Russell were publicized. Hollywood columnists maintained that the actor's plots came from stories he had heard old-timers tell during his boyhood on the frontier. Acquaintances noted that he even began to talk to the press in the vernacular of the West rather than the language of a Shakespearean actor.

An English journalist from *Pictures and Picturegoer* spent a day with Hart's unit in the Mojave Desert and reported: "As many as two to three hundred people accompany Mr. Hart on his location trips and pitch their camp for a week or a fortnight. . . . Everybody bunks in tents, and a chuck-wagon is taken along to serve as a kind of perambulating cafeteria." The Englishman noticed that plenty of beef, beans, and potatoes were served to the film crew and that a fraternal spirit existed among its workers. During the day, there were demonstrations of fancy roping, riding, boxing, and wrestling, and at night the men played poker or shot craps around a campfire.

Fans eager to recover their own memories of frontier times were enthralled by Hart's screen re-creations. His great stone face became a symbol of manliness, and according to an account from Tacoma,

Washington, women saw the cowboy star as a "perfectly adorable bad man." Hart "didn't have to speak," said Louella Parsons, "he had only to be the grim silent type. He could ride with the best of them over the purple sage." The blend of religious sentiment and romantic adventure in Hart's pictures soothed an anxiety-ridden nation as America sought to stay out of World War I during 1915 and 1916.

Future writer Jean Dalrymple went to the movies every Saturday afternoon as a child at a theater on 181st Street in New York. "I was in love with Bill Hart," Dalrymple said. "My father had given me a typewriter on my birthday, because I was writing scenarios. I sold one when I was about twelve to Bill Hart, my great love." Hart sent the girl fifty dollars for her script, complimenting her on her knack and saying that he intended to use one of her scenes in a movie.

In 1917 the Cowboys' Reunion Association in Las Vegas, New Mexico, voted William S. Hart and Dustin Farnum the most popular cowboys in the world. In France Hart came to be known as "Rio Jim," and throughout Europe his image on the screen helped shape the myth of the American West and establish the cowboy as a lasting hero. Children in Spain hid behind theater seats and shot imaginary pistols at the screen in imitation of Hart's stance.

In his private life Bill Hart was far from the adventurer or the racy O. Henry–type character he portrayed in the movies. Self-educated though he was, Bill had become an avid reader, a lover of the arts, and a man of exalted notions. Away on location, he sometimes went nightclubbing with his crew, but in Los Angeles he was a stay-at-home. He did not consider himself a lady's man but admitted to being a sentimentalist where women were concerned. "The chief reason for my success was my mother," he said. "I went to her with my troubles and came to her for advice." He could be stubborn, hated to be swindled, had a persecution complex, and was loath to forgive when he felt slighted, which was often.

By the spring of 1917 Hart had grown so dissatisfied with his arrangement with Triangle that he was prepared to do battle. He made three more pictures for the company between January and early May of that year, but by March 22 he had begun negotiating with Adolph Zukor, who was prepared to pay him $4,000 a week if he signed a contract with Famous Players. "I was flabbergasted!" Hart said. "Here was an offer that was reliable." Triangle responded with a counteroffer, mentioning $6,000 or $7,000 a week for Bill's services. "I had to watch where I put my feet," Hart said. "I was not sure I was awake!" He had dinner with Harry Aitken and a new vice president of Triangle at the Beverly Hills Hotel, and Aitken surprised the actor by saying, "Well, Hart, how about nine thousand, and we'll settle right now." The next morning Hart said that he would sign with Triangle for $10,000 a week, and four days later he did, since Zukor would go no higher than $6,000 a week.

Then Triangle began to renege, asking Hart to postpone his increased salary for three or four weeks. Bill made *The Desert Man* for the company, his first association with Lambert Hillyer, who wrote the screenplay; later Hillyer would direct Hart in some of his best work. When *The Desert Man* was finished, Triangle's executives requested four more weeks' grace, promising to start Bill's bigger salary as soon as he finished one more picture. Hart agreed to the postponement on one condition—that the company give him Fritz. Bill calculated that because of the delay in getting his salary raised Fritz cost him $42,500.

Earlier Ince had refused to sell Fritz to Hart, aware that the horse helped keep the star from defecting to a rival company. Ince never liked Fritz and thought that Hart's six-foot-two-inch frame looked ridiculous astride the small pony. Adolph Zukor remembered that "Bill's feet almost touched the ground" when he rode the little pinto, and Zukor admitted that there was criticism of "so big a man on so little a horse." Some of the Hollywood cowboys said that Hart preferred riding the pony because he was afraid of horses, but the mawkish star responded that a westerner's love for his horse amounted "to a religion."

Wolf Lowry went into production at Triangle as winter was ending in 1917, with Hart directing and playing the title role. "*Wolf Lowry* has more tragic force than most of its kind," *Moving Picture World* reported when the movie was released in June 1917. The reviewer saw Hart's character as relying "largely upon brute strength for dominance of men and situations, a survival of the cave man, with a submerged strain of tenderness for womankind." With the United States at war with Germany, the critic reflected current attitudes by saying that Hart gave "expression to the frontier bully," who showed "a German-like faith in the rule of force."

Bill made one more picture for Triangle, *The Cold Deck*, completed on May 5, 1917, at a cost of $22,000. The story had come to Hart on two sheets of note paper, written in longhand. He and writer Jack Hawkes expanded the sketch to feature length in two days, and the scenario was rushed into production. *The Cold Deck*'s plot had some weak places, but the picture offered sufficient action mixed with pathos to satisfy most Western movie fans.

When Triangle's management asked for another delay before starting Bill's promised salary increase, the star refused. Instead he agreed to make a five-week, coast-to-coast tour to promote his pictures and sell bonds during the First Liberty Loan Drive. Hart traveled east on a special train and appeared in thirty-four cities in thirty-one days. "At Needles, California, the hand-shaking ovations started and never stopped until I reached home," Hart recalled. At Raton, New Mexico, a boisterous stream of cowboys ran through the train after midnight looking for Hart, to the disgust of sleeping passengers. In Dodge City, Kansas, what seemed like the community's entire population turned out to welcome the star. "Every citizen who owned one had a forty-five belt full of lead on his hip," Hart said. "The good priest of the town unstrapped his hardware and presented it to me in the name of the citizens of Dodge City." Hart claimed that the gun was one taken from the body of the last outlaw shot on Dodge's Front Street. In Kansas City Hart made twenty speeches in three hours, then boarded the train for St. Louis, where he led a parade and talked in various parks and public squares on horseback.

The tour marked the first time Hart had been away from Hollywood in three years, and the pace was grueling. He spoke in depots, hotels, and theaters and many times appeared in two cities on the same day. "I was almost tumbling over for want of sleep," the actor said, but he was astounded by the tributes fans paid him. A midwestern lady, past ninety, waited for the cowboy star for hours, and when a car drove up with Hart inside, she asked to kiss his hand.

Hart hugged the woman and kissed her cheek before escorting her into the theater. At every stop he shook hands with hundreds of people, and streets were crowded wherever he went.

In front of a theater in the Bronx, an assembled throng tore the top off the limousine in which Hart was riding. Film exhibitor Marcus Loew presented the actor with a large silver cup at one of the theaters in Manhattan, and Hart rode in a parade with musical comedy star Lillian Russell. When the parade broke up, the crowd was so rowdy that soldiers had to be called out to restore order. "I was thrown about like a cork," Hart said.

Ince was in New York at the time Hart made his appearances there, and when the two met, Hart discovered that Triangle was trying to force Ince out of the partnership. Hart had always yielded before the force of Ince's personality, but he had come to realize how shrewd and opportunistic his old friend had grown. After a stall of more than ten weeks on his salary increase, Bill was angry enough to argue when Tom offered justifications for the delay. "I explained briefly that I had been in pictures three years," Hart said, "and that I had nothing to show for my work, outside of my popularity." At fifty-two, time was running out if he ever hoped to become rich.

Ince placated his unhappy star for an hour, then handed him a document to sign. So persuasive was Tom's charm that Bill signed the agreement, although he later claimed that he had no idea what he was signing. The bond tour continued with Hart making fifteen to twenty speeches a day to riotous acclaim. After stops in Boston, New Haven, Philadelphia, Baltimore, and Wilmington, the special train started west.

Bill spent three days in Chicago, during which he sat next to Louella Parsons at a banquet where the waiters all dressed as cowboys. Parsons was kind to the Western star in her newspaper article, and the two got along so well that she invited Bill to her home. "By this time I had a small child," Parsons said. "There was great excitement in the neighborhood: William S. Hart, the famous cowboy, was coming. . . . My daughter trooped in with all the children, and there were many in the neighborhood." Hart's friendship with the newspaper woman lasted until his death, although Parsons later remembered him as "the biggest ham in the world" and said that "he was an actor off and on the screen."

On the morning of his third day in Chicago, Hart received two telegrams—one from Ince, the other from Harry Aitken. Both men were en route to Chicago from New York by train and wanted to see him. Aitken arrived first and informed Hart that Ince was severing his connection with Triangle but that Hart's big salary would commence as soon as the star returned to California. Aitken promised Hart that he would be in complete control of his pictures if he stayed with Triangle. Hart insisted that should Ince be forced out of the company, he would have the right to quit, since he felt that his first obligation was to Ince.

At Spokane, Washington, on June 3, Hart was greeted at the depot by a crowd of shrieking girls who had pushed past the station's gateman. The smiling actor emerged from the train and was instantly surrounded by a mob of gushing females. Hart told the press, "I am enjoying this trip immensely, and I like the experience of meeting people who are interested enough to want to meet me." In Portland, Oregon, the actor strolled into the Thornton Hotel decked out in cowboy regalia. "He is quiet and reflective," a local newspaper reported, "and he talks of ideals and visions rather than his thrillers. . . . He talks slowly and leaves the impression that he takes life seriously."

Hart never made mention of any matrimonial plans and disavowed that he had love-making intentions. He referred to himself in speeches as "not a freak of any kind—just a good Indian of white parentage." He told fans that acting the life of the West kept him young and said that motion pictures, although still in their infancy, had established themselves to such a degree that spoken drama would never again pose a threat to their popularity.

In San Francisco the press referred to the star as "the idol of all true Americans." While he was in the Golden Gate City, Hart heard from Ince in New York, and in a dictatorial manner Ince told the actor to stay in San Francisco until he heard from him again. "It was an order," Hart said, "but when I resented it, [Ince] quickly switched to pleading and I quickly forgave him." Over the producer's protests Hart kept to his schedule and returned to Los Angeles.

Hart soon uncovered the source of Ince's alarm. "All of the principal producers and distributors had their representatives in Los Angeles to see me," Hart said. "I could not only write my own ticket, I could write as many tickets as I wanted to write." Adolph Zukor and Samuel Goldwyn were only two of the studio executives eager to do business with Hart, and no offer made was for less than $10,000 a week. Suddenly Bill realized that he had reached a level of stardom equal to Charlie Chaplin, Mary Pickford, and Douglas Fairbanks.

Ince called Hart daily from New York begging for his continued allegiance. Meanwhile Triangle representatives came to Hart with weekly checks in the amount he had been promised in March. Since Ince had split with Triangle, Hart had sent in his resignation as well, but the company continued to tempt him with money, which he refused to accept. For four weeks the star went without salary. "Friendship was costing me dearly," Hart said.

On June 29, 1917, Ince signed a contract with Artcraft, part of Zukor's aggregate that operated as an arm of Famous Players. Ince agreed to deliver Hart to Artcraft within thirty days. Under the agreement that Ince negotiated, the cowboy star would make sixteen pictures for Zukor's company with a guarantee of $150,000 for each one, plus a percentage of the profits, which Hart and Ince would share. "I felt a bit hurt at Tom going in for wholesale producing," Hart said. "I had a talk with Tom and told him I wanted to work by myself." It was stipulated that Hart would have his own production company within the Zukor empire, and the first meeting of William S. Hart Productions took place on July 14, 1917.

Soon Triangle flooded the market with Hart's old pictures, some of them released under several different titles, which the public found confusing. Two-reelers were built up to five, and one five-reeler, released as *A Lion of the Hills*, was created wholly from discarded film shot during earlier productions. "I never knew who was responsible for this picture," Hart said, "nor did I ever work in any such picture." He was furious when he started getting letters from fans all over the country, many of them children, complaining that they had gone to see one of his movies only to discover that they had seen it before under another name. "I went after the offenders," said Hart, "and while it cost me a great deal of money, my attorneys were influential in getting an order from the Federal Trade Commission that does away with this practice."

By the time William S. Hart began making movies for Artcraft, director John Ford had entered the Western field at Universal with Harry Carey as his star. Another New Yorker but fourteen years younger than Hart, Carey was a more natural actor, and his early Western character, Cheyenne Harry, dressed in an old flannel shirt and patched overalls, looked like a working cowhand. Cheyenne Harry was as much rogue as hero. Tom Mix, who began making Westerns in 1911, was also gaining in popularity and in the 1920s would surpass Hart as a box office attraction. Mix had worked at the 101 Ranch in Oklahoma, was a better horseman than Bill, and used his roping skills and boyish personality to make Westerns that were full of thrills and adventure. A limited actor, Mix became famous for flashy dress, daredevil stunts, and good-natured pranks. Unlike Hart, he took neither himself nor the West seriously, but Mix won audiences with his undiluted showmanship.

Despite growing competition, in 1917 William S. Hart stood as the undisputed superstar of silent Westerns, hailed for his determination to impart realism to the screen. Convinced that the public shared his love for the West and that there was "nothing on earth as humanly appealing as the American cowboy," Hart continued to give audiences images of frontier life that blended action, sentimentality, and melodrama with his unique slant on Victorian morality. For another decade the star would represent the virile, taciturn Western hero and a lethal moral force to mass audiences. "If motion pictures never did any more than perpetuate some of the things in our American life that are being lost in the dust of time," Hart said, "they would be worth their weight in gold."

Despite his arcane theatrics, Hart brought stature to Western movies, filled them with ramshackle frontier towns, authentic trappings, and a sense of dirt and desert heat and created a mood of romantic realism comparable to what Charles M. Russell and Frederic Remington achieved in paintings. "I believe in the picture that tells a real story," Hart said. "I mean by that a story of human beings . . .

with all the frailties, depths and shallows, sympathies, desires, errors, and good qualities that are so inextricably mixed in most of us."

In 1918 the Buffalo, New York, *Commercial* hailed Hart as the "Buffalo Bill of the film world." Nearly four and a half decades later, respected film historians George N. Fenin and William K. Everson dedicated their history of Western movies to Hart, maintaining that he was "the finest Western star and director of them all, and the best friend the West ever had." Beyond question Hart involved himself with his productions far more actively than Broncho Billy Anderson or Tom Mix did theirs, for he served as actor, often director, and sometimes story writer.

With much of his finest work behind him, Hart entered Hollywood's celebrated ranks by joining Adolph Zukor's powerful dominion. Under the terms Ince had worked out with Famous Players, the cowboy star would have his own office, his own production staff, a highly favorable financial arrangement, and the benefits of Zukor's publicity machinery and comprehensive distribution system. While Hart got along well with Zukor, he and Ince argued incessantly from the time his first picture for Artcraft went before the cameras. The enmity that had been building between the two for months finally broke their friendship and ended in a venomous lawsuit. Always a loner, Hart seemed to grow increasingly unhappy as his career progressed, despite his enormous popularity. He felt betrayed, frequently persecuted, and chose to recoil into the days when, he maintained, cowboys were loyal and Indians pure and noble. The West, Bill said in retirement, has been "my hobby and more—almost my life itself for many years. I love it. I love the people who make it or have made it what it is. I love its traditions and its codes, its freedom, unconventionality, and its bigness." As the film industry consolidated and his bitterness grew once he was shut out by corporate powers, Hart's personality became more negative and his views were increasingly colored by a nostalgia for the bygone frontier. When he could no longer re-create the old West on film, he did so in his imagination from the solitude of Horseshoe Ranch, his private sanctuary.

WILLIAM HART

854 TRIANGLE-FILM

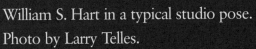

William S. Hart in a typical studio pose.
Photo by Larry Telles.

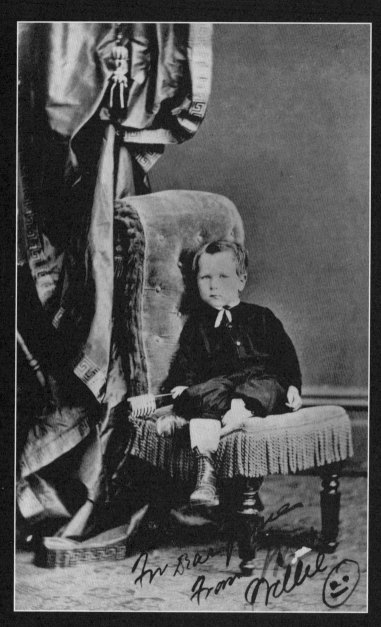

Hart as a child, inscribed to Jane Novak.
Courtesy of Mickell Seltzer.

Producer Thomas H. Ince at the time of his association with Hart.
Courtesy of the Academy of Motion Picture Arts and Sciences.

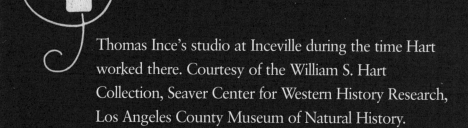

Thomas Ince's studio at Inceville during the time Hart
worked there. Courtesy of the William S. Hart
Collection, Seaver Center for Western History Research,
Los Angeles County Museum of Natural History.

Hart with actress Mary Pickford. Courtesy of the William S. Hart
Collection, Seaver Center for Western History Research,
Los Angeles County Museum of Natural History.

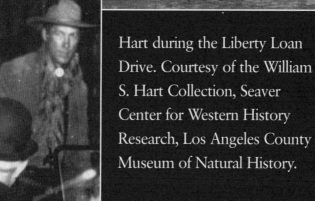

Hart during the Liberty Loan
Drive. Courtesy of the William
S. Hart Collection, Seaver
Center for Western History
Research, Los Angeles County
Museum of Natural History.

Hart with silent film actress Ann Little. Courtesy of the William S.
Hart Collection, Seaver Center for Western History Research,
Los Angeles County Museum of Natural History.

 Hart and his horse Fritz,
inscribed "For Our Jane,
From Fritz and Bill Hart." Courtesy of Mickell Seltzer.

Hart and his future wife, Winifred Westover, in
John Petticoats. Courtesy of the William S. Hart
Collection, Seaver Center for Western History
Research, Los Angeles County Museum of Natural History.

Hart in *Wagon Tracks*. Courtesy of the William S. Hart
Collection, Seaver Center for Western History Research,
Los Angeles County Museum of Natural History.

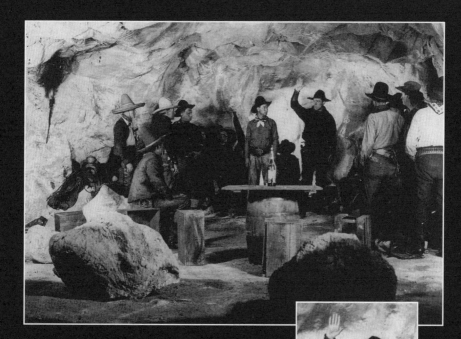

Hart, as Black Deering, voting not to commit another robbery in *The Toll Gate*. Courtesy of the William S. Hart Collection, Seaver Center for Western History Research, Los Angeles County Museum of Natural History.

Hart in typical studio poses, 1921.
Photos by Larry Telles.

Bill Hart
and his famous
Pinto Pony

To My Old Friends, The Screen Public:

Dear Folks:

AFTER two years absence, I'm back in motion pictures and mighty glad to be back too. I want you folks to know how much I've missed you all and how happy I am that we're to be together from now on.

My heart is all set on having you agree with me that this new picture of mine, "Wild Bill Hickok," is the best film in which I have ever appeared. I've spent two years writing and polishing this story and digging into the history books to get things straight.

"Wild Bill," you know, was a real man, the daggonedest, most lovable two-gun man that ever lived. Back in the days when the West was young and wild, "Wild Bill" fought and loved and adventured with such famous frontiersmen as Bat Masterson and Wyatt Earp. Calamity Jane, the most notorious woman of the day, was his friend. He was a personal friend of General Sherman and General Custer, and the proudest moment of his life was when he shook hands with Abe Lincoln. All that is in my picture.

The scene of "Wild Bill Hickok" is Dodge City, Kansas, "the toughest town west of the Mississippi" at the time of my story. Lots of action is what you folks want, I figure, and there's plenty in this picture. One of the fight scenes is the greatest ever, in my belief. And there's a love story too. And a big part in the story for my Pinto Pony, who is fat and sassy as ever, thank you.

William S. Hart

ADOLPH ZUKOR PRESENTS

WILLIAM S. HART
IN
"Wild Bill Hickok"

By WILLIAM S. HART   Directed by CLIFF SMITH
Scenario by J. G. HAWKS   A William S. Hart Production

Country of Origin
U. S. A.   *A Paramount Picture*

Hart's letter, "To My Old Friends, The Screen Public," 1923.

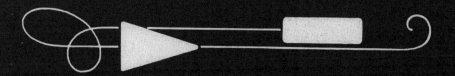

The scene of "Wild Bill Hickok" is Dodge City, Kansas, "the toughest town west of the Mississippi" at the time of my story. Lots of action is what you folks want, I figure, and there's plenty in this picture. One of the fight scenes is the greatest ever, in my belief. And there's a love story too. And a big part in the story for my Pinto Pony, who is fat and sassy as ever, thank you.

William S. Hart

William S. Hart

Ljunggrens Konstförlag, Stockholm.
N:o 278

Hart in a typical studio pose, 1923.
Photo by Larry Telles.

Hart, Jane Novak, and artist James
Montgomery Flagg at a rodeo in
Saugus. Courtesy of Mickell Seltzer.

William Hart

1102
FÖRLAG NORDISK KONST STOCKHOLM

Hart in a typical studio pose.
Photo by Larry Telles.

Artcraft Star

Producing pictures for Artcraft gave Hart the prestige and money that his box office standing warranted. At Famous Players–Lasky, the soft-spoken but powerful Adolph Zukor was building the greatest production-distribution-exhibition combine of the silent era. Hungarian by birth and recently out of the fur business, Zukor was an entrepreneur and administrative head rather than a skilled filmmaker. Under his guidance the studio's theater chain grew to more than two thousand houses. Through block booking, Famous Players and its successor, Paramount, forced theaters to take the company's mediocre films along with its good, booked even before a script was shot and sold on the strength of the studio's stars. Heading his own production company within Zukor's empire assured Hart that his movies would reach a worldwide audience at premium prices.

Hart was eager to prove his merit under the new arrangement, but he had no story except one that he had had in mind for a long time, a plot stemming from his love for Fritz. The star wrote a treatment of the idea in three days and turned it over to Harvey Thew, one of Famous Players' writers. Thew completed a scenario within three more days, and in late July 1917 *The Narrow Trail* went before the cameras. Almost immediately Hart and Ince argued over the allotment of overhead costs, and in the clash that followed the star's anger at his former friend spewed like venom.

With Hart acting as producer under Ince's loose supervision, Lambert Hillyer directed *The Narrow Trail*, and Joe August continued as cameraman. Hillyer, still in his midtwenties, had been a track star at

Drake University. He became a newspaperman in New York and later a short story writer. Hillyer would direct twenty-five of Hart's Artcraft movies and write sixteen of them. He was also a crack shot with a rifle and supposedly fired real bullets at the cowboy star during pictures they made, at least once shooting a glass out of Bill's hand for the camera.

Fritz was seen in *The Narrow Trail* as King, the leader of a herd of wild horses. In the movie's opening sequence the pony is captured by the hero against an austere but beautiful landscape. Then the film quickly becomes a review of what Hart had done before: action, sentiment, and an outlaw reformed by a doe-eyed woman whom he thinks is the "most wonderful being he has ever seen."

A bigger budget permitted *The Narrow Trail* to be shot on a grander scale than Hart had had at his disposal at Triangle. The chases are grander, the brawl involves more extras, and outdoor settings are more majestic. Hart's age shows; the bags under his eyes give him a fatigued look, and his cheeks appear more sunken than before. But the film was a promising start at Artcraft, and Zukor's publicists proved resourceful in ballyhooing it as something special—not just mere entertainment but a vehicle for moral instruction. "William S. Hart pictures are always inspiring," trade papers announced. "They make folks breathe deeper." Advertisements for the movie proclaimed, "Better a painted pony than a painted woman." (One does wonder toward the end of the picture whether Fritz or Sylvia Breamer, the leading lady, is going to hold Hart's affection, for Fritz persists in nosing his master amorously.)

When *The Narrow Trail* was released in late December, Hart made personal appearances with Fritz to promote the picture, and most critics agreed that it was one of the actor's best. According to *Moving Picture World*, "Every Father, Mother, and Mother's Son is boosting William S. Hart because he tells a true tale of the Wild West." The *New York Dramatic Mirror* reported that *The Narrow Trail* was "a film offering of exceptional merit, if suspense and climax go to constitute merit. The story builds with quickening tempo to a crescendo finish which leaves one breathless, and through all the hurry and agitato of the movement it unfolds a simple tale of the heart."

The pace of moviemaking at Artcraft was nearly as frantic for Hart as it had been at Triangle. *The Silent Man* went into production almost immediately after *The Narrow Trail* wrapped, and the second film was actually released first. Although Hart is credited, Lambert Hillyer directed *The Silent Man*, as he did all of Hart's films made under the star's initial Artcraft contract. When Ince and Hart left Triangle, Hillyer, Joe August, and Gardner Sullivan went with them to Artcraft, but Sullivan and Hillyer were soon sued by Triangle for breach of contract. Even though their former employers could not stop them from working, they did prevent the writer and the director from receiving screen credit.

Meanwhile Hart and Ince fought over Fritz. Ince still did not like the pony, for reasons Hart never understood, and he refused to let Hart ride the pinto in his next fifteen pictures. When Ince insisted that Hart use another horse, the actor said, "I began to doubt either his or my own sanity." During the weeks between Hart's last work for Triangle and the start of *The Narrow Trail*, Fritz had been taken from his corral at Inceville and kept in an indoor stall on Washington Boulevard, not far from Ince's new studio. Hart was unhappy about the treatment Fritz received and had battled fiercely for permission to use him in *The Narrow Trail*. Once the movie was made, the star was furious when Ince refused to let him use the horse in any of his pictures for the next two years. "Perhaps our row about the pony might have been patched up had I not found that I was being charged a proportionate share of the overhead expense of running Tom's own studio," Hart said. "I was dumbfounded."

The rupture between the old friends soon became permanent. Hart only saw Ince three or four times for a few minutes each during the making of his next fifteen pictures, although Ince continued to act in a supervisory capacity. "All our quarreling—and there was a heap of it—was done through E. H. Allen, my studio manager," Hart said. Hart had leased the old Mabel Normand studio in East Hollywood from Mack Sennett and worked there for four years.

Much to his dismay, the cowboy star rode a different horse in *The Silent Man*, a mount Ince considered a more appropriate size. The crew spent a week in a small town in the Mojave Desert making the picture, and the location work added to *The Silent Man*'s impact. The composition on the exterior shots is excellent, and Joe August used backlighting to singular effect. The movie contains numerous close-ups of Hart, and "somehow the old scout just looks you in the eye and makes you believe it," *Wid's* reported in December 1917, when the picture opened at the Rialto Theater in New York.

Hart suffered some bruises and lacerations doing stunts for *The Silent Man* and, at the age of fifty-three, he seemed to have discovered women. He described Vola Vale, his leading lady in the movie, as small but "alive and full of vivacity and sweetness. . . . She's the sort of girl any ordinary puncher off the range would simply fall head over heels in love with at the very first sight of her."

There are no indications that Hart had ever dated anybody—certainly no one seriously. In 1917 he and Mary Ellen were living together in the Rex Arms Apartments in Los Angeles. Although Hart's declared income for the year was $18,400, he appeared to have little social life. Hollywood was still a small town, where everyone in the picture business knew everybody else, but Hart found making deep friendships difficult. He admired the vigor of former President Theodore Roosevelt, kept up a lively correspondence with a number of people across the country, but spent most of his time working. "On the screen Hart was honest and blunt-spoken," Adolph Zukor wrote in his autobiography. "In real life he was the same."

Hart's strongest attachments were always to pets and children. He maintained that a man's treatment of animals was an index to his character. "If a man can truthfully say that he is as good as his horse," he declared, "he is a pretty good man. If you and I can live up to our good instincts as well as a good horse or a good dog lives up to his, we have accomplished something to be proud of."

The star was courtly and deferential toward women and placed virtuous ladies on a pedestal. When Hart overheard an actor in his unit insult a young female extra on the set, the ill-mannered fellow never worked at the studio again. Yet Hart seemed unnatural with women other than Mary Ellen—too artificial for lasting intimacy and gentlemanly to the point of phoniness.

By 1918 Hart's pictures were among the largest grossing in the industry. The star claimed that the essence of good acting was to be able to feel the part, live the character, and try to think as the person he was playing would. "If the role is that of a bad man, all my feelings are those of a desperate character throughout the play," Hart said. "When the picture is complete, I relax and become myself again." Actors in Hart's movies spoke lines during scenes that involved dialogue, even though the words were not recorded. "They completed our performance," he said. "Sometimes we used music while playing scenes, but seldom."

In *Wolves of the Rail*, Hart played a train robber who goes straight as a promise to his dying mother and cleans up the railroad line. The Western was undiluted melodrama, but critics conceded that the cowboy performer had never been in finer form. *Blue Blazes Rawden*, in which Hart played the boss of a crew of Canadian lumberjacks, followed in February 1918. Without his western accessories, the actor succumbs to broader, more overwrought gestures that did not seem to annoy contemporary critics but strike present viewers as ludicrous. So does the syrupy story of a mother's love and the subsequent softening of her daredevil son's heart.

By the time *The Tiger Man* went before the cameras in December 1917, many of the cowboys working on Hart's movies had been called into the armed forces and were being trained for combat in France. Since the picture required an unusually large number of expert horsemen to play outlaws, soldiers, and members of a sheriff's posse, Hart's studio manager advertised for skilled riders. Eighty percent of the men hired later admitted that they had lied about their equestrian skills to get the job. "They looked all right," Hart said, but their inadequacies were evident from the first chase on level ground. "It was hopeless!" he said. "There were soldiers, cowboys, and sheriff's men scattered all over the mesa." Finally, the production crew, everyone except those turning the cranks of cameras, suited up and served as doubles. Hart, playing an outlaw, did his own rides, then changed clothes and joined the sheriff's posse to chase himself.

Bill's leading lady in both *The Tiger Man* and *Selfish Yates* was Jane Novak, a tiny wisp of a blond girl, whose sister Eva was also in silent movies. Jane later became Hart's first big public love affair, and her winning ways made her a favorite with movie crews. "The first time Jane came to my studio to work," Hart said, "I thought she was a little girl." And he treated her as one. Novak and actress Vola Vale were close friends, and the two of them frequently upset Bill's dignity by playing pranks on him. He nicknamed them the Pest and the Nuisance; Jane was the Pest. But Novak was a splendid actress, and she played the reforming influence in five of Hart's movies with radiance.

Urban reviewers were starting to complain about the repetition in Hart's Westerns, even though they admitted that his pictures still drew standing-room-only crowds during most engagements. "There is no doubt that Hart can do well the part he almost invariably plays," a *New York Times* critic wrote in May 1918, "but one would think that artistic ambition, if nothing else, would prompt him to try something different."

In February 1918 Hart, his sister Mary Ellen, and a production unit went on location to Donner Lake, near Truckee, California, in the Sierras, where the crew filmed exteriors for *Shark Monroe*. This time Hart played the captain of a sealing schooner on the coast of Alaska and had to drive a dog team. "I discovered that it was just the same as driving steers," the actor said. Most of *Shark Monroe*'s action takes place on shipboard, but its star again emerged as the "rough, strong man of primitive ways and stern manner," according to the *New York Times* review.

In 1917 Bill had been featured in an all-star production consisting of patriotic episodes for the Second Liberty Loan Drive, and in April 1918 he toured the western United States speaking on behalf of the Third Liberty Loan campaign, while Mary Pickford, Douglas Fairbanks, and Charles Chaplin did the same in the East. The four-week tour began for Bill in San Diego and included stops in Salt Lake City, Butte, Seattle, Spokane, Portland, and San Francisco. Bill proved a forceful public speaker and met with ovations everywhere he appeared. "The Third Liberty Loan will go over so big it will make the Kaiser stagger," Hart told a gathering in Salt Lake City. "The west has never been so thoroughly knit on a single issue as it is on the question of America's responsibilities in the war." He was touched to see so many young men in uniform, was impressed by the staunch support the Mormons gave the war effort, and was disturbed when he saw a camp of alien prisoners, surrounded by a high wire fence and "an ugly-looking gun" on a platform at each corner of the compound that confined them. Hart frequently wore his cowpuncher outfit to make speeches during the tour, and in Portland, Oregon, he was asked to talk to a body of high school students. "It was such a gathering as angels would have grouped," he said.

Hart was always sentimental about children but seemed wary of his growing number of female fans. When he checked into a hotel in Seattle, he told the switchboard operator, "Don't let any women bother me on the phone." Hart was never the lady's man he fancied himself, but he had a certain appeal to the opposite sex. "I think it was because he had that little-boy quality that women like," Louella Parsons recalled, and "that he was always sad and unhappy."

On April 26, as the Third Liberty Loan tour was coming to an end, a man wrote Hart from San Francisco, saying that he and his wife had heard the cowboy star speak the night before in their local auditorium. "Your appeal, personality, and Americanism so impressed the good wife," the letter read, "that she has requested me to say she is going to strain a point and take one more $500 bond in this third call." Hart sold millions of dollars worth of bonds during the tour, and his own subscription reputedly totaled $105,000, one of the largest amounts received from a member of the motion picture community.

Hart returned to Los Angeles and prepared to film *Riddle Gawne*, in which he played a western rancher bent on finding the killer of his younger brother. Lon Chaney, who would later score tremendous hits in the silent picture versions of *The Hunchback of Notre Dame* and *The Phantom of the Opera*, was the villain in the picture. The company camped out for three weeks in June 1918 at Brent's Crags in the Santa Clara mountains, about one hundred miles from Hollywood, filming exteriors. The men slept in tents and ate from tin dishes food that a cowboy cook prepared for them. With *Riddle Gawne* Hart began a practice that he would repeat many times: he proposed marriage to his leading lady, in this case lovely Katherine MacDonald. Convinced that he was in love with MacDonald, Hart asked her to marry him a dozen times without success. Those who knew Hart best found his many proposals humorous, and no one, including the ladies involved, was sure how serious he was.

The Border Wireless, a war movie, was released a month before World War I ended. Hart's crew went to San Ysidro on the Mexican border, where the Eleventh Cavalry of the U.S. Army was camped, to photograph scenes for the picture. The star again played an outlaw with a price on his head, but the character reforms, overwhelms Mexican bandits, and stalks German spies to prove himself fit for the army.

As the war in Europe entered its final weeks, Hart considered forming a regiment of rough riders for service in France and told the press that he intended to recruit the men from the ranks of the motion picture studios. "I was simply crazy to go to war," Hart said later. "I had found out that horsemen were badly needed as dispatch bearers right at the front when wires were torn up between the main body of the army and the front-line trenches. My heart beat high with hope." Almost fifty-four years old, Hart was an unlikely candidate for active duty in combat zones, and nothing came of the plan.

Instead, the star agreed to serve as a major spokesman for the Fourth Liberty Loan Drive, covering the territory from Chicago east. Mary Ellen and actress Natalie Talmadge accompanied him to New York, where he began making speeches in mid-October 1918. A reporter who interviewed Hart in his hotel room noticed a bouquet of yellow dahlias "arranged with a woman's hand" and "a neatness and indescribable air" that made the newspaperman suspect a woman's presence. "She is Miss Mary Hart," the journalist wrote on October 20, "who keeps house for her brother and looks after him generally." Another press observer said, "Hart did not shoot anyone when I saw him. He was in fact eating a nut sundae in a Times Square soda emporium."

Bill, in cowboy attire, claimed the distinction of addressing the largest crowd ever assembled in Manhattan's financial district. "For blocks up and down Wall Street, for blocks up and down Broad Street, and even around on Pine Street, the streets were jammed with humanity," the star recalled, "and every building seemed to be alive—

all windows being packed with people." When he spoke from the steps of the Astor Library, traffic for the four blocks between Thirty-eighth and Forty-second Streets came to a standstill. "Everybody loves Big Bill Hart," the Buffalo, New York, *Enquirer* reported.

Bill confessed that speaking before such huge crowds made his knees shake and his voice tremble. "I thought of my father and mother," he said, "and how proud they would be if they could only have lived to see me so honored." He made a nostalgic walk past the old Manhattan Athletic Club track, where he had once won races, and the house where he had lived as a boy. When he reached the basement steps of his old home, he stopped and uncovered his head, remembering family ties that were no more.

In City Hall Square a mangled soldier was carried to the platform from which Hart spoke. Hart said that he immediately saw that the young man was a Native American, and he took a chance by speaking to the fellow in Sioux. The youth's body straightened, and tears flowed down his cheeks. Hart asked the boy if he was in pain, then could speak no more, since he, too, was full of emotion. As the actor gripped the Sioux's shoulder, their eyes exchanged a moment of tenderness. "And to this broken soldier of the trenches," Hart recalled in a burst of drama, "must have come a vision of the faraway prairies and the stoicism of his people, for he said in Sioux—slowly, deliberately, proudly—'Our fathers were brave men.'"

In his speeches Hart told an adoring public that no American must ever say they "hoped" the Allies would win the war; they must say "We've got to win this war." "All I want to tell you is to buy bonds. Buy, buy, buy, buy! Buy until it hurts like hell!" Patriotic to the core, Hart had no trouble viewing the Great War as a clear fight to save the world for democracy.

During his stay in Manhattan, Hart at last had occasion to meet Bat Masterson, the legendary frontier marshal. The two had exchanged letters and compliments for years, but on his trip east in 1918, Hart went to the *Morning Telegraph* office expressly to visit his idol. "I would rather see Bat Masterson than any man in the United States," he said. Masterson was equally effusive about Hart. "He knows how to ride and he knows how to shoot on the screen," the former western lawman said, "and he is the real thing outside of pictures." Masterson later dropped by Hart's hotel for a chat. "We talked for two hours and it seemed like five minutes," Hart said. He was thrilled to get to know the old sheriff personally, found him a soft-spoken, unpretentious person, and referred to Masterson in his autobiography as "a great American citizen."

The flu epidemic of 1918 was raging at the time, and a quarantine caused Hart's speaking dates in Philadelphia, Washington, D.C., and Boston to be canceled at the last minute. On the way to Providence, Rhode Island, Hart's train passed through towns that had coffins stacked high at the station, awaiting shipment to burial plots around the country.

Hart was getting into his cowboy clothes to speak in towns close to Providence when his manager announced that he had been ordered back to New York. Woodrow Wilson was to talk at the Metropolitan Opera House, and Hart had been chosen to introduce the president. Hart's party rushed to catch a train for Manhattan, but Wilson developed a conflict and had to cancel the engagement. Hart appeared at the gala anyway, along with Enrico Caruso, Fritz Kreisler, and Will Rogers.

Evangelist Billy Sunday came to see Hart during the actor's trip east, and the two men became friends, although Hart did not consider himself a religious person. He said that the preacher's disposition was such that he treated Sunday like he would have treated "a brother cowboy." Although Hart had made no pretense at having been a working cowboy early in his career, as his reputation grew he claimed to have herded cattle in Kansas with his father when he was young.

Branding Broadway, the story of a westerner going east to straighten out a rich man's wayward son, was to be Bill's next picture, so he took advantage of his time in New York to film scenes for the movie. One sequence, which climaxed with a fight, took place in a fancy Broadway restaurant. The night the footage was shot, the stuntmen that Hart normally used in such scenes brought in a newcomer that Hart could tell was a professional boxer from his ear marks. The bruiser, whom Hart was supposed to trounce, understood none of the movie tricks for faking blows and fought like a demon. "Every time he hit me," the star said, "I let out a grunt that was almost a roar of pain." To make matters worse, the boxer was stone deaf and didn't hear Lambert Hillyer when the director yelled for him to get knocked down.

Another sequence for the picture was filmed at Forty-second Street and Fifth Avenue late one afternoon, with cameras placed in taxis parked at the curb and in second-floor windows. The action called for Hart, as a displaced westerner, to grow confused in the traffic and ask a policeman to take him across the street. During the take, as the officer was leading Hart by the arm and traffic was held up, a woman grabbed hold of the cowboy actor, ripped out her book and pencil, and asked him for his autograph.

In yet another scene Hart was to grab a mounted policeman's horse, chase a taxi up Sixth Avenue, and overtake the man he was after in Central Park. The chase was filmed at six o'clock in the morning to avoid heavy traffic, but by the time Hart reached the park, a sizable crowd had gathered. Since Jack, the horse Hart had used since Fritz's forced retirement, had been left in California, Hart had to request a substitute. The borrowed steed turned out to be a Kentucky racehorse, and before cheering fans, the horse ran away with the actor. "How that horse did run!" Hart remembered. "We passed the taxi that I was to catch as though it was some sort of a June bug. . . . It was horrible!" Eventually Hart slid off the saddle and sat in the middle of Central Park's bridle path and cried.

Chicago was the final stop on Hart's Fourth Liberty Loan tour, and he claimed that the Windy City was a hard town in which to sell bonds because of its large German population. "I won't say [Chicago] was pro-German, because I do not know," he said, "but in many sections it was pro-unAmerican." Hart closed his part of the drive at the Chicago Athletic Club, where members "showed their one hundred per cent Americanism" by a generous purchase of bonds. "Every dollar I've got—and some I haven't—are invested in Liberty bonds," the actor told a Chicago reporter. In all, the actor collected $16 million for the U.S. government during his tour through the East.

Hart's next picture after *Branding Broadway* was *Breed of Men*, which had scenes set in Chicago, most of them in the stockyards.

When Hillyer sought permission for his crew to film there, the stockyard officials were less than cordial, still reeling from the injury that Upton Sinclair's novel *The Jungle*, published in 1906, and a subsequent movie had caused the meatpacking industry. Bill interceded with the stockyard supervisors and finally secured authorization to shoot the scenes needed, but even the cow pen workers expressed hostility toward the filmmakers. "Many of those cowhands had good memories [of the old days before meatpacking reform] and were bitter at what had taken place," Hart said.

Bill returned to Los Angeles in early November and immediately went to work finishing *Branding Broadway* and *Breed of Men*. When the Broadway picture, a comedy, opened at the Rialto Theater in Manhattan, the *New York Times* reviewer was less than enthusiastic. "William S. Hart cannot keep his story from taking itself seriously," the *Times* critic wrote, "and when such a story takes itself seriously it becomes a bore." *Moving Picture World* was kinder to *Breed of Men*, yet its critic said that the story lacked most of the essential ingredients of drama, particularly any element of suspense.

Hart announced in mid-November 1918 that he might retire from motion pictures at the expiration of his present Artcraft contract. But later in the month major renovations were made on the William S. Hart Studio, which indicated that the star would not be forsaking the movie business any time soon. A solid roof was built over the studio's stages, making it possible for ten sets to be arranged within a space of 60-by-110 feet. Film companies were getting away from the idea of mixing sunlight and electric light, since the combination tended to result in a grainy quality. Paul Conlon, who had been publicity director for actor Fatty Arbuckle, joined Hart's staff in that capacity late in 1918 and served Hart well until the end of the cowboy star's career.

"With the coming of peace," Hart said, "millions of our American boys are returning home exulting in their new-born strength. Whether or not these soldiers return to their former occupations, they will retain the glorifying love of the great outdoors which has come to them through many months of the most arduous military training." Hart was convinced that this renewed vigor ensured a successful future for Western movies.

Hart's popularity stood at its zenith. Among his many fans was President Wilson, and the chief executive often showed Bill's Westerns in the Blue Room of the White House for himself, Mrs. Wilson, and a few invited guests. In December 1918, when the *George Washington* sailed for France, carrying President Wilson and the American delegates to the Paris Peace Conference, four Douglas Fairbanks movies, three William S. Hart and three Mary Pickford movies, and D. W. Griffith's *The Great Love* were on board for the passengers' entertainment.

During New Year's week that year, Hart and his company were in San Francisco filming scenes at San Quentin prison for *The Poppy Girl's Husband*. In the movie Hart played Hairpin Harry Dutton, a convict in the tenth year of a fourteen-year sentence for burglary. Hart was not fond of the picture's title, but the script was based on one of Jules Boyle's Boston Blackie stories, and, because of the copyright, the title had to be used. Juanita Hansen, whom Hart described as a "delectable young person who exerts a charm that sort of befuddles you and mixes you up," played his leading lady.

Hart's role in *The Poppy Girl's Husband* was a radical departure for him, but most reviewers found the movie among the best of his recent vehicles. P. S. Harrison, writing for *Motion Picture News*, said: "William S. Hart should be proud of this picture; the story calls for mostly emotional work, but he acquits himself in that line, and although the tax on his acting is rather heavy, he hardly ever crossed the line of naturalness."

While in the Bay area, Bill met Mary Pickford on a ferry going over to Oakland. Pickford informed him that she, Douglas Fairbanks, and Charlie Chaplin were tired of the unfair treatment actors had received from studio heads and had met in the Alexandria Hotel to discuss plans for forming a motion picture distribution company of their own. They wanted Hart and director D. W. Griffith to be part of the organization.

When Bill returned to Los Angeles, Fairbanks paid a visit to his studio, and the two men had a lengthy talk about the benefits the proposed company would have for independent producers. Three months of meetings followed to discuss the configuration of what in April

1919 became United Artists. All but Hart wanted the "Big Five"—Pickford, Fairbanks, Chaplin, Griffith, and Hart—to be in complete control of the new company. "On account of my liking for Mr. Zukor and the excellent treatment I had always received from him," Hart said, "I was strong for an alliance with Famous Players and talked for it on all occasions." The others firmly opposed the idea. Another point of contention was whether the Big Five should supply their own money for the company or it should be financed by outside capital. Hart, who was tight with the dollar and had no desire to risk $125,000 of his own funds, was the only one who held out for external financing. The other four even offered to put up an additional $25,000 each to cover Hart's share of the financing if he would join them in forming the company, but Hart refused. "I bade them all an affectionate goodbye and withdrew," the reluctant star said.

Hart later claimed that the prolonged discussions over the organization of United Artists got to be a burden for everyone involved and had continued at the expense of his much-needed rest. In addition to his movie work, Bill was writing a series of books for boys. *Pinto Ben and Other Stories*, issued by Britton Publishing Company in April 1919, was successful enough to entice Hart to draft more yarns for publication, some of which appeared first in serialized form. The *Pinto Ben* collection included two stories by Bill (one in verse about his favorite horse, the other about an Indian) and a third story by Mary Ellen about an English bulldog, each of which had been printed earlier in newspapers or magazines. Hart's attachment to animals was obvious in the book, and in its introduction Pinto Ben speaks. "I'm for anything the boss does even if it ain't good," the pony declares. "He likes me an' I like him."

Hart's love of boys remained equally strong, and in many ways Hart had the mind of a child. Each year, as Christmas approached, he spent weeks gathering toys and distributing them to needy children. He talked to boys' groups, and his advice to them in July 1919 was: "Be American through and through. . . . Any boys bred in this wonderful country of ours has advantages that no other boys in the world have."

Hart was so busy with various projects in the spring of 1919 that he turned down the government's invitation to assist with the Victory

Loan Drive. Feeling guilty about having to decline, he recruited thirty of his cowpunchers to help him stage a holdup of the Victory Loan Special as the train made its way from San Francisco down to the San Fernando Valley. The mock robbery was well covered by the Associated Press and gave the Victory Loan Drive valuable publicity.

In February 1919 the star was filming *The Money Corral*, one of his own stories, and getting ready to start *Square Deal Sanderson* the next month. *The Money Corral* involved location work at Fraley Point, Montana, and included a western rodeo, with most of the current rodeo champions present. During the making of the picture, Hart refereed a fight between a pugilist and an Australian boxing kangaroo as a publicity gag. "The hopping Corbett knocked out the 'pug' in four rounds," the press reported.

Jane Novak, the stunning blond who had worked in two of Hart's earlier films, was again his leading lady. "We all surely do love her around this studio," the cowboy star wrote in May to a Nebraska friend. "If anyone wanted to start a real, honest-to-God riot right quick, all they would have to do would be to seriously interfere with Jane." The actress was married at the time and frequently brought her baby daughter to the set. Film crews, including Hart, teased Novak a great deal, but the men were all immensely fond of her.

Ann Little, an outdoor woman who rode horses expertly, played opposite Hart in *Square Deal Sanderson*, a production that required Hart's unit to spend two weeks in the Mojave Desert. *Square Deal Sanderson* was a straightforward action movie and included a cattle roundup and plenty of fast riding and shooting. Hart played a cowboy who saves a girl's ranch by posing as her brother. In a dramatic moment the heroine is rescued when the title character throws a lasso over the transom of a door and half strangles a villain on the other side. "Considering the hundreds of thousands of feet of cowboy melodrama that have been produced since the days of Broncho Billy Anderson," *Wid's* remarked when the film opened in June 1919, "it is something of an accomplishment to find a new stunt for a thrilling climax. Bill Hart found one for *Square Deal Sanderson* and it goes over big."

In May Hart was back in the Mojave Desert shooting *Wagon Tracks*, another of his own stories. The picture was a romantic treatment of the

Santa Fe Trail around 1850, and Hart modeled his role after Kit Carson. He admitted that he had gathered his material from hearsay. While playing on the stage in Kansas City, he had visited old Westport and claimed that he discussed travels over the Santa Fe Trail with some old settlers there. In Hart's view the trail into Mexican territory was less an artery of commerce than a "sand-rimmed wilderness" over which pioneers journeyed to build a new empire. One of the picture's titles refers to a train of covered wagons as the "white-sailed Armada of an unconquerable race" on its way to Santa Fe, "the Threshold of the Land of Promise."

Hart maintained that he put all he knew of wagon trains into *Wagon Tracks*, yet the movie is a collage of clichés. Its band of Kiowas, inclined to be friendly, all wear Plains Indian warbonnets and demand "a life for a life" when one of their warriors is killed by a white man. Hart's character, dressed in buckskin and coonskin cap, looms as the indomitable pathfinder, convinced that the western landscape "brings God close," yet ready to help his nation fulfill its manifest destiny by leading more settlers into the Southwest.

C. Gardner Sullivan wrote the scenario for *Wagon Tracks*, based on Hart's outline. River and boat scenes for the movie were filmed around Sacramento, and much of the work with horses was done near Victorville, California. Hart's studio manager advertised for the large number of cowboys and extras that were needed in the picture, and the women hired spent more than a week in the desert wearing sunbonnets and long dresses. "I liked to work with Bill Hart," said Mrs. Jim Rush, one of the background people in *Wagon Tracks*. "His pictures were always big pictures, and we had more days than we did anywhere else—especially when we went on location."

Hart's age is detracting in the movie, and the cowboys he worked with often joked that the star must have eaten alum the night before shooting close-ups to make his lips so tight. Bill's playful attitude toward Jane Novak, again his leading lady, had become boyishly flirtatious and at times downright immature. Returning home from location by train, the star poured a glass of water down Novak's neck in the dining car. "No man in the world reveres Jane more than Bill Hart," he told a friend. "To me she represents the highest type of womanhood."

The cowboy actor opposed any publicity regarding his personal life, and for the most part he managed to keep his sister Mary Ellen out of the public eye. Despite his fame, Hart considered his life difficult—full of burdens and obligations to others, with little time for private pleasures or romantic entanglements. He did not consider himself handsome, and as time went on he doted on how the giants in the motion picture business exploited and persecuted him. Even in his films true friendships are rare; more often his characters are betrayed, as Hart felt he had been by Thomas Ince and others. Under the star's genial, courtly exterior was an angry man, and it did not take much to send Hart into tirades or despair. When a woman bumped into his new car and dented a fender, Hillyer remembered that Hart was furious and difficult to live with for two days.

Hart had one more picture to make under his initial agreement with Artcraft and Ince. To finish the contract, he selected another script by Gardner Sullivan, *John Petticoats*, filmed in New Orleans during early June 1919. In the movie Hart played a lumberjack who inherits his uncle's dress shop in the French Quarter and has trouble mixing with members of the fashionable society who are his customers.

Hart's publicity director had a field day arranging magazine layouts with funny pictures of the cowboy star mingling with beautiful models amid the feminine finery in the clothing store. Hart's leading lady in the picture was Winifred Westover, another attractive actress to whom Hart paid more than casual attention off-camera. "I had never been out of California before and to be in New Orleans playing opposite Mr. Hart was enough to send me into raptures," Westover remembered. "It was terribly hot and we worked hard all day, but every evening brought an excursion into an enchanted world. Mr. Hart knew some charming people who were lovely to us. Then we explored all the picturesque corners of the old French town, dined in queer places, and had a beautiful time. We were such pals."

John Petticoats' plot contained a suicide attempt and was rife with psychological motivations that were never Hart's strength as an actor. The movie proved a disappointment on its release, and Hart's persistent collie dog expression seemed out of place. "Perhaps Mr. Hart is tired of his spurs and chaps," a reviewer speculated in the

Chicago Tribune. "Perhaps since so many imitators have arisen to do him flattery he longs to start off on a new tack."

The new direction Bill most wanted was to break his alliance with Thomas Ince, which had become increasingly unpleasant. While in New Orleans making *John Petticoats*, the actor received word that Ince had filched his production company's account books during his absence. "I'll be damned!" Bill said, as if the news signaled the final blow to their relationship. Hart wanted no part of Ince in any further negotiations. His contract with Artcraft was due to expire on July 14, 1919, and already he had two promising offers awaiting his decision.

During the location work on *Wagon Tracks*, Douglas Fairbanks had come to see Hart, informing him that United Artists was formed and fully financed. The new distribution company's backers would be willing to fund Hart in the making of nine pictures and would release them on a profit-sharing basis, with Hart receiving 75 percent of the gross and a guarantee of $300,000 per picture. As assurance of the company's earnestness, once the contract was signed, United Artists would put up the full amount of the guarantee on the final picture and allow Hart to draw interest on the sum until the money involved was paid him in full. "I could see that this was a marvelous contract," Hart said. "Its face value meant a fortune."

The actor felt an obligation to give Zukor an opportunity to meet United Artists' offer. "Mr. Zukor was always most fair in his business talks with me," Hart said. "He stated just what he would do if I would continue to release my pictures through his company." But Zukor's best offer was 70 percent of the gross and a guarantee of $200,000 per movie, an increase of only $50,000 more per movie than Hart's expiring contract. There seemed little choice but for the star to sign with United Artists. "I walked the streets at night," Hart said. "I worried. . . . I had my constant adviser, my sister Mary, walking the floor of her room."

In the end Bill's loyalty to Famous Players won out, and he ordered William Grossman, his attorney, to wire Zukor that he would accept his terms. Hart's previous arrangement with Ince was no longer part of the deal. A final meeting with Ince, Ince's wife, and the former friends' lawyers was held at the William S. Hart Studio, during which

Ince claimed some $125,000 more than Bill thought he was entitled to. "There was quite a nervous tension throughout the proceedings," the actor remembered, with Ince and Hart sitting on opposite sides of a table ignoring one another. A prolonged legal battle followed.

Hart's disposition in the summer of 1919 was not good. He much preferred making pictures to corporate administration, yet he found himself becoming embroiled in company matters. To the guileless star, honor was the greatest principle a man could live by—"as essential as the air you breathe," he said. But he felt surrounded by disreputable types and baffling issues. In the aftermath of World War I, the country had fallen heir to complex world problems and faced internal strife that Hart lacked the capacity to understand. "Local conditions out here at this time are very bad," he wrote in August 1919. "All of the electric line employees, both city and interurban, are on strike, and this morning they were joined by the employees of all the steam railroad terminals. . . . On all sides one hears of nothing but formation of new unions and strikes." In his naive way Hart wondered if the country's voting in Prohibition and denying workmen their beer and wine was not responsible for the massive dissatisfaction. "A man deprived of something to which he has long been accustomed without ever having had the opportunity to voice his opinion (his vote) is apt to be more easy of approach by agitators," he said. "I also wonder, as another factor, if the terrific income tax (which is confiscation in effect) does not cause big corporations to double and treble their prices to pull up their net incomes." For Hart, the rising cost of living was "the root and branch" of the country's postwar turmoil.

Underneath the onus of stardom was a simple, fanciful man of narrow perspective. In Hart's view millions of American boys had left the "crowded confines of the big cities" to fight in the trenches in France. In the "melting pot of war they discovered the joy of living. Their soft, underdeveloped bodies became suddenly and miraculously marvels of strength and endurance. They had become once again regular he-men; they had regained their American birthright." In his mind the country should be teeming with optimism, not torn with internal dissention.

Personally, professionally, and politically, Hart's paranoia was growing. "Merely living in America doesn't make an American," he wrote in December 1919. "If a man doesn't vote for the Right, doesn't uphold the laws, and doesn't honor the Stars and Stripes as his ONLY flag, he's an alien—an outsider at heart, no matter where he was born. You can tell such snakes by their rattle. Keep your eye on them—their bite is poisonous!"

Concurrently, his view of the bygone frontier seemed to become more rigid and his pronouncements on life in the old West increasingly pontifical. "I know the innate fairness of any man who has ever worked among or around cattle," he said. "The only cause of wearing guns low was to take some of the weight off the belly," he wrote a friend. Hart claimed to be an authority on George Armstrong Custer and to possess information about the much-discussed Custer massacre that was not known outside official circles. To Hart, Custer was a brave, ambitious, opinionated, hardheaded man; had he lived he would have been court-martialed. The real heroes in the Battle of Little Big Horn were the Indians, who personified the fundamental premises of life. "There never lived a better-natured or finer man than the Indian," the actor said. "The Indian of the plains—the full-blooded red men, without any taint or admixture of Spanish or Mexican strain—naturally is gentle, kind, and honorable to a fault." Time and again Hart repeated, "I know by personal experience much of the actual life of our frontier days."

The press and the public accepted his authority and came to view the star as the epitome of rugged manliness, as well as a living symbol of the untamed West. With the motion picture business ranked fifth among the industries of the United States, Paul Conlon, Hart's director of publicity, estimated in 1919 that six million people all over the world saw a William S. Hart movie every day. Hart's image behind two flashing six-guns became as much a representation of vibrant Americanism as James Montgomery Flagg's famous poster of Uncle Sam pointing a finger forward and saying, "I Want You" on a recruitment placard for the armed forces first issued in 1917.

Hart was not only the man who gave faithful portrayals of the old West, he was viewed—along with Daniel Boone, Davy Crockett, and

Buffalo Bill—as an embodiment of America's frontier heritage. In July 1918 the *Los Angeles Evening Herald* stated that in Hart's presence "one can distinguish the true man of the plains, living at a time when these unpopulated stretches of dry prairie were the romping grounds for the Indian, the cattle thief, the bandit, and in fact every unreliable human who could sit a horse." Two months later *Motion Picture Magazine* declared, "William S. Hart knows and understands Indians as well as he does his own race. He was brought up among the Indians when he was a boy, taught by them, lived with them." The Hart legend grew until it became fact. Phillip Schuler, an old actor from the East who went to Hollywood when his voice failed, later wrote, "I recall the first days of Bill Hart—how he thrilled the cast by firing a pistol bullet into a post and then, at twenty paces, fired another into the same hole. His feats with guns were incredible and none were faked. Likewise his horsemanship."

By the end of World War I, William S. Hart's mystique had grown into a composite of Uncle Sam, the chivalrous cowboy, the western trailblazer, a preserver of basic American values, the true spirit of the great West, and every young person's grandfather. Far more than a world-famous actor and filmmaker, Hart had become an icon and had gained a place in American history.

Artcraft Contract Renewed

Under the terms of his second contract with Artcraft, Hart made nine more pictures for release though Famous Players–Lasky, with no time limit and no restrictions on footage. Hart was his own producer, but Famous Players put up the money and was responsible for advertising. By 1919 Hart was one of the highest paid stars in Hollywood and was considered "an original" by Adolph Zukor. Hart had decided to renew his agreement with Zukor and Lasky because they had always been fair with him and kept their word. "I want my next two years in pictures to be free from worry about business," the star said, "so that I can devote my time to making good photo-dramas."

Determined to produce films his way or not at all, Hart's first step after freeing himself from Ince's control was to bring Fritz out of retirement. "The only horse I ever knew in pictures that could do and did do anything and everything himself was Fritz," Hart said. "There were no platforms used when I jumped Fritz, nor was he blindfolded. I just urged him and he jumped." With the passage of time, Fritz seemed to have become increasingly human to Hart. The actor "never claimed that Fritz could actually talk—at least in English to human beings," Zukor wrote in his memoirs, but the horse did look sympathetic when Hart spoke to him.

During his two-year hiatus from movies, Fritz had taken up with a mare named Cactus Kate, which Hart bought to keep the pinto company. Bill had been told that Cactus Kate was a mean-dispositioned horse and that nobody had been able to ride her. Undaunted, Bill had the mare saddled and led her by the bridle for a mile or two.

Then he had a cowboy mount her, and Kate made no attempt to buck or act up. Bill later told Zukor that Cactus Kate had helped Fritz "over many a rough spot."

The William S. Hart Studio was located at 6404 Sunset Boulevard, among the orchards of East Hollywood, near the Hollywood Athletic Club. The studio stood in a gully, and according to one observer, the place was like "a breath of the prairies." The prop room was filled with saddles, bridles, spurs, bits, boots, chaps, hats, and guns and smelled of rawhide. "Never fake anything!" was a dictum at the Hart studio. Since Bill insisted on authenticity, there were no painted backdrops used in his movies. Bricks, lumber, cement, and wallpaper needed for constructing sets had to be real.

Although employees at the studio understood that Hart was the boss, the cowboys who worked there enjoyed a great deal of fun, with Hart often participating. The men sometimes held kangaroo courts, and Hart liked to sit as judge at those sessions and render punishments. Once Hart himself was convicted of loaning an actress five dollars, which she lost in a crap game. The rule was that if a leading lady was loaned money, the amount must be larger. The penalty for this offense was a whipping with a pair of leather chaps. Although Hart was an indefatigable worker, there was time at his studio for pie-eating contests, dunking young actresses, and laughter between takes.

A reporter once asked the cowboy star why he bothered about details so much, pointing out that the general public would not know whether his movies were accurate or not. "Yes, but I would," Hart said with a haughty air. More than ever Hart felt the need to bring the fading West to the screen for a new generation. Although his films had become predictable, he refused to spice them with superfluous action and foolhardy stunts such as Tom Mix and other Western stars did. He wanted his movies to remain genuine, clean, and instructive in moral values for America's youth.

The actor claimed to do his own horse falls and often got hurt making pictures. Hart was frequently seen around the studio with a bandaged hand or walking with a limp. "There's a lot of danger in this game," he said. Once he thought his knee was broken, but an x-ray showed that a fragment of bone had chipped off and gotten lodged in a muscle. The actor denied using the "Running W," in which a length of cable was attached to a horse's legs and also fastened to a stationary object, so that the animal's feet were snapped out from under him when the horse and rider reached the extent of the cable. "It was a dastardly thing to do to an animal," said Hart, who estimated that in about 20 percent of such falls the horse's neck was broken.

Eventually most of the costumes used in Hart's movies came from Western Costume in Hollywood. For pictures set before 1865, Hart carried a Colt 36 as his weapon. Location work had become vital to his productions, and he was ever alert to the beauty and grandeur of natural scenery.

While the "Little Giant of the Film Industry," as the diminutive Zukor was called, spent most of his time in New York, he enjoyed visiting Hart's sets or dropping by the studio for a talk when he was in Los Angeles. "Mr. Zukor was often in my office at seven in the morning," Hart recalled. "I always called him Mr. Zukor. There was something about him that demanded your respect."

Eugene Zukor, Adolph's son, also held a position at Famous Players after World War I, and years later he remembered William S. Hart as "the John Wayne of that era," although the older star's approach was more limited than Wayne's. "There was not much direction in a Hart picture," the younger Zukor said. "He jumped on a horse and he got off of him. That was about the extent of the dramatization." The assessment was harsh, but Eugene Zukor did not consider Hart the asset to Artcraft that his father did. "It was better to have him on your team than not," the mogul's son maintained, but "Hart never was that important an individual that the business would shake and shiver if anything happened to him."

Sand, the first picture Hart made under his renewed contract with Famous Players, was a railroad story, filmed in September and October 1919 on the desert outside Victorville. The movie offered a series of thrilling episodes, lots of fast riding, and a leap from a cliff into a river by Hart. Lambert Hillyer was again Bill's director, and Joe August continued as his cameraman. Hart's publicist claimed that thousands of the star's fans had asked about Fritz, and advertisements made much of the fact that *Sand* would mark the pinto's return to the screen.

"*Sand* has sand," *Moving Picture World* announced when the Western was released in February 1920. "It is a typical Hart picture, only somewhat better than those he has been making for the last year or so." Some reviewers thought the movie lacked vigor and that the story seemed unduly protracted. President Wilson, however, said that *Sand* was his favorite Hart film.

Three years before filming *Sand*, Bill had written a story that he liked, but he could not come up with a satisfactory ending for it. The plot had an effective climax, but then the narrative dissipated and went nowhere. None of the writers he consulted could find a solution. While Bill was in Victorville making *Sand*, his sister Mary Ellen visited and said, "Will, I think I have an ending for your story." Bill listened to her, thought Mary Ellen's conclusion was a "corker," and *The Toll Gate* became his next picture. Bill and his director collaborated on a script, and Bill considered the result one of his best efforts.

The Toll Gate provided Hart with an archetypal vehicle as a good bad man. In the movie he played Black Deering, the leader of a hunted gang of outlaws. Although eager to quit his life of crime, Deering reluctantly agrees to one last train robbery, only to be captured and taken into custody. He escapes, heads for the Mexican border, and on the way seeks shelter in the cabin of Mary Brown, an abandoned wife with a small child. When Mary protects Deering from the sheriff's posse, the outlaw recognizes true goodness and his reformation is complete. Feeling unworthy of the woman, Deering pays for his crimes at a symbolic toll gate and rides off to spend his life alone, no longer a desperate man.

The Toll Gate was in production for six months, much of it filmed around Sonora, in the Sierras of northern California, with Hart supervising every detail. In the movie Hart had to jump off a seventy-two-foot cliff into a river to save Mary Brown's little son from drowning. The star was not hurt in the fall, but he claimed that he and Fritz nearly lost their lives shooting another sequence in the picture. The filmmakers used a swift-running stream that tunneled through a mountain as the entrance to the bandits' cave. Hillyer, August, and their assistants had reconnoitered the cavern on a raft the day before the footage was shot, measuring for depth with a long pole. Joe August reported about eight feet of water in the underground stream, except for one stretch of about thirty feet where he could not touch bottom. The underground chamber was some six feet wide at the precarious point, with an arched roof about the same height. The camera was placed at the upstream end of the tunnel, and nine horses with riders—Fritz and Hart leading—were to swim against the current with the men carrying torches to give the crew enough light to photograph them.

The water was icy cold but shallow where the horsemen entered the cave, and not until they reached the center of the tunnel did their mounts begin swimming. Fritz had gone only a short distance across the pool when Hart felt the pony's feet strike something. The obstacle proved to be a slippery ledge projected into the water from the side of the cave. When Fritz tried to climb the ledge, he fell over backward, taking Hart with him. "Down, down, down we plunged into the bottomless depths," Hart recalled. "Over and over the frantic horse turned." After what seemed like an eternity, horse and rider surfaced. In desperation Fritz tried to climb the wall of the cave but tumbled over backward again and was swept into a whirlpool. "I sure thought my beloved pinto was gone," Hart wrote in his autobiography, but the pony managed to right himself. Fighting his way back toward the entrance of the cave, Fritz was finally able to touch bottom and regain his footing.

Bill's leading lady in *The Toll Gate* was Anna Q. Nilsson, one of Hollywood's first imports from Sweden. Nilsson was a competent actress, but a riding accident and the coming of sound pictures cut her career short. (She would appear as one of the "waxworks," who played bridge with Norma Desmond, in Billy Wilder's 1950 classic, *Sunset Boulevard.*) Hart supposedly proposed to Nilsson, and for a brief time the two were said to be engaged, but no wedding took place.

The Toll Gate was held over for a second week in many of the first-run theaters where it played and became Bill's biggest moneymaker. "Hart resumes his old character of the good bad-man reformed and regenerated by the inevitable innocent woman," the *New York Times* reported when the Western opened at the Rivoli Theater in Manhattan, "though this time he rises to even greater heights than before and, in the last scene, sends the woman from him back to 'her people,' where she will be 'happier' than she could be with such an outcast as he."

As *The Toll Gate* neared completion, Hart received a court summons that he found embarrassing. Shy around women and shocked by the behavior of his more aggressive female fans, Hart had remarked only a short time before his court date, "I'd rather buck a broncho any day than try to talk about the fair sex." The case against the star, filed in a Los Angeles court in November 1919, was a paternity suit. Elizabeth MacCauley of Brookline, Massachusetts, claimed that she had met Hart three years before in Syracuse, New York, and that he had seduced her and fathered her child. McCauley said that she had kept the baby hidden for fear the actor might kidnap the child. The woman stated that she had earned her living as a nurse but had become ill and needed financial assistance. To support her case the woman turned over letters that Hart had allegedly written to her attorney.

Hart was scheduled to film a railroad sequence on the day the trial began, and his company had chartered a train and arranged for a hundred people to be on hand to shoot scenes on a track that ran between Los Angeles and San Pedro. Hart maintained that he had never heard of Elizabeth MacCauley, and he became angry when his lawyer advised him that he must comply with the subpoena. He busied himself with the train work on the morning of the court date, then got into a waiting car and started for the courthouse in his makeup and cowboy clothes. When MacCauley was asked under oath if she could identify her seducer, the thirty-five- to forty-year-old woman replied, "Certainly I know him. Everybody knows him. He is William S. Hart." The courtroom erupted with laughter, and the case was ultimately dismissed. "No one outside of myself and those who battled for me so loyally can ever imagine what stupendous difficulties there were to overcome," the star said.

Apart from Bill's habit of proposing marriage to his leading ladies, rumors had circulated from time to time that he kept a series of mistresses in private. The actor was also said to have had a brief engagement to Margaret Evans, the daughter of a Montana rancher, during his speaking tour for the Fourth Liberty Loan Drive, but Bill claimed there was no such person and that the report was a press story. A woman calling herself Bepie wrote Hart at the Rex Arms Apartments about the time of the MacCauley case saying, "You told me last December to 'get over it' and I've surely tried." But the writer insisted that it was "no use at all" for her to try to forget Hart. Whether the letter came from an overzealous fan or an illicit flirtation is not known.

Hart often talked about his vision of the ideal woman—one who would become his helpmate and be "waiting at the home threshold each evening to smooth away the cares of a hard business day." Hart maintained that he once thought he had found a perfect companion. He invited the woman and her mother on a camping trip to Yosemite, and the women showed up with seven trunks and two French maids. The outing proved a disaster. The mother was shocked when she discovered that she was expected to sleep in a tent, and the girlfriend complained of being stiff as a board from horseback riding by the end of the trip. "No, it's the outdoor girl for me any time," Hart said. "I reckon the ideal girl for me, if she exists, would be the breeziest, sunniest, and wholesomest outdoor girl that ever rode a broncho. She might have a heap of freckles and perhaps a few callused spots on her hands from paddling a canoe, but she'd be a mighty good pal."

None of his assertions of romance sound particularly convincing. Hart never demonstrated a deep commitment to the notion of love or matrimony, and he appeared content with an asexual existence. When he talked of romantic involvements, he was vague, lighthearted, or melodramatically sentimental. Once at the Ritz Hotel in New York, a clerk put the actor in the bridal suite, since there was no other space available befitting his celebrity. Hart was amused at the accommodations and told Adolph Zukor that he was staying in the "bridle" suite.

Prude that he was, it is unlikely that Hart had passionate, much less carnal affairs. He voiced frequent dismay over the rebellion in manners and morals that marked the 1920s, and he believed more than ever that his kind of pictures were needed to show the nation's youth a righteous path amid the current confusion.

Hart was deeply vexed by the behavior and world conditions in the postwar era. He professed to have no set views on politics and said that he was neither for nor against the League of Nations. He was concerned about the turmoil in Mexico and felt that American troops would probably have to be sent south of the border again to restore order there. Hart's experience with Mexicans was limited, but he admired those who worked in his pictures. "The best horseman I know is a Mexican who can scarcely speak English," the actor said. "I have known him to break several almost unbreakable horses and never use quirt or spur."

Hart wanted to believe that World War I had been fought for a purpose and that the United States had been strengthened and cleansed by the experience. In *The Cradle of Courage*, released in October 1920, Bill played a man who at one time had been the finest safecracker in San Francisco. When war came, the crook was drafted into the American Expeditionary Force, and he returned home from France with a distinguished war record and a changed attitude toward life. In Hart's opinion the crook had regained "his manhood in the melting pot of the Cradle of Courage," and he viewed his movie as a valuable lesson for a period struggling to find stability.

By 1920 Bill earned around $8,400 a week in a time of nominal taxes. (Lambert Hillyer made $150 a week, while Joe August drew $125.) Hart ranked among the five most popular Hollywood screen stars, along with Charles Chaplin, Mary Pickford, Douglas Fairbanks, and Wallace Reid. Yet he was still living in a rented apartment with his sister Mary Ellen and their biscuit-colored bulldog, Congo. The star bought his suits ready-made and usually wore them with a Stetson hat. He lived quietly, drank moderately, enjoyed an infrequent game of poker, and made a morning ritual of reading George McManus's cartoon "Bringing Up Father" in the *Examiner*. Yet he spent most of his time at home silent and moody. Acquaintances remarked that a sad droop to his mouth revealed an unhappy, lonely man.

Hart's public persona, however, was quite different. "He comes into a room in that loving fashion," a journalist wrote in 1920, "just like a big clumsy, lumbering Newfoundland dog." At his office Hart sat in a swivel chair at a rolltop desk, most often wore a clean white shirt with gray pants and plain black shoes, and gave the appearance of the polite gentleman, except for an occasional "damn" or "hell" in his speech.

Hart understood the importance of publicity as well as any star of his day, and when not busy with a picture, he made himself available for judging beauty contests, making speeches, or anything that could be hyped into media fanfare. He once gave a talk in sign language to some Seneca Indians in Buffalo, New York, an event the press covered in detail, and the mawkish actor welcomed any chance to expound on "Measuring Up to Animals" as his personal credo. "I don't care to have anything to do with a man who doesn't like dogs," he said.

One evening Adolph Zukor, his son Eugene, and Jesse Lasky were aboard a Pullman car traveling from Los Angeles to San Francisco. An hour or so after they had left the Pasadena station, the train suddenly stopped out in the middle of nowhere. Word spead from car to car that bandits were holding up the passengers. While people hid wallets and jewelry in the seats, Adolph Zukor looked out the window and saw western bad men lining the track. "A tall man and a little man, six-shooters drawn, came into the car," the mogul recalled. "The taller wore a slouch hat and a bandana over the lower part of his face. The shorter had on a huge sombrero and a mask." Both headed straight for the elder Zukor, who quickly recognized them as William S. Hart and California theater owner Sid Grauman. The other passengers in due course were told that the holdup was a gag and that the train crew had been in on the prank.

Throughout 1920 Hart received fan mail from all over the world, an estimated average of three hundred letters a day. Babies were named after him, and his Westerns were the rage in both hemispheres. "It pleases the community at large to look upon me as a square man," Bill wrote Adolph Zukor in January 1920. He had genuine affection for his public, tried to live up to their image of him, and claimed that their loyalty meant more to him than money.

But Hart's immense popularity was about to fade. The moral revolution of the flamboyant 1920s eventually made his preachy films seem naive, and Hart lacked the capacity to alter his formula. Barricaded from close involvement outside his restricted world, Hart had little chance for emotional growth, and his movies reflected an arrested development that became more apparent as he entered advanced age. Hart talked frequently about retiring at the end of his Artcraft contract. "I think five years is about the limit for a star in motion pictures," he said, but he could not bring himself to relinquish the exalted status that masked his fragile private identity.

In March 1920 Hart was back in western garb playing "Sierra" Bill, the leader of a band of outlaws during the California gold rush, in *The Testing Block*. Hart argued that the current crisis in motion pictures lay in the weakness of available scripts, and his solution was to involve himself more in writing his movies. "In my opinion," Hart said, "it is much easier for a man of limited education to write for the screen than to write fiction for reading, as brilliant dialogue and proper atmospheric and descriptive language is not necessary in pictures. It is the plot and action that count." *The Testing Block* was based on Hart's original idea, although the scenario was drafted by Lambert Hillyer.

During the shooting of the film, a company of nearly fifty people was housed at the Grand Central Hotel in Felton and at the Dickinson Hotel in Ben Lomond in the California redwood country. A one-street frontier town was constructed about ten miles from Felton, which included log houses, tawdry-looking shacks, a saloon and dance hall, a general store, a sheriff's office, and a hotel as the community's only two-story building. For over ten days it rained, during which the crew could not shoot a single scene. Much of the filming on the picture needed to be done at night, and the heaviest, brightest lights available were placed among the giant redwoods so that the company could do its work. It was still drizzling intermittently when the first shots were taken, and drops constantly fell from the overhanging branches. Despite the cold and dampness, the crew worked from seven o'clock in the evening until five o'clock the next morning to make up for lost time.

The Testing Block's plot called for Hart to fight eight members of his gang, one at a time, around a campfire. "Those who fought first were the lucky ones," Hart said. "Those who were kept waiting were unlucky. They nearly perished with the cold." One of the first men to fight the star was an ex-heavyweight champion who was on his wedding trip; the man's bride, bundled up in a thick coat, sat watching while her husband received a black eye. By the end of the ordeal, Hart was also a sorry-looking sight, having battled one opponent after another, only to wind up fighting a twenty-five-year-old Indian at four o'clock in the morning.

Eva Novak, Jane's younger sister, was Hart's leading lady in the picture, and Hart rewarded her with his customary proposal of marriage, which the actress tactfully declined. Eva came to Hollywood a bit later than Jane, but some thought she was even prettier than her sister.

At six reels *The Testing Block* was Bill's longest movie to date, and it fared well at the box office and with critics. "William S. Hart as the tigerish outlaw, 'Sierra' Bill, is a figure so powerful and distinct as to need no other centering of attention than that provided by his own personality," *Moving Picture World* reported. "His dress is new, his attitude more intensely animal than ever before, his expression of the lawless male one to be remembered."

Meanwhile Hart and Ince were preparing to do battle in court. Hart claimed that Ince owed him money, and Ince filed a cross-complaint. J. Parker Read, Ince's friend and business associate, also brought suit against Hart, alleging that Hart owed him a commission on the star's initial contract with Famous Players. Ince testified against Hart for several days in the Read lawsuit, but eventually the case was thrown out of court. Hart ultimately received a settlement of $88,779 from Ince, but legal fees consumed much of that. In addition, Hart had operating expenses. While court reporters filled twenty-five volumes with transcripts of testimony in his cases with Ince and Read, a $5,000-a-week overhead mounted at the William S. Hart Studio, where facilities sat idle for two months.

To Hart, Ince had become an Iago, who practiced "submarine warfare which never knows the sunlight but deals knife thrusts in the dark." Bill warned Adolph Zukor that Tom was trying to use Famous Players–Lasky in the same underhanded way he had used Triangle and at the same time attempting to cause a rift between Famous

Players and himself. Ince "devotes all of his time, in conjunction with his man, Read, to scheming and the furthering of his own interests," Hart wrote Zukor on January 3, 1920. "I have refused to be robbed, all the vitrol in their bottle is directed against me."

With the money Hart received from Ince, he bought a nine-room house in Hollywood. Located at 8341 DeLongpre, a block off Sunset Boulevard, Hart's home was in the same neighborhood as the residences of actor Wallace Reid (who later died of drug addiction), director William Desmond Taylor (who was murdered in his home on Alvarado Street, a block away), and Ernest Torrence (who would play the king of the beggars in the silent screen version of *The Hunchback of Notre Dame*).

In 1920 Hart also purchased his 220-acre Horseshoe Ranch outside Newhall, twenty-five miles north of Los Angeles. The town of Newhall was frequently used as a movie location, and Hart's property was just seven miles west of Saugus, where Western actor Harry Carey had a three-thousand-acre working ranch, with sixty Navajo Indians living on the land and facilities available for rodeos. Like Hart, Carey was a New Yorker by birth, but he had fallen in love with the West and opted to live a western lifestyle. A decade later Carey claimed that he only made movies to earn the money to buy fence posts for his spread. Carey's wife, Olive, often explained her husband's absences by telling visitors, "Sorry, Harry's out playing cowboy."

The Carey ranch became a center for the Hollywood crowd connected with Western movies. Hart and Carey were friends, although they were such different personalities that Harry found Bill amusing. "My dad was like talking to the next-door farmer," said Harry Carey, Jr., a later Western actor, "and William S. Hart was just the opposite— very theatrical." The minute Hart came on Carey's ranch, he started acting macho and affectedly "western." Hart visited the Careys once during Christmas season, and Carey brought out a jug of grappa, an Italian moonshine, and two tumblers. Carey asked Hart if he would like a drink. "By God, yes," Hart said. "I was weaned on that stuff!" Harry poured them both a glassful, and Bill took a big swallow. Soon he couldn't get his breath; blood rushed to his head, and tears filled his eyes. He made the same mistake another time by sampling the chili peppers Olive Carey kept in a bowl on their dining room table. "Hart turned purple," Harry Carey, Jr., remembered. "Sweat started glistening on his forehead, and he blew the peppers all over the table."

Carey's circle, which included Will Rogers, Charlie Russell, and cowboy star Hoot Gibson, delighted in ultramasculine mannerisms that the younger Carey found intimidating as a boy. "All of those guys, including my father, were huge bullshitters," said Harry Carey, Jr. "They all exaggerated the truth. But Hart was always 'on.' I never saw any humor in him. I much preferred Will Rogers, who had a magnetic quality and never talked down to people."

In 1925 Hart would build a mansion on his Horseshoe Ranch and spend most of his time there. Even before that he entertained a few close Hollywood friends like Will Rogers, Harold Lloyd, and Pola Negri at the ranch on Sunday afternoons. "We loved the excursions to the old West we had grown up with in novels and old movies," Negri said. "Bill worked very hard to give [his] place an air of authenticity."

Discouraged with moviemaking and finding suitable Western scripts harder to come by, Hart turned more of his attention to writing stories for boys. His campfire stories appeared in sixteen weekly installments in *The Citizen Patriot* during 1920. Subjects were selected from questions the actor had been asked by his young fans through the years and included his views on cowboy clothes, Indian sign language, Indian games, signal fires, branding cattle, six-shooters, horsemanship, cattle stampedes, capturing wild stallions, and how to ride a bucking bronco. Hart's second book, *Injun and Whitey Strike Out for Themselves*, was published by Houghton Mifflin in 1921, and *Injun and Whitey to the Rescue* came out a year later. In his writing Hart emphasized frontier virtues, set forth as plain, practical lessons in living. "We must not forget that we are writing for boys," Hart wrote his editor. He wanted to entertain young readers but also to win their affection and instruct them in such matters as hygiene, diet, and fair play. He gave hundreds of copies of his books to newsboys, aware that the publicity he received from their newspapers would be invaluable. He also had copies printed in Braille for distribution to the blind.

During the summer of 1920, Hart made *O'Malley of the Mounted* in the mountains near Chatsworth, California. Hart played a sergeant in the Northwest Mounted Police and suffered bruises and four broken ribs during the filming, which made fight scenes difficult for him. The director waited to shoot the biggest scrap until the rest of the movie was finished, and special care was taken to guard against injuring Hart further. Since the actor's opponent in the fight had been warned not to hit him in the body, the fellow had no choice but to direct his blows at the star's head. "That man hit every spot on my face four hundred times," Hart maintained. The next afternoon Hart and Hillyer ran the footage in a studio projection room, only to discover that it was ruined with static. The entire fight had to be done over, with Hart in agony the whole time.

Eva Novak again played Hart's leading lady in *O'Malley of the Mounted*, and in one scene, considered too difficult for the delicate actress, she had to be doubled. "I never saw a cowboy double for a girl who didn't go one hundred per cent nutty when he got the skirts on," Hart said. Hank Potts, a small but tough man, substituted for Novak, and with skirts on he became "the wildest 'cowjane' that ever came off the prairie," Bill said.

Reviews of *O'Malley* were more kind than complimentary. "Bill Hart is like the old family physician—you have great faith in what he prescribes," *Wid's* said when the picture was released. "And you can always depend on him." The *New York Times* agreed: "Hart . . . is an institution, and nothing new may be said about him. People like him or they don't." Both responses resonated indifference.

Hart talked often about retiring at the end of his current contract. Already he felt slighted by Artcraft and complained that he came last among Famous Players' stars in trade paper coverage. "I make consistently good stories," he reminded Adolph Zukor. "I represent (and have the field to myself) the vanished and vanishing West, which all Americans love, and they love me for reproducing it in a truthful manner."

Hart was never tempted to go back on the stage, even though he said that Broadway producers had offered him as much as $15,000 a week to do so, more money than he ever dreamed existed in New York. He told reporters that by the time he had finished his second Artcraft contract he expected to have enough money to live comfortably and felt that he had earned the right to relax. "Boys," he wrote in his campfire stories, "when I retire from the motion picture screen, I am going to make a tour of the world and then settle down on a big Western ranch for the rest of my days. Life in the great outdoors is the birthright of every human being."

Although critics seemed to be tiring of Hart's pictures, his fans remained loyal. The star averaged fifteen hundred letters a week from admirers, and he spent between $8,000 and $10,000 a year sending out photographs of himself. Hart appeared to be every American boy's favorite, but he also received requests for still photographs from Cuba, Peru, Australia, Japan, and throughout Europe. Most of his fans preferred him in Westerns, and a New Yorker complimented the actor on his ability "to show the struggle to overcome the 'devil within' in such a manner as to leave its impress upon the many 'down and outs' who see your pictures." Any time more than a few months passed without a new William S. Hart movie in the theaters, admirers wrote him demanding an explanation.

After William F. Cody's death in 1917, William S. Hart became the most publicized living symbol of the American frontier. "Buffalo Bill is dead," the *Portland Oregonian* declared in March 1920. "But Bill Hart still remains. And not even in his palmiest days—the days of his plainsmanship or the days of his showmanship—did the famous former have an audience so great or a following so enthusiastic as the famous latter."

Two months later Hart was nominated for sheriff on the Democratic ticket in Hood River country, Oregon. The following September, the *Newsboys' World* said, "Sometimes there's a lot of difference between a real cowboy and a movie actor who plays the part; but after you have spent an hour or so with William S. Hart, you realize that he is one actor who knows the West and could be elected sheriff of the Panhandle if he cared to run for that office." More than a personification of the old West, Hart had become "a man who represents humanity," according to the *Picture Show*.

Hart's pose as a westerner intensified as his career started to decline. During press interviews, the star's use of cowboy language became so improvident that many observers found him comical, and movie executives began to snicker behind his back. Hart taught Jesse Lasky, Jr., the "quick draw" he used in films, and when Adolph Zukor's daughter married, Hart sent her a mounted silver bridle as a wedding gift, aware that she liked to ride horses. In the popular press Hart's exaggerated image approached caricature: "No horse is too wild for 'Bill' to ride," *Boy's Cinema* proclaimed in the early 1920s. But the slick, streamlined Westerns of Tom Mix, Hoot Gibson, and Buck Jones were soon to overtake him.

Despite the slowdown in his production of movies, the old actor claimed to be overloaded with work and running at top speed day and night—planning future film projects, writing stories for boys, discussing a series of books for Bobbs-Merrill, making personal appearances, taking care of his ranch, entertaining Boy Scout troupes that toured his studio, talking to YMCA groups, and dealing with "the usual problems and lawsuits sandwiched in between." He was still disturbed that his early films were being reissued under different titles, and in October 1920, Hart filed two suits in the Superior Court of Los Angeles, asking for an injunction to stop the practice and $250,000 in damages. "Through the cooperation of the newspapers," he said, "I am exposing a shameful deception which is now being perpetrated on unsuspecting theatergoers throughout the United States." Although illegal, pirated versions of the star's films continued to be shown.

To escape the harsh weather in Montana, Charlie and Nancy Russell had begun spending winters in southern California, and although the commotion of urban Los Angeles bothered the cowboy artist, he enjoyed spending time in the area with friends like Will Rogers, Harry Carey, and William S. Hart. "Charlie Russell was down here a short time ago and I had several long talks with him," Bill wrote a friend in April 1920. "He is the same old Charlie; success has not changed him a bit."

Wyatt Earp, the legendary peace officer of Dodge City and Tombstone, began a correspondence with Hart in 1920, initially to inquire about the possibility of making a motion picture depicting his exploits in the lawless West, including the famous gunfight at O.K. Corral, in a less sensational way than his career had been treated in previous accounts. Earp enjoyed visiting movie sets and tried to correct film-makers when he noticed mistakes in Western pictures. Earp's friends later claimed that he spent hours trying to teach William S. Hart the fast draw but that the actor proved so inept and dropped his gun so often that a blanket had to be spread out on the ground for padding. Nonetheless, the contact with a man who helped tame the West added to Hart's credentials, and the actor delighted in boasting of their friendship.

Soon after Hart moved into the house on DeLongpre, he received a number of letters from a Madeline Banks that intimate an ardent love affair. Addressing him as "Lover Man," Banks wrote Hart, "Darling man, is this love of ours quite the most wonderful thing in the world? I think so. . . .I only want you to take me in your arms, my darling." What happened to Madeline is not known, nor is the genuineness of her ardor.

Hart informed Adolph Zukor that he needed to make at least four pictures a year or he would suffer financially. By 1920 Hart's movies were costing $100,000 or more to produce, but the overhead at his studio continued whether or not he was turning out films. In the late summer of 1920 Hart filmed *The Whistle*, a different kind of story for him, one that dealt with the clash between capital and labor in a New England town around 1914. "This should stand out as one of the finest contributions William S. Hart has given the screen," *Photoplay* maintained when the picture was released in July 1921. Although Hart's portrayal in *The Whistle* lent dignity to the theme of labor exploitation, the movie was not the fare fans expected from him, and it did not do well at the box office.

Bill had three more pictures to make under his contract with Artcraft (which by then operated under the Paramount banner), and he wanted all three to be "pippins." He realized that he had to go after "big stuff with punches in it, a lot of heart interest and a few stunts." Exhibitors demanded more Westerns, so in November 1920 Hart and twenty-five members of his company left for Sacramento to begin filming *White Oak*, an action Western, with Hart playing a river gambler seeking revenge on his sister's seducer. Paramount's advertisements for the movie were lurid, yet the kind that filled theaters: "When hostile Indians stalked the wagon trains, and none but the quickest-trigger man was safe . . . came White Oak Miller riding over the plains! Riding on a quest your heart will thrill to see!"

The waterfront at Sacramento substituted for the Mississippi for *White Oak*'s river sequences. Hart had a number of scenes in the water, and since several days of rain had put the production behind schedule, many of those were not shot until December, when cakes of ice were floating down the Sacramento River. Hart developed a severe cold as a result, but he had to move on to Victorville for the movie's desert scenes. When his temperature rose to 103 degrees, a doctor was called, and Hart was ordered to bed for three days, while his company sat idle.

"Cowboys are children," the actor said, "from eight to eighty, age makes no difference. They are boys just the same." During the wait for Hart to recuperate, a freight train side-tracked in the vicinity of the movie's location, and one of its oil tanks proved full of bootleg Mexican wine. The cowboys working on the picture managed to siphon out enough of the wine with a garden hose to fill buckets, garbage pails, horses' nosebags, and every other available container. "For two whole days and nights the carnival lasted," Hart maintained. "The streets of the town became a public dance hall." With the situation completely out of hand, local residents telephoned the sheriff in San Bernardino, who dispatched twenty deputies to the scene to arrest the merrymakers.

Mary Ellen Hart came to Victorville to look after her brother, and she often accompanied him out to the day's set, where she carefully brushed some of the dust from his hair between takes. Mary Ellen was Hart's business partner as well as his sister, and she seemed to become more possessive of Hart as the years went by.

Maude Cheatham visited the *White Oak* set in the desert and described the experience for *Motion Picture Magazine* as "so exciting" and "so thrillingly real" that she looked on breathlessly as the scenes unfolded. "Every day for three weeks the cameras clicked," she wrote, with Hart's "keen eyes shaded by a big sombrero, silently watching every detail." At the end of the day's shooting the cameras were packed in wagons, and automobiles carried the players down a winding road to the little town where they were housed.

"So long as I live I shall never tire of playing cowboy roles," Hart said in 1921, but the public's enthusiasm for his brand of Westerns had crested. Bill asked Zukor to let him finish his contract with *Travelin' On*, released in March 1922. "It is psychologically fitted to be so—and in my opinion is the best picture I have ever made," Hart said. *Travelin' On* cost about $165,000, and Hart said that rather than try to hold down costs, he had "gone the limit on everything rather than take the chance of turning out inferior work." Yet critics found the movie slow and below par.

Hart had become displeased with Paramount and felt that its executives were treating him badly. He complained that his box office had declined because his films were released during the summer months, when business was bad, since theaters were not air-conditioned. Bill was convinced that Adolph Zukor's attitude toward him had changed, and he insisted that his recent releases—each seven reels—were too long and would have fared better had they been cut.

At fifty-seven, Hart's seniority was written in his face and his energy was low. The pace of his films had grown slower and their narratives more redundant. His acting seemed increasingly strained, and his last pictures lacked compelling tension. His characters were either too pure or too vile, in either case too trite to please movie audiences whose tastes were becoming more sophisticated. Younger moviegoers preferred the audacious riding, breezy showmanship, and glib manner of Tom Mix, the flashier dress of Hoot Gibson and Ken Maynard, and the comedy of Buck Jones. More mature viewers admired the work of Harry Carey and John Ford and would soon embrace Western spectacles such as *The Covered Wagon* (1923) and *The Iron Horse* (1924). While Hart continued to whine about managerial neglect and imagined abuses, the vogue in motion pictures was moving away from his moralistic themes. The simple truth was that Hart's day in motion pictures had passed.

Romance and Marriage

In January 1921 twenty-four-year-old Jane Novak had a three-year-old daughter and was in the process of a divorce. The actress had already made four movies with William S. Hart, and Hart wanted her again for *Three Word Brand*, the final release under his renewed Artcraft contract. Hart described Novak to Adolph Zukor as "a girl who has worked her way up to an enviable position. . . . She is one of the very best actresses on the screen. She is young . . . and exquisitely beautiful. She is modest, unassuming, and a little child could control her." Hart assured Zukor that Novak was in great demand and said that he thought so much of her ability that his studio was willing to pay her current salary, $750 a week, even though $500 a week was the highest the company had gone before. "Miss Novak appears to be one of the few who by their popularity with the public can command such salaries," Hart said.

As had become his practice, Hart had asked Jane to marry him after her separation, and she had accepted his proposal. The two planned to wed shortly after September 18, 1921, when Novak would be free. Bill pointed out to Zukor the publicity value, both for his next film and for the actress's budding career, in having *Three Word Brand* ready for release around October 1, when Jane would become his wife. "Of course," the cowboy star added, "there is always the chance of a girl changing her mind, but in this case I do not think she will do so, as we are very fond of each other. She is a girl of irreproachable character—sweet and wonderful in every way."

Three Word Brand went into production in the late winter and was finished in the early spring of 1921. Hart played triple roles in the Western—a father and his twin sons. To save the boys during an Indian attack, the westerning father blows himself to bits with gunpowder. (Despite Hart's avowed respect for Native Americans, *Three Word Brand* and many of his other movies portrayed Indians as savages.) The twin sons are adopted by different people and grow to manhood in Utah as strangers. One becomes a ranch owner, and the other is elected governor of the state. Jane Novak played the love interest of the rancher, who is reunited with his brother when they both become involved in a question of water rights. The picture offers interesting backgrounds and atmosphere, but it barely broke even at the box office, causing Paramount executives to decide that Hart's brand of Westerns was dead.

Tired from the relentless pace of moviemaking and free of his Artcraft commitment, Bill gave up his studio and planned to enjoy a long rest. He intended to marry, raise a family, develop his ranch in Newhall, do some writing, and eventually make a few independently produced films. Still, after four years of constant work, seeing the William S. Hart Studio dismantled was a painful experience for the aging actor. "When, one calm spring morning, the last truck pulled away from the old place, I felt that something had gone out of my life," he said.

That spring he devoted himself to Jane. "Oh Jane, dear Jane, if I could only stretch out my arms and reach you," he wrote Novak in April 1921, while she was in New York City on a month's vacation and shopping spree. "No two people on earth ever loved so strongly, purely, and unselfishly. We belong to each other; we are one and the same body, one and the same soul. . . . It all seems so bald and impotent to try to write what I feel."

Jane Novak was born and raised in St. Louis and had moved to Hollywood in 1916. Soon after coming to California, she met William S. Hart at the Miramar Hotel in Santa Monica. "From then on we were friends," she said, and eventually Hart and Novak's brother Joe, an assistant cameraman, became close friends. "Everybody called him Willie," Jane said of Hart. "I didn't; he would have hit me if I'd called him Willie. I called him 'B' mostly. Just his initial, just plain ole 'B.'"

Novak remembered the cowboy star as a lonely man, devoted to his sister Mamie. "I think that he used to feel sad that Mamie didn't have a lot of friends around," Novak said. "Mamie wasn't really a well person. People that she liked, she loved. She kept as close to them as she could, but that wasn't very close. Mamie was not a very outgoing person." Novak never saw Mary Ellen do any cooking; mostly she stayed in her bedroom when Bill had company. "She was a very inward person," Novak said. "Willie took good care of her. I don't know why she never married. . . . She was sort of a closed person."

Acquaintances remembered Jane Novak as lovely and delicate, with clear skin and graceful hands. "She looked like she never washed a dish," Harry Carey, Jr., said. Jane always seemed quiet and retiring, but although she was sweet dispositioned, she had a mind of her own. She did not overdress to draw attention to herself and had a shy laugh that was part of her charm. Friends said that Bill treated her like a little girl; he was always tender and gallant and thoughtful with her.

"So Bill Hart is to marry Jane Novak!" *Picture Play* exclaimed in August 1921. "Anyway, that's what folks say." The periodical's reporter first met Jane on the set of one of Hart's movies, and on that occasion Hart spent most of his time between setups teasing Novak unmercifully. When the cowboys working on the picture hid Jane's slipper on a cabin rafter, Bill climbed up and got it for her. Jane was struck by how nice and unassuming the venerable actor was with people.

When Novak accompanied Hart to the opening of *Three Word Brand*, she noticed grease spots on his vest and tie as fans filed past them in the lobby to shake their hands. She later voiced surprise at the soiled clothing, since he was always so immaculately dressed when they went out to dinner. "Well, it's this way," Hart told her. "My public rather expects me to look common." Mary Ellen claimed that whenever she laid out fresh clothes for her brother, he dipped his fingers into the gravy bowl and flicked gravy onto his front before going out to meet fans.

During their engagement, Novak visited Hart's house in Hollywood and found it "very comfortable." She also went with him to his ranch, where they rode horses. Bill was fond of Jane's daughter, Mickey, whom he called Bubbles, and the couple usually took the child to the ranch with them. "Mickey loved horses," Jane said. "She never rode; she was too young for that." Hart bought a little crib for Bubbles and kept it at the ranch house for her naps.

"My heart is full to the bursting point with happiness," Bill wrote Martha McKelvie, a Nebraska friend, during his engagement to Novak. "The past few hazy blue days have turned into glorious ones, and the blue mountains have taken the red of the sun on their crests and all the ills of the world seem to have gone down with that wonderful orb. . . . Who can look upon that face, who can look into those eyes, and doubt. . . . Love is a very great thing."

Silent pictures' man of stone and steel, Hollywood's eternal bachelor, at age fifty-six, appeared to have found romantic bliss. Hart had been the hope of unmarried women, misunderstood wives, and jilted matrons, but most of them had adored him from afar. Mary Ellen described to reporters the many disconsolate women who had camped on their doorstep, waiting to waylay their hero and pour out their anguish to him. Hart had remained the gentleman and treated these lovesick ladies with courtesy, but his emotions seemed frozen. Jane Novak apparently had awakened an ardor in the wintry actor that surpassed anything he had ever experienced, and his response was joyfully adolescent.

"I cannot live without you," Bill wrote Jane in April 1921, while she was in Manhattan with Mary Ellen. "I am nothing but a shell of a man walking around. All my whole being is with you. . . . I am positively aching for you, a dull physical and mental ache. . . . I just can't exist without you." Bill wrote Novak every day during the month she was away and eased his loneliness by visiting her brother Joe and his wife, Ann, checking on "little Bubbles," and taking Congo, his bulldog, for long walks. Since Jane's divorce was still pending, Bill had not accompanied her to New York, insisting that they must avoid damaging publicity. He urged Jane to see as many Broadway shows as possible, dine at the best restaurants, and buy lots of pretty things—dresses, hats, shoes, whatever she wanted. "I hope you go broke in a week," he wrote her, "so I can send you another check."

One evening, paying a call on Jane's brother, Bill ran into Jane's husband romping with Bubbles on the lawn. The little girl saw Bill's car drive up, and, thinking Congo was inside, she screamed with delight and ran to greet him. Apparently the encounter with Bubbles's father was none too pleasant, for Bill wrote Jane, "I hope I never meet him again—under any circumstances—but especially when he has the baby. . . . He is just an obscure corner loafer, and he is aching for notoriety. If it has to come, I want to have him where he will suffer for his dirty tricks. . . . On account of the baby I never want to mix with him personally if I can help it. . . . I haven't the slightest doubt but what he would welcome any sort of a row. That would put him in the limelight as an injured husband and suffering father, which on account of our prominence he could easily do in any newspaper in the country, if we gave him a chance." Hart assured Jane that he would be on the first train east were it not for her marital status. "I just ache for you," he wrote. "But I cannot [join you]; it would ruin everything— and place you in an awkward position. . . . If I started for New York, it would be known before I got on the train."

Hart purchased forty additional feet of property adjacent to his house on DeLongpre while Jane and Mary Ellen were in New York and attended a rodeo at his ranch, taking Joe and Ann with him. "All the cowboys I ever knew were in it," Hart wrote his beloved. "It was frightfully dusty, and we left early to escape the crowd. . . . The inside of the house is all clean and waiting for you to say what you want in it—and how you want it arranged."

Tom Mix had recently helped Jane's sister Eva get ten weeks' work at the Fox studio, earning $400 a week. Hart told Jane that he had figured out why he had once fallen in love with Eva. "She was you," he wrote, for Eva was "half Jane in looks and speech. . . . I always was in love with my Jane, and while it never occurred to me that I could ever get you, the love that I've subconsciously felt for you kept me from loving, really loving anyone else—until I met Eva." But he thought Eva wore too much makeup. "I like to see girls powdered up and touched up a little," he told Jane. "It seems to be so feminine. But there is a limit."

Hart wrote Jane that their monthlong separation had been good for them, since she had admitted that she loved him in one of her early letters from New York. "It was the first time after over three years that you ever laid bare your heart to me," he said. "It has made you confess that we are yet to have our first kiss. . . . I know you love me, and I know I am the love of your life. . . . And when we meet we will have our first kiss—and when we are united by God, my sweetheart will be the same as she is today." Hart admitted that he wished he were younger for his "darling girl's sake." He said that he loved her so much that he was suffering from "blind staggers" and feared he might die of love. "I do not expect to die," he wrote Jane. "I am healthy and strong, but I am so much older than you it is only to be expected I should go first." Yet he assured her that his love was so great that he would "crawl after her" if he were "crippled and dying to the ends of the earth. It is beyond the power of anything human to ever separate us."

When Bill talked of their future together, it was always Jane and Mamie and little Bubbles. When he bought the additional property in Hollywood, he urged Jane and Mamie to talk over what they wanted to do with it in the way of improvements. "I will have fifty feet from the cement drive," he said, "and I want to fix it just as you and Mamie want it." He assured Jane that they would never be parted again. "Where you go, I go," he said, "until death do us part. Oh, my darling, we will be so happy—you and Bubbles and Mamie and I—for we all love each other so dearly." He counseled Jane not to be afraid of letting Mamie know that she loved him. "She will worship you for it," he said. "I have often thought that Mamie saw you were holding back."

Bill promised that he could never be jealous of Jane's actions, for it was not in her "to do wrong—even in thought." "Your mind is clear and sweet and wholesome," he wrote. Since Jane liked New York, he said they would divide their time between Manhattan and Los Angeles once they were married, until she decided which home she wanted. It was his duty, he wrote, to care for her and protect her. "Every fiber of my whole being is trembling and on fire for you, my mate."

The love-struck actor took comfort in knowing that Mamie was with Jane on her New York holiday. "I know that no harm can come to you or Mamie as long as you are together," he said. "I want you to see all the life you can; I want you to enjoy yourself. I want you to have all the liberty that any girl is entitled to, but I would be lower than a beast of the field if I did not want you to be with a party and not one person and that person any man that was ever born of woman. . . . For you to be embarrassed would make all the earth go red for me and cause me to lose my reason. . . . I'd rather die a million times by the torture of the Spanish Inquisition than to feel the pangs of an unfaithful love."

Threatened with numerous scandals and rapid transition, Hollywood studios had gone into a temporary slump. "I don't see how Famous Players or any company can be any too solid and safe with so much dissatisfaction," Hart wrote in 1921. He was relieved to be on the sidelines. If Jane wanted to continue working after they were married, that was all right with him; he would even help her select the best studio. But, he said, "your money worries in this life are ended. It does not matter what your obligations are or how much money you need to fulfill them. It is yours—I care absolutely nothing for money. I have toiled through poverty all my life with only one aim—to earn money to make those I love happy. . . . It is only the last few years that I can do things for those I love. I always had the inclination but never the means. . . . My darling can work and star or not work and star—just as she wishes."

While Jane was away, Bill spent a great deal of time at his ranch, usually taking Joe, Ann, and Bubbles along. "The horses follow me around just the same as dogs would," he wrote Jane. Fritz not only had Cactus Kate as a companion, Bill had also bought Lizabeth, a mule, to keep the horses company. Hart had begun acquiring a menagerie of dogs at the ranch, one of which was named Wolf. "Fritz and Kate and Wolf are all waiting for you," he wrote Novak. "I will not touch the inside of our Newhall home. You must do it. If you only put a wood box in the corner and a horse blanket on the bed, I'm happy."

Mamie talked Jane into buying a fur coat that cost $1,500 while they were in New York, and Bill seemed delighted when he learned of the purchase. He sent her another check and told her to go to Tiffany's and buy herself a platinum and diamond bracelet. "This is not a request, it is an order," he said. "Mamie will go with you." He told Jane not to think any more about earning money. "I have it and you are me," he said. "I love you. I worship you. . . . It is my happiness to do things for you. . . . You must not rob me of the joy of giving you pretty things."

Bill spent most of his evenings with Joe and Ann and Bubbles during Jane and Mamie's absence, and occasionally the four of them went over to Jane's mother's house for dinner. Bubbles usually sat beside Hart at the table, while Congo slept in a corner. Sometimes Bill, Joe, Ann, and Eva went bowling or to a movie. Many evenings Bill stayed home alone. "It is not human this separation," he wrote Jane. "I can't do anything. I can't go anywhere. I just go home and stay by myself. It would seem like a sacrilege if I tried not to be lonesome." With Jane and Mamie away, he had not been feeling well. "I hurt all over," he said, "and my head is actually wobbly. . . . I am going to cut down on my drinking and smoking." Hart vowed to limit his smoking to four cigars a day and restrict himself to either wine at dinner or one cocktail before dinner.

Hart was overjoyed when he learned that Jane would have a chance to visit his farm in Westport. "I know you'll love it," he said. "It is so pretty and full of memories. . . . How our little mother would have loved to see you in those rooms. How she would have smiled and kissed you and asked you to be good to me. I can see her doing it!" In his solitude the reclusive actor ruminated over his life: the lessons he had learned from his father, the years of poverty and struggle, but especially his little sister who had died. "Oh, Jane, how she would have loved you," he wrote. "How she would have clung to you. She was God's own embodiment of love and affection. For years after she went away I used to write with grease paint on the mirror of my dressing room what seemed most to fit the call of my soul. . . . It almost killed my little mother and Mamie and me when she went away. We were in a daze. She was so young, so good, so full of the joy of living. It was a tragedy—the more cruel because it came from God and crippled our lives."

Loneliness gradually spawned depression, and in his despair Hart reviewed the hurts he had suffered—the betrayals, the lawyers' fees, the hangers-on, the petty annoyances. "It is simply astounding what crooks there are in the world," he wrote Jane, "and the sad part of it is they get away with it." At present Famous Players was two and a half months behind in their statements of earnings to him. "Of course, I have no reason to suspect anything wrong," he said, "but when the money is in securities and the securities are in a vault, it's better for us."

Jane's husband was threatening trouble, and Bill feared that any false move might endanger his fiancée's appeal for sole custody of Bubbles. Also aggravating to Bill were scurrilous letters he had received from a woman in Indianapolis. He was trying to locate her address so that he could instruct his lawyer to look into the situation and have the woman put in jail for misuse of the mail. Mainly Hart was lonely and unhappy and, for the first time in his adult life, idle. Even his celebrity had become a source of complaint. "I am a marked man," he said. "I cannot go across the street. Everyone knows me."

Charlie and Nancy Russell had recently been in Los Angeles, trying to find a place to buy for her father. Bill suggested an available house, but Nancy didn't like it. A trifle miffed, Bill wrote Jane, "I'm through recommending places. Let 'em get out and find them, same as we have to do. Charlie did not see the place at all. Nancy's devotion to Charlie is marvelous, but is she not Charlie? Does Charlie live at all?" It is a telling comment on the artist's marriage but perhaps also revealing about Hart's perception of women.

Mary Ellen became ill during her stay in New York—first with a cold, then with something sufficiently chronic that she could no longer accompany Jane on shopping excursions. Bill commented in his letters that Mamie's system was "being poisoned somewhere" and that doctors were trying to find the cause. Most likely Mary Ellen was none too pleased about Bill's sudden burst of adoration for Jane and sensed that her brother might be slipping from her grasp. Whether friction developed between Mary Ellen and Jane on the trip is not known, but an aloofness apparently set in. "You love Bubbles, and I love Mamie," Hart wrote his fiancée shortly before she returned to California. "That does not lessen our love for each other. How could I be capable of loving you if I did not love a sister who had made a sacrifice for me and her parents and loved me all her life?"

Hart's impassioned letters to Novak continued day after day during her holiday, and he finally begged her to come home, whether Mamie was well enough to travel or not. "I look at your picture over the bed and I just choke up," he said. "You are my world and you are not here. I love you up to the sky and back again and all 'round the hills. . . . What a blue-eyed baby vamp you are. Is it any wonder that I have fallen so hard?" He said that he had gone back to the letter in which Jane had confessed her love for him and picked it up time and again. "I crushed it to my heart and then to my lips and kissed it a hundred times. And I am not ashamed to say it was wet with tears." Repeatedly Bill said that he was not capable of putting into words all the emotion he felt for her. "It is all too intimate—too close—too big! . . . Unless I hear something from you soon about coming home, I'll be a lunatic."

He longed for their first kiss—"and a million more on top of it"— and wondered why they had not kissed long ago. "When you come home," Bill said, "we'll just put our arms around each other and not talk for hours—just you and me and Bubbles. . . . Do you realize, my darling, that in about eighteen weeks we can be side by side all the time and sleep in each other's arms.?" He vowed that God had given them their love for one another and said that casting it aside "would be like desecrating a church."

Years ago Hart had spoken some lines from the stage that he said he did not understand as a man, only as an actor. He told Jane that he now knew what they meant. The lines were penned by Victor Hugo: "I love her as the lion loves blood, as the sea bird loves the ocean, and as the eagle loves the sun." Hart wrote Jane on May 10, 1921, "If I had to say those lines now, I could close my eyes and say them to you whom I worship, and an audience would be hushed and stilled with wonder!" Soon she would be coming home, he said. "We can hold each other close and not talk for hours and hours. And the lowland people and the mountain people and the travelers by land and sea can live their lives, and the smoke of civilization can rise and be blown away by the four winds of heaven, and little babies can lie asleep in their cribs, and the wolf, the deer, the fox, and the coyotes can wander where the snow clings to the branches of the trees, and still we will stand oblivious to all save the fire of an unextinguishable love."

Such melodrama does not portend a mature, lasting relationship, and Hart's romance with Jane Novak ran into trouble within a month after her return to Hollywood. Probably her very proximity was the cause, but acquaintances and business associates also pointed out to Hart the dangers of marrying a divorced actress so much younger than himself. A whisper campaign had started in the film colony even before Jane was back from New York. "I must tell you that what I was told, and what came from different quarters seeming to prove it, nearly drove me insane," Bill wrote his fiancée on May 3. "I defy any man on earth to suffer as I suffered. Night after night I would sit at the table and not eat. . . . And then I'd leave and walk about and try to find a way out but there was no way."

When Mary Ellen came home from her trip with Jane, Bill had her coldness to deal with. Night after night they sat across the table from one another, staring at each other without speaking. Clearly Mary Ellen did not favor his marriage, and Natalie Talmadge had been recruited to add her opposition. Jane Novak's daughter, Mickey, was convinced that Mary Ellen was responsible for putting an end to her mother's brief engagement to Hart. Jane later said that wherever she and "B" went, they always took Mamie with them. But in New York the spinster sister had mostly stayed in the hotel, becoming increasingly quiet and distant. Probably Jane's report to Bill of the growing resentment Mary Ellen showed her did not sit well with him.

Bill felt a strong obligation to Mamie. They had lived together for so long. She was his companion, his business partner, his adviser, his only close family, and she was totally dependent on him economically and emotionally. Jane said that she never knew Bill's other living sister, Frances, although Frances's granddaughters used to visit Bill and Mamie occasionally. Bill told Jane that he did not love his other sister and that she had never loved him. She "never did one-tenth of her duty," he wrote Novak. "I had to furnish money . . . to care for our mother and Mamie. She does not belong in my life."

For whatever reason, Hart's engagement to Jane Novak was over by late June 1921. Bill was bitter and unhappy about the breakup, feeling nothing inside, he said, but a dull ache. "It is just a case of 'be a man' and wait for time—that dimmer of all ills of the heart," he wrote his friend Martha McKelvie in Nebraska on July 26. "I know and feel that I have never deserved such unhappiness, which has been thoughtlessly and needlessly thrust upon me. Our Jane is and can be an angel—or she can be a sulky, self-centered, cruel girl—and without cause." He was so distraught, he told McKelvie, that he could say no more. Then he added a postscript: "It was finished about seven weeks ago—nothing can alter it. The book is closed."

In September, free of romantic encumbrances, Hart made a trip to New York. While there, he saw Will Rogers in the *Ziegfeld Follies* and spent several evenings chatting with the folksy entertainer, whom he considered the greatest humorist since Mark Twain, in Rogers's dressing room. Afterward they went to Dinty Moore's for a late supper. "It was like the old stage days," Hart said.

Hart also visited the sixty-seven-year-old Bat Masterson during his stay in Manhattan. The two men had their picture taken together on the roof of the *Telegraph* building and another downstairs in Masterson's office. A few days later, Masterson died. Bill considered the old peace officer and Wyatt Earp the last of the great western gunfighters who had upheld law and order and helped mold a new country. "To know Mr. Masterson was to love him," Hart wrote in *My Life East and West*. "What he did for the Western frontier is recorded. May flowers always nod their heads and the winds blow gently over the graves of this man and his kind!"

On his way back to Los Angeles, Hart spent a few days in Chicago with Jack Dempsey. Dempsey invited Hart to a dinner that was being given in his honor, and later they traipsed around the city together, wherever a boxing match was being held. "We would enter in the dark," Hart said, "and in some places leave before the lights were thrown on at the end of a round," so as not to be recognized. One evening Hart and Dempsey were joined by heavyweight champion Jim Corbett, and Hart said they parted "when the streets were light." The cowboy actor adored boxing, and there is little doubt that he was most comfortable in a male world.

Meanwhile fans wondered who was going to take William S. Hart's place in Western movies. "His successor will have to blaze a new trail and show us yet another phase of the vast West," Elsie Codd wrote in the English magazine *Pictures and Picturegoer*. "That West is not always lonely and aloof. It has also its domestic aspects." But Codd acknowledged that it was "to Hart alone that we owe the Western's present status as a film classic. He has revived for us, truthfully and realistically, much of the glamour and romantic atmosphere of that bygone roaring age."

When asked about his retirement, Hart answered that there would always be plenty to keep a man who owned a big ranch occupied. He said that he wanted to travel and do more writing. "I'd like to give the public some idea of the true history of the West," he said, "not the kind the college professors dig up after years of research amongst the long-forgotten archives of dusty libraries, but a yarn written by one who knows the West as a man knows his own wife, one who has heard the stories of countless old-timers gathered round the campfires at night, and who has shared his blanket with Indian braves."

Hart continued to keep up a lively correspondence. Andy Adams, author of the Western classic, *The Log of a Cowboy*, wrote Hart in 1921 from Colorado Springs, endorsing the actor's approach to moviemaking. "We have all seen the same thing," Adams said, "where the only note that rang true in a Western picture was the horses. . . . The movies may yet break down the barriers of the East, who insists that its West must be wild and wooly. My conception of the West always leant toward things valid, not the lurid. The West was not reclaimed by its Alkali Ikes or Rattlesnake Petes, but by entirely different men."

J. C. Miller wrote Hart from the 101 Ranch in July 1921, telling him of an exhibition the Ponca Indians and some neighboring tribes were planning for early September. Oklahoma pioneers from before 1886 were going to hold a reunion at the same time, and the 101 Ranch was slated to put on some riding and roping contests as entertainment. For the occasion Miller planned to build a frontier town, complete with saloon, dance hall, and livery stable, that would be reminiscent of pioneer days. The rancher wanted to know if Hart would like to make a movie using the facilities he intended to construct, or perhaps come to the celebration as a guest and simply enjoy the fun. "I feel that a William S. Hart and a 101 Ranch picture combined would go over like Ringling Brothers and Barnum and

Bailey," Miller said, "and would make both of us some money." Hart declined the offer, explaining that he was absorbed in private matters.

Hart leased an office on Hollywood Boulevard over the Apollo Theater and spent most of his days there between ten o'clock in the morning and four o'clock in the afternoon. He was shocked by the Fatty Arbuckle scandal in the fall of 1921, and Will Hays's tour of Hollywood the next year and subsequent appointment as movie censor made the industry aware that more bad publicity could cause serious harm. "The press is eager for news," Hart said. "The damaging news has been spread all over the world. . . . The time is fast approaching, however, when this honorable profession will be forced to clean house." Hart's complaint about "unregenerate traitors" and corrupt lawyers became constant, for his films continued to be pirated and wrested from his control.

Throughout his courtship of Jane Novak, Hart had been in contact with Winifred Westover, his leading lady in *John Petticoats*. Westover, another golden-haired, blue-eyed beauty, had recently returned to the United States from six months of picture making in Sweden. In May 1921 Bill justified his writing Winifred to Jane by saying, "That little girl has been constant in the face of no encouragement so long. Nothing has changed her. Nothing has even been able to enter her life that it is honestly pathetic, and she is trying to be game and white. I'm so glad you understand. I love you for it."

Hart had been responsible for introducing Winifred to Thora Holm, who came to Los Angeles looking for a player to take back to Sweden. Hart thought the experience of making movies abroad would be good for the young actress. Westover went to Stockholm with her mother and made three pictures there. Most people she met in Sweden were convinced that William S. Hart was a bandit in real life, and they made fun of Winifred when she tried to tell them that he was a kind, generous actor who had befriended her. She had nothing but respect for the man. "I hunted up all his pictures and would sit right down in front so as to be near him," Westover told reporters.

Bill and Winifred corresponded all the time she was in Europe and most of the year she spent in New York afterward. While Hart was in Manhattan during September 1921, he telephoned her. "I was so surprised and so happy that I nearly dropped the phone," Westover said. Hart saw a great deal of Winifred during his visit to New York, mostly escorting her to dinner and shows. But they also went dancing and took long walks, during which they talked and held hands and renewed the friendship they had enjoyed in New Orleans while making *John Petticoats.* "It was all very wonderful until he left," Winifred said, "then how I hated New York; it had grown drear, dead."

Westover was about to sign a five-year contract with Lewis J. Selznick when she received a wire from Hart saying not to sign until she had received a letter from him. Winifred thought perhaps Hart wanted her to appear in his next picture. But when his letter came, it contained a proposal of marriage. "I was very, very, very happy," the young actress said, and she immediately wired him her acceptance. Hart sent Winifred an exquisite diamond wristwatch as an engagement present, and she quickly went shopping for a trousseau. Six days after receiving Hart's proposal of marriage, Winifred and her mother boarded a train for California. They arrived in Los Angeles on the afternoon of December 5, 1921, and two days later, at six o'clock in the evening, Winifred Westover and William S. Hart were married in Hollywood's Little Church Around the Corner. Bill had turned fifty-seven the day before; Winifred was twenty-two.

The bride later said that Hart had tried to back out of the marriage, but she pursued him with unyielding persistence. She blithely showed reporters her white chiffon wedding gown, trimmed with heavy embroidery, crystal beads, and a long fringed sash, and told them of her groom's promise to honeymoon in San Francisco, where she had grown up. At the wedding Winifred wore a veil and carried a huge bouquet of orange blossoms, and guests threw "pounds of rice" at the couple as they left the church. "I have the love and tender devotion of the best man in the whole wide world," the new Mrs. Hart said. "We're so in love with each other and so happy that it seems almost too beautiful to be true."

After a whirlwind trip to northern California, the newlyweds settled into Hart's house on DeLongpre. A reporter who interviewed Winifred shortly after their marriage found the lacy, beribboned pillows heaped on their bed amusing. "You should see [Bill] carefully lifting them off at night as if he thought they might break," Winifred said with a giggle, "but when I tease him, he pelts me with one, and, presto, there's a pillow fight on."

The actress said that she was less interested in pursuing a career now that she had married but added that she probably would play a part in her husband's next picture. Meanwhile she was taking harp lessons (because she found out that Bill's favorite instrument was the harp) and planning a rose garden, a fountain, and a teahouse to enhance the property her husband had recently bought. "Grandmother used to say I had the makings of a good old maid," Winifred told fan magazine writers, "for I never cared for boys. Billy is my first sweetheart. . . . I never dreamed he would ever love me." She maintained that her life would be centered on her husband and that she was ready to devote herself to him completely. "I'd probably be the despair of the suffragettes," Winifred said. "I think it is heavenly to have a lord and master and be a little clinging vine."

In a letter to Adolph Zukor thanking him for the flowers he had sent when he learned of the marriage, Bill expressed his supreme happiness. "I never dreamed there was such joy like mine in the world," he wrote. "My little girl wife is one of the most wonderful, sensible, loving human beings that God ever made." The movie colony was shocked by the news that Bill Hart had finally taken a wife. "Is William Hart married?" the *New York Tribune* asked; then the newspaper conjectured that several thousand flappers would have their lives upset until that question was answered.

A month after their wedding, Bill bought his bride a bunch of American Beauty roses to celebrate their anniversary. "Bill won't let me change this house a bit," Winifred complained. "Anyway he's going to let me build a place all my own—back on our place in Connecticut. I'm to design the house and furnish it. . . . I'm going to have a real colonial mansion there—stately drawing rooms and lovely bedrooms. . . . I'm going to have white staircases, real old-fashioned carved chandeliers, and a blue room." The couple planned to spend six months of the year in the East and six months in Los Angeles.

After Bill's marriage, Mary Ellen had moved to the ranch house in Newhall. "We want her with us as much as she can be," Winifred said, "but it's nice for everyone to have a little place that is their own. . . . Bill built an awfully nice house up there." Mary Ellen had not been feeling well, and her brother explained her move by saying that the drier, more invigorating air at the ranch would help her gain back her strength.

Then came the report that Winifred was pregnant and expecting a baby in September. "It sure will be a strange feeling for me to be an honest to God daddy," Bill wrote Martha McKelvie. His bride assured reporters that both she and her husband adored children and intended to have a large family. "She's a good kid," Hart said of his wife, while she referred to him as "my little creampuff."

But within a month after their marriage, there were signs of trouble. "It was like finding Bill Hart tied up in pink baby ribbon," said journalist Adela Rogers St. Johns, who was fond of Westover and critical of Hart. "We had had difficulties," Winifred said of her relationship with Bill, "but I am sure that if it had not been for the return of his sister, Miss Mary Hart, we would have been able to adjust our troubles. But after that, nothing I ever did seemed to please him—or rather, his sister."

In May 1922, after less than six months of marriage, Bill ordered Winifred out of his house. "I might have been a ten-year-old child as far as the position I held in my husband's home was concerned," the angry wife told reporters. "Everything was done according to the desires of his sister." Winifred later claimed that her husband knocked her down, and the press reported that Hart beat her and dragged her around by the hair. Hart swore "before God" that he had never laid a hand on his wife.

"It was following a long conference between my husband and his sister that I was finally ordered to leave," Winifred said. "I could hardly believe my ears. It appeared incredible that a man with any idea of chivalry would order his wife, about to become a mother in a few months, out of her home. I thought he was joking until he sternly reiterated his order. . . . And what added to the humiliation was the fact that guests were present at the time."

Winifred went to live with her mother in a bungalow in Santa Monica. When reporters showed up at the house to question her, they were met with angry words and given a choice of leaving quietly or being evicted from the premises. "I loved my husband with a passionate and sublime devotion that comes to a woman but once in her lifetime," Winifred said later. "It was a love based upon respect for his remarkable accomplishments and his seemingly genuine affection and universal kindness. . . . I cannot believe that he didn't love me once."

Bill maintained that Mary Ellen had never lived in his Hollywood home during his marriage and did not return there until half a year after he and Winifred had separated. In a letter to Martha McKelvie, however, Hart said that Mary Ellen "stays up at the little ranch most of the time," which leads to the suspicion that she was hovering about more than he was willing to admit. Hart also told McKelvie to be careful how she wrote him. "You know I'm branded as a wife beater!" he said. "They went so far they sort of make themselves look foolish."

William S. Hart, Jr., was born on September 6, 1922, but his father did not see the child until eight days later, when he visited his estranged wife's home in Santa Monica. "The poor little tyke will have to grow up without knowing what a real father means," Winifred said. Hart contended that he tried on several occasions to have the boy with him, hoping to build a paternal relationship. "I have been refused," he said, "and told I can only see my son at his mother's home and cannot take him out."

Bill wanted to end the marriage quietly, but legal proceedings and money disputes dragged on until February 11, 1927, when Winifred was granted a divorce in Reno, Nevada. The actor was charged with extreme cruelty and willful abandonment. "For three years this woman and her dirt lawyer branded me throughout the world as a brutal wife beater and offered to get a divorce for fifty thousand dollars more," Hart said. "For three years I begged her for the sake of our son to deny these charges. She remained silent until my lawyer forced her to admit the truth in court. Yes! the lady is a deeply tenacious nature." He agreed to a cash settlement to Winifred of $200,000 and later referred to the marriage as "our unfortunate union," a simple case of incompatibility. At the time of the divorce the cowboy star was estimated to be worth $3 million, having recently earned approximately $10,000 a week.

Hart agreed to his former wife's having sole care, control, and custody of their son. "I love my boy," he said. "He is my great pride and joy." Hart set up a trust fund of $100,000 for the support and education of his son, but he saw very little of the child. He often said that he would have liked to have done more for the boy financially but that he did not trust Winifred to use the money properly. In every discussion of his matrimonial woes, Hart inserted his delight and love for his son. "God, but he's a wonderful kiddie," Bill said. "It is my fondest hope that, when my son grows to young manhood, he will follow in the footsteps of one of his great-grandfathers, and show an aptitude for the profession of law. It is a manly, honorable calling, one that can always be used for good. It's pathway and training lead to the highest gifts of our Republic." During the months and years that his divorce was pending, Hart told reporters that he had had enough of mud-slinging and would only comment that his separation from his wife was permanent. "There is no other man and no other woman," he said. "It is simply a case of not being able to get along together—or agree. There can be no scandal for there is none, nor will there be any grounds for any."

Hart did not work for two years after the completion of *Three Word Brand* and said that he could not think of making movies until his troubles with Winifred were settled, even though he had been urged "on all sides to find forgetfulness in the studio." By the fall of 1922 he had a story in mind and began making plans for a return to the screen. "If I don't make pictures for Famous Players–Lasky's Paramount distribution, I will not make pictures at all," he said. "It is Paramount or nothing. . . . It is just affection and trust on both sides."

But Paramount's executives had grown wary of Hart's old-fashioned approach to making Westerns and had doubts about his continuing appeal at the box office. Jesse Lasky felt that the aging star needed supervision and that Paramount must exercise firm control over his pictures. "We all feel if Hart will cooperate with us and let us use our judgment and experience, we can give Sales Department the kind of Hart pictures they want," Lasky wrote. "If Hart will not agree to above plan . . . , then there is no way in which we can protect situation and get quality of picture Sales Department requires."

By 1923 Hollywood's big studio system was crystallizing, with Paramount leading the way. The movie industry had changed rapidly, and William S. Hart was locked into an antiquated mode that was out of touch with current practices in distribution and marketing. The star was not prepared to lighten his plots or accept the mandates Paramount heaped on him, and he felt victimized by men he had once trusted. Set in his ways and reclusive by nature, Hart became increasingly isolated in his advanced years and retreated deeper into nostalgic visions of the vanishing West, until fable and celebrity became his principal reality.

Back to Work

By the early summer of 1923, when Hart began making *Wild Bill Hickok*, Lambert Hillyer was busy with other commitments, directing such stars as Lon Chaney, Florence Vidor, and Tom Mix, and cameraman Joseph August was also unavailable. Zukor and Lasky insisted that Hart base his future productions at the Famous Players–Lasky Studio, and Hart conceded, having had a pleasant association with the company in the past. He renewed his contract with Famous Players, agreeing to make nine more pictures for Paramount to distribute, but with an additional clause. Under the new arrangement, either party could cancel the contract with the completion of any one of the pictures.

Clifford Smith, Hart's old assistant during his Triangle days, directed *Wild Bill Hickok*, but Hart quickly fell into despair during the filming. "I found everything so different at the studio that I realized what a great mistake I had made," he said. "Where before I had gone ahead and made my picture as any tenant that was renting space should do, the heads of my staff were now constantly receiving orders and instructions as to how they should carry on their work." Hart was furious and told his staff to pay no attention to these dictates. "I thought surely it was all a mistake," Hart said, "that it would all blow over and adjust itself. But it did not do so—it became worse."

Hart found himself dealing with Charles Eyton, the studio manager, on issue after issue, and the veteran star resented Eyton's intrusive manner. He notified studio executives that his experiences as a boy combined with his training as an actor and the success he had had with sixty-four earlier movies more than qualified him to make films his own way. *Wild Bill Hickok* was a Western story he had originated and one he thought he understood well. "'Wild Bill' was a real man," said Hart, "the daggonedest, most lovable two-gun man that ever lived." Hart did not claim to have known Hickok personally but said that he remembered his father and others talking about him.

Hart emphasized heroics in his screen biography of Hickok, but at the same time he fashioned a drama that suited his talents. The picture included a characterization of Bat Masterson during his early years as a hunter of desperadoes, and one of the movie's principal sets depicted Dodge City, Kansas, during the town's balmiest days. Hart escaped some of the studio's control by returning to Victorville for location work on the film, and two streets were added to the town near the train station to make it look like frontier Dodge. "At times we had 400 people on the set," Hart said, "and we got some splendid stuff." Passengers getting off trains that came through Victorville were startled to see that the Wild West had come back to life. At one point Bill did some fast gunplay in a street fight for the picture, and shooting the sequence created quite a stir among onlookers.

Although fans were excited about Hart's return to the screen, the reviews of *Wild Bill Hickok* were mixed. When the film opened in December 1923 at the Rialto Theater in Manhattan, the *New York Times* reviewer said that watching William S. Hart's performance made one feel "almost ten years younger—as if one were again living in the days of screen ineptitude. Mr. Hart is enthusiastic about his shooting and his sobbing. It is sad enough to witness the tearful grief of a big man; but it is agony to sit through Mr. Hart's weeping and shaking." To the *Times* critic, *Wild Bill Hickok* was a fatuous movie. "Nobody connected with this picture seems to have the vaguest notion of the chief character. Wild Bill did not strut around with his chest out. Nor did he pose as a hero. He was a good shot and a bad actor, who loved whisky and fighting. . . . It is just as if Mr. Hart took the whole motion picture public to be very young school children."

Still, the Western drew large audiences at the Rialto, and other notices were kinder. The *New York American* said that the movie "neither sagged nor bogged" and displayed Hart's "priceless pugilistic figure immaculately." Farther west the movie fared even better. The

Milwaukee Journal declared, "Never has Bill Hart's trusty six-gun spoken so eloquently as in these scenes, nor the pinto pony performed more heroic service for his master." Diehard fans noted a sober quality and a polish in the film that had been lacking in Hart's earlier work.

Few defended *Wild Bill Hickok*'s historical inaccuracies, for it was clear that Hart's romantic indulgences followed an image of the famous gunfighter that dime novelists had already established. The mistakes in the movie were glaring, all the more annoying since they came from a man who had built his reputation on presenting the old West authentically.

Courtland Manning, who actually saw Wild Bill Hickok during the 1870s at the Academy Theater in Buffalo, New York, with Buffalo Bill Cody and Texas Jack Omohundro in Ned Buntline's *The Scouts of the Prairie*, wrote Hart his recollections of that occasion in February 1924, after seeing the screen biography. "Wild Bill made his entrance from a cabin surrounded by Buffalo Bill, Texas Jack, and Ned Buntline," Manning recalled. "They had to pull him from the cabin door and push him into a chair at a table centre stage, where he sat with a big gun dangling from each hand, his eyes staring wildly across the footlights. At his cue he was so frightened he could scarcely articulate. . . . He was better in the last act while using his shooting irons on the pesky redskins. He was with the show but a short time, then returned to his western home, declaring he was done with play acting."

When *Wild Bill Hickok* played Oklahoma City in 1923, western lawman Bill Tilghman was coaxed out of retirement to make personal appearances during the movie's run there. Tilghman was billed by the management as "about the last survivor of the Hickok crowd." But the public response to the picture in Oklahoma was tepid.

Bill expressed satisfaction with the reviews *Wild Bill Hickok* received, conveniently overlooking the blast from the *New York Times*. "We knew we had turned out a fine picture," he said, "but we also knew that New York was the Mecca of the amusement world. It was wonderful to know we had conquered."

Jesse Lasky at Famous Players was less selective in his response to the criticism that Hart's film had generated and wired Hart that it was a mistake for the actor to continue writing his own stories. Lasky pointed out that current audiences were mainly interested in seeing well-known novels and plays on the screen, and he advised Hart to move away from morbid themes and semitragic endings in the future. "Audiences everywhere like to see at least a ray of hope for a brighter tomorrow," Lasky said. "Audiences felt *Wild Bill* was without this ray of hope."

Hart was dazed by the suggestion. "I could not think coherently or get a grip on myself," he said. "Try as I might, I could not pull myself out of the trance-like feeling." Lengthy letters and telegrams were exchanged, with Lasky assuring Hart that he had exhibitors' reports to substantiate his reproaches. To continue its affiliation with the cowboy star, Lasky said, Famous Players would have to exercise control over story selection, the writing of scenarios and the way they were treated in production, and casting. Hart replied that if the studio intended to tell him what stories he could film and dictate how they should be made, he and Famous Players should end their agreement and "save a lot of fuss and worry on both sides." Lasky accepted the proposal, and it was decided that *Singer Jim McKee* would be Hart's last picture for release under the Paramount emblem.

Meanwhile Bill had returned to his life of bachelorhood, with Mary Ellen and Congo, his feeble old dog, to keep him company and a Japanese butler and maid to serve his needs. Mamie spent more time than ever in what friends called Mary Ellen's Tea Room. "That was sort of her parking spot," Jane Novak recalled later, "[but] I don't ever remember Mamie drinking tea." Neither Hart nor his sister gave parties, and they rarely socialized with the fashionable Hollywood crowd, although Hart served on the initial board of trustees for the Motion Picture Relief Fund and participated in an occasional charity benefit. Hart increasing came to view himself as the foremost authority on the frontier West, and he filled his house on DeLongpre (where future actor Joel McCrea is rumored to have been his paperboy) with a collection of historic guns and Indian rugs, blankets, and handicrafts.

Bill's fantasies about the old West and its heroes had grown into an obsession. Bat Masterson, he said, was "the whitest man that ever breathed, but also the quickest on the draw. And, believe me, that meant something in the days when every man who valued his life and his worldly possessions had to be a lightning artist in the use of his gun. . . . It was not long before [Bat] was the terror of every outlaw in the surrounding country. He was so fast with the trigger, so sure of his aim, that with a single movement of his hand he'd wing his man without even removing his gun from the holster."

Hart devoted more time to writing, and his book *Told under a White Oak Tree* was published by Houghton Mifflin late in 1922. The next year *A Lighter of Flames*, his novel about Patrick Henry, was completed and published by Grosset and Dunlap. Hart had written the Patrick Henry story first as a screenplay, emphasizing the romance of the American revolutionary hero's life rather than his notable deeds. Hart hoped that a movie would eventually be made from the book and talked about the project for several years, but plans for filming the story were ultimately scrapped.

Bill clearly did not favor the emerging studio system, which virtually eliminated the independent producer, and he was baffled by Paramount's current business practices and its executives' market-oriented decisions and concept of efficiency. Fan letters blinded him to the fact that tastes in movies had changed. Wyatt Earp wrote Hart that he liked *Wild Bill Hickok* so much that he saw the picture twice. Sid Grauman said in a note to Hart that the picture had packed his Metropolitan Theater, which had a seating capacity of four thousand, during afternoon and evening showings. The editor of the *Topeka State Journal* wrote his congratulations that Hart had avoided the "sex appeal stuff" and the "avalanche of sickening sheiks" that had glutted Hollywood's recent output. "I am sure there are enough he-men left in the country to thoroughly enjoy the William S. Hart pictures," the Kansas editor said.

Paramount's choice in Westerns during the late 1920s was either those based on Zane Grey's novels or epics such as *The Covered Wagon*, most of which made a considerable amount of money for the company. Hart thought *The Covered Wagon* was "a good picture to those who do not know. . . . But to those who do know or have studied the frontier days, it is a sad affair." His objections to the film were multiple: "Jim Bridger made a senile, undersized old bum, when at that time he was forty-four years old; bulls swimming with neck yokes on, a wagon train corralled in a blind box canyon in a hostile Indian country." Hart was seldom generous to his competition.

Although Hart felt slighted by Paramount, his ego was stroked by an offer to appear at Cheyenne's Frontier Days, which attracted daily crowds of between 12,000 and 18,000, according to officials. Colt's Fire Arms Company requested an arrangement whereby they could use the old cowboy star's photograph on postcards and advertising posters for distribution in South America, with a statement to the effect that the actor used or recommended Colt's firearms. Aware that there was money to be made from the deal, Hart replied, "I have always withheld from any such form of advertising, but—with a Colt Gun—that's different." Two months later Hart signed an agreement with Kingfisher Company of New York, granting the firm permission to use his name on certain brands of boys' clothing.

More than ever Hart flaunted his superstar status to ease his growing disappointments. "This being a hero with the public is an awfully hard thing to live up to," he wrote Adolph Zukor from the Waldorf-Astoria Hotel in New York. "I've just been rushed to death every minute of my stay here." He prided himself on being a model of masculinity to thousands of American boys, who saw him as a tower of strength and honesty, a man with the courage to put things right no matter what the odds. Even the young son of Will Hays, Hollywood's new censorship czar, was a dedicated Bill Hart fan, and like many a fading star, Hart had no doubt that his public wanted to see more of him on the screen. Feeling abused and lonely, the aging actor let public adoration substitute for personal intimacy.

Bill took special delight in his frequent correspondence with Wyatt Earp and his wife, and after the couple settled in southern California, Hart and the Earps visited occasionally. Earp wrote Bill on July 7, 1923: "During the past few years, many wrong impressions of the early days of Tombstone and myself have been created by writers who are not informed correctly, and this has caused me a concern which I feel deeply. . . . I realize that I am not going to live to the age of Methuselah, and any wrong impression I want made right before I go away. The screen could do all this, I know, with yourself as the master mind." Earp maintained that he had taken the right course as Tombstone's peace officer during a turbulent time when the courts could not convict wrongdoers and the territory's legal process failed to function.

While many viewed Hart as the master of Western movies and frontier history, others came to look upon the sad-faced star as a buffoon, largely because of his exaggerated stance. In 1922 Buster Keaton burlesqued the hammy cowboy actor savagely in his two-reel comedy *The Frozen North*. Rather than portray Hart as a Dudley Do-Right character, Keaton played him as a bully, a thief, a seducer, and a murderer, all in a highly stylized manner. Hart refused to speak to the comedian for years.

In 1923 Hart mistakenly thought he was still operating from a position of strength in his negotiations with Paramount. If Zukor and Lasky no longer wanted him, he was certain that Metro or one of the other major studios would. But Hollywood in the 1920s was a sleepy village, and news traveled fast. Word had spread that William S. Hart's old-style Westerns were a drug on the market, and no studio in town seemed willing to risk financing his pictures.

Bill began work on *Singer Jim McKee* under a cloud, with Clifford Smith again directing. The production company went up to the California mining region to shoot exteriors, and Phyllis Haver, formerly one of Mack Sennett's bathing beauties, played Hart's leading lady. Bill planned to retire Fritz once the picture was finished, and he wanted to end the pony's career with something spectacular. In the Western, as Hart gallops along the edge of a cliff playing an escaping bandit, his horse is shot, and pinto and rider tumble and roll into a gorge below. It was a dangerous stunt, since Bill planned to take the fall from the top of a precipice. The drop was about twelve feet, and the distance horse and rider would roll was something like one hundred fifty feet. "I knew the little horse could do it," Hart said, "but there was that fear that I knew I had of injuring him. I knew I could not do him justice and help him as I should. . . . If there is any over-anxiety or affection for the mount and fear of injuring him, it is bad, very bad, for both horse and rider." After talking to mechanics at the studio, the decision was made to use a dummy horse rather than risk hurting Fritz. Studio workmen spent five weeks creating a pony that looked like the pinto. "Every measurement was perfect," Hart said. "The mane and tail were real horsehair. We had an artist paint all the markings. Every joint worked on springs. The head swung in the most natural manner, and the weight was within a hundred pounds of what Fritz himself would weigh."

The scene was shot toward the end of location work on *Singer Jim McKee*. Hart rode Fritz at a gallop to the edge of the cliff, then the dummy horse was substituted, held in an upright position with piano wires so that Hart could mount. "It took about thirty carpenters and helpers to get the mechanical horse to the top of the precipice and get him set up," Hart said. With the camera grinding and Hart astride the mechanical steed, the wire was cut and over the cliff horse and rider went. Hart was shaken up quite a bit, but his injuries were mostly scratches and bruises. He claimed that the scene on film was so realistic that he had to appear before a censorship board in New York City to explain how the sequence was shot before the censors would allow the footage to be shown to the public.

The title character in the movie breaks into song at inopportune moments, making the picture's incoherent plot seem all the more absurd. *Singer Jim McKee* may possibly be the worst film the cowboy star ever made. He was entirely too old to play a youthful hero who pursues and wins the love of a mere girl, and the Western rambles and includes most of the clichés from Hart's earlier movies. The stern, stalwart man of Inceville Westerns now seemed shriveled and preposterous. "If William S. Hart . . . had only intended his latest picture, *Singer Jim McKee*, as a valiant satire of his previous pantomimic efforts, we would say that he had been quite successful," the reviewer for the *New York Times* said. "We are afraid that this picture does not even come up to the old-fashioned standard of Mr. Hart's previous film, *Wild Bill Hickok*."

Some critics remained respectful of Hart's approach. "Here is not only a western picture," the *Los Angeles Evening Herald* contended, "but a picture that is the west itself." When *Singer Jim McKee* opened at the Metropolitan Theater in Los Angeles, the advertising was minimal, and Hart was devastated to learn that the management there only planned to run the Western for two days. He went to the theater on opening night and found the house packed. "Don't believe what

you hear, Mr. Hart," an usherette told him. "All of the girls in the theater just love the picture."

Soprano Mary Garden was singing with the Chicago Civic Opera
Company on tour in Los Angeles at the time. Bill arranged for *Singer
Jim McKee* to be shown privately for the diva and her friends, and he
maintained that the distinguished party was enthusiastic in its praise
of the picture. Garden, as flamboyant a figure as the cowboy actor
was reserved, said that she admired Bill Hart so much that she would
be glad to marry him. Needless to say, she never did.

Hart continued to believe that *Singer Jim McKee* did tremendous
business, played to full houses, and received unanimous praise from
critics. It was a great picture, he told the Paramount hierarchy; the
naysaying was merely a plot to destroy him. He had three or four
more stories in mind that he thought would make strong motion
pictures, but it was clear that Paramount had lost confidence in him.
"The whole trend of happenings seems to point to the fact that the
Famous Players–Lasky Corporation does not take kindly to my making my own productions as I always did," Hart wrote Jesse Lasky on
December 4, 1923. Bill talked the situation over with Mary Ellen and
concluded that he had to make pictures his way or not at all. "I came
back to the studio, gathered my stuff together, and read the letter
[terminating the agreement] to them."

Unwilling simply to act in films and give up his role as producer, Hart
contacted First National and was told to talk to Mr. Rowland, a company representative, who was staying at the Ambassador Hotel. Rowland said that he would be happy to see Hart and discuss a contract but
that he was leaving Los Angeles for the weekend and would call when
he returned. Hart never heard from him again. A contract for four pictures with Marcus Loew, head of Metro, also fell through. Hart's publicist, Scoop Conlon, told the cowboy star that malicious propaganda
was being circulated about the failure of his recent movies; Conlon had
encountered it everywhere he went. "I am qualified to make Western
pictures," Hart told the press. "I will have to be shown why and where
I am wrong before I can intelligently try to change my ways."

Hart went to his ranch and spent days walking through the hills. In
time he decided that perhaps he had been wrong to be so unbending

with Famous Players. Maybe there was merit in the position Lasky, and apparently Zukor, had taken. Hart went to see Lasky in his office. "I have decided to give in a whole lot," he said. "You all can supervise my stories, providing I have the last word, and I will be glad to consult with you on any reasonable thing concerning my productions." Lasky reminded Hart that the company's sales division must be closely involved in the selection and treatment of stories. Hart argued that to allow the sales people to have power over content would "stifle all imagination or inspiration" and put an end to creativity. But Lasky held firm; if Hart worked for Famous Players, he would have to yield completely to the studio's policies. After twenty minutes of talk Hart knew that he was beaten and bid Lasky a final good-bye. "We shook hands and parted," Hart said. "When I came out, I staggered as I walked. . . . All that had been bright now seemed to take on a darkened hue."

By January 1924, deeply hurt that even the gentlemanly Adolph Zukor seemed to have turned against him, Hart moved his remaining things out of the Famous Players facilities. The dejected actor became distrustful of everyone. He felt unjustifiably scorned, beleaguered with trials and lawsuits, hounded by the government for back taxes and his estranged wife for additional child support, and confronted with disloyalty on all sides. Convinced that gossipmongers had ruined him, Hart voiced nothing but contempt for Hollywood society. He felt rejected and humiliated and vented his suffering in anger. "The Jews have crucified me!" he exclaimed to friends with his arms outstretched in a dramatic pose. His nature was unforgiving; his self-pity eternal. The faded star's only hope for contentment appeared to be a retreat into seclusion. Perhaps at his ranch he could find tranquillity if not happiness.

Hart added to his land in Newhall, supervised the remodeling of his ranch house, and made repairs on the corral and barns. He set up an office on the property and began planning a permanent home there. Newhall at the time consisted of three or four stores, a post office, and a few dirt streets, set in a cup of hills. The section of the Southern Pacific Railroad that ran through the town had been used in countless movies, and bands of Indians, hired to appear in prologues at nearby Hollywood theaters, had until recently camped in Cahuenga

Pass. At the ranch Hart surrounded himself with his western memo-rabilia and a growing assortment of animals, which he found more trustworthy than people. "I reckon I like horses best," the actor said. "They're more intelligent." But he also loved Congo, who slept at the foot of his bed.

Saturday Evening Post illustrator James Montgomery Flagg, cre-ator of the famous World War I recruitment poster, came to Holly-wood in 1924 with his bride, and Flagg painted Hart's portrait on Fritz during that time. "I was sort of in the dumps," Bill said, "and the few weeks that Jim and Dorothy spent with us did me a lot of good." Flagg started the painting at the ranch but finished it in Hollywood. "Fortunately, he had put in all of his time [at the ranch] working on Fritz and could finish him from memory," Hart recalled. "But my end of it was not so easy. Instead of a live horse, I got a saw-horse with a pre-Volstead whiskey barrel on top of it." Flagg had a keen wit, and the sight of the illustrious hero of Western movies perched on a whis-key keg in a Hollywood garden caused him to laugh and make end-less quips. Meanwhile Hart complained that his face was weary from holding a ferocious grimace so long. The illustrator would remain a close friend and later painted Mary Ellen's portrait.

Will Rogers had been supportive of Hart during his recent troubles with Paramount and had been at the train station to see Hart off when he went to New York for a final conference with Adolph Zukor. Bill visited Will at his ranch at the far end of Sunset Boulevard when Will was in Los Angeles. Like Hart, Rogers loved horses and rode horse-back over the Santa Monica hills. He also collected guns, saddles, and Navajo rugs and was a friend of Charlie Russell, Harry Carey, and James Montgomery Flagg.

Bill broke his foot in October 1924 and suffered the inconven-ience of wearing a cast up to his knee. Mary Ellen had not been well, suffering from a car accident, which caused her brother worry, and she spent more than a year in bed. Hart continued to see little of his son, although he often talked about the "wonderful sensation" of being a father. "I saw my little chap a month ago," Bill wrote Thomas Ince in 1924, shortly before the producer's death, "and when he put his arms around my neck and kissed me, my cup was full." For young

Bill's third birthday, his father sent him a drum encrusted with gold and silver and rosewood sticks to beat it, the cost of which was $650.

In February 1925 the cowboy star made a trip east to appear in a Lambs Club gala at the Metropolitan Opera House. Not sure what to do on a bill that included Al Jolson, Will Rogers, Eddie Cantor, Weber and Fields, John Philip Sousa, and General John J. Pershing, Hart decided to tell a story about Wild Bill Hickok and concluded the yarn by executing a quick draw and firing two six-shooters, loaded with blanks, into the audience. He received a great ovation for his effort and was called before the curtain to take bows sixteen times. "It was one of the proudest moments of my life," Hart said. "I had tried to act as I thought Hickok would have done."

Hart told the press that one of his keenest regrets was that the last of the famous western characters were disappearing. "Who shall tell their story?" he asked. "In my own modest way, in my pictures and in my interviews, I have tried to bring to these forgotten heroes some seed of recognition by a modern generation. Historians have missed much that was characteristic, much that was supremely human and potent in its influence upon the development of the West."

Hart received a letter from Wyatt Earp shortly after his Lambs Club appearance, telling him that a friend had just completed a draft of the frontier marshal's life story. "I wonder whether you still would be inclined to film the production," Earp wrote. "If it goes on the screen at all, I would not want anyone but you to play the role and to put it there." Two of the original coaches used in the stage line between Tombstone and Benson, Arizona, had recently been found, and Earp thought they would add authenticity to the picture. "I am sure that if the story were exploited on the screen by you, it would do much toward setting me right before a public which has always been fed . . . lies about me," Earp said.

Bill answered that it made his "hair want to stand straight up" when he read things about the West that were not true. "I can readily imagine what it must mean to one like yourself who has been through it all to have false stories printed about yourself," he wrote the ailing Earp.

Meanwhile Hart's collection of western accoutrements had grown to include more than forty buffalo coats and robes that he claimed had been worn by officers and soldiers in the Indian Wars of the 1870s and 1880s. He owned guns that supposedly had belonged to Bat Masterson, Billy the Kid, and other frontier notables. "When he showed me the guns," Adolph Zukor recalled, "he made me stand back a little. He wouldn't let anyone else handle them." And his collection of western paintings had grown impressive.

Hart became an ardent worker for the Society for the Prevention of Cruelty to Animals and was a spokesperson for the conservation of natural resources. He helped establish a lodge for boys and continued to designate himself a moral beacon to the nation's youth. "Work hard and play hard," was his advice to boys, "but it must be work that is fun and play that teaches."

Although Hart's standing with Hollywood studios had plummeted, his eminence with the public, particularly in the hinterlands, remained high. His fan mail averaged three hundred letters a day, and he still sent out as many as four thousand photographs of himself each month. The veteran actor scored well in 1925, when the *Nebraska Farmer* sent out a ballot asking readers to list their favorite movie stars, and parents across the country saw the cowboy actor's bad men turning good as great lessons in teaching children the superiority of right over wrong. No less a critic than George Bernard Shaw said in 1925 that William S. Hart had "done everything that can be done in dramatic dumb show and athletic stunting and played all the possible variations of it." The inference, of course, was that Hart had fulfilled his mission and perhaps ought to retire.

But moviemaking was what Hart loved best, and he felt only half alive when he was not busy with a new project. In July 1925 the announcement was made that Hart would star in a new picture, which would be distributed by United Artists, the company he had earlier declined to join. "I am about to start production on a big picture," he wrote on July 11, "and every moment of my waking time is occupied and a whole lot of the sleeping ones also." Fans were ecstatic when they learned that Hart was planning another comeback. "The youth of this land will not only hail with joy your return," H. S. Ryerson of the Los Angeles County Conservation Association wrote Hart, "but I feel that they will be inspired to better things as a result of the type of pictures you invariably produce." *Picture Play, Movie Weekly, Photoplay, Smart Set,* and *Vanity Fair* all saluted the announced project, and when Hart and twenty-five mounted cowboys appeared in the Greater Movie Season Parade on July 31, throngs of spectators accorded the old cowboy star enormous ovations as he passed. "Were I six Bill Harts I could not begin to do all the things that I have to do in connection with my picture," the actor told the press.

Filming on *Tumbleweeds,* his last movie, began on August 10, 1925, at a time when Charlie Chaplin's comedy *The Gold Rush* was breaking attendance records on an extended booking at the Strand Theater on Broadway. Bill was pleased with some night scenes for his picture, shot toward the end of August, and a United Artists publicist was already ballyhooing *Tumbleweeds* as "far and away the biggest Western made in a long time," one that had "everything in it—comedy, romance, drama, conflict, beauty of investiture, fine cast, and Bill never looked as well in all his experience." United Artists' exploitation men were placing press kits that promoted Hart's comeback in every town they went into.

Hart told reporters that the film he was making was "a stupendous affair," as big an epic as *The Covered Wagon,* and was costing him practically all the money he had. In addition to his own funds, Hart borrowed $100,000 from bankers to finance the Western. "One of the most dangerous things in life is to lose your courage," he said. "If your courage goes, you are whipped—your enemy and the world soon know it." He felt that his courage had been "hammered down" by his recent quarrel with Paramount. "The hard facts of exterior circumstance had sadly depleted my fighting spirit," he said.

Bill's contract with United Artists had come just in time to revitalize him. He was overjoyed to be working again. King Baggott, *Tumbleweeds'* director, told his star, somewhat apologetically, that the first shots for the picture would be taken at 5:30 A.M. Bill was on the set, made up and ready to work, at five o'clock. "While we waited for the rising sun, the morning air was like a long, cool drink," Hart said. "I love acting. I love the art of making motion pictures. It is the breath of life to me!"

The story of *Tumbleweeds* is set in 1889, during the opening of the Cherokee Strip to settlement. Hart had gotten the idea for the picture from his friend Harry Carey. C. Gardner Sullivan, whom Hart had worked with so successfully at Inceville and later, wrote the screenplay, and Joe August returned as Hart's cameraman. August and his crew made the Oklahoma homesteaders' dash across the sloping prairie truly spectacular. Nineteen cameras were trained on the land rush, re-created at La Agoura Rancho, some forty miles outside Hollywood. The sequence intercuts long shots and action with close-ups and details that capture human emotions.

Hart's character in the picture, Don Carver, is accused of being a "sooner"—someone who staked a claim before the time set by military authorities—but the charge proves false, perpetrated by the heroine's conniving half brother. Carver ends up with his land, and before the final fade-out, the young woman he has been wooing consents to be his wife.

A well-crafted picture, *Tumbleweeds* cost over $312,000 and required the services of nearly a thousand extras, almost as many horses, hundreds of wagons, buggies, buckboards, and prairie schooners, and a herd of cattle and other livestock. Simply feeding everyone on the set became a problem. To add a special touch, Hart gave his friend Charles Siringo, a Pinkerton detective who had tracked down members of the Wild Bunch, a small part in the movie's barroom scene and street celebration. Many of the exteriors were filmed on the back lot of the Universal Studio in the San Fernando Valley, and August managed to achieve a dusty, windswept atmosphere in the movie that was appropriate for its setting.

By the middle of October 1925, *Tumbleweeds* was ready for editing. The film has relatively few titles, since Hart wanted the emphasis to be on action. "As someone said in the laboratory, if you winked, you missed a scene," Hart told reporters. "That is my idea of a picture—speed and verve and punch." Joseph M. Schenck, then head of United Artists, wanted to cut the film from seven reels to five, but Hart held firm. Hart said that he fully expected to lose $75,000 on the movie but loved what he thought it represented—the last of the West.

When *Tumbleweeds* premiered at the Strand Theater in Manhattan during Christmas season, 1925, every billboard available to United Artists was used to promote the film. The night it opened, Hart received dozens of wires congratulating him on his success. "It is hard to find adjectives to describe the joy they gave me," he said. Hart knew that *Tumbleweeds* was the biggest picture he had ever made, and he was confident of a positive reception.

But the film received only passable notices in New York. Everyone agreed that the land rush sequence was thrilling, but much of the movie was hokum. The *New York Times* said that Hart emphasized the "righteousness" of his character and stalked as if "he dared the villains to do anything in this story." Some reviewers found Hart's acting unbearably artificial and stagey. "*Tumbleweeds . . .* happens to be extremely good in spite of the vexatious presence of William S. Hart," said *Dallas Morning News* critic John Rosenfield. Hart's "staple pose of 'looking noble' has lost its savor. He is about as dynamic as the Indian head on the Buffalo nickel."

Hart went to San Francisco for the opening of the movie on the West Coast and came away elated. "I firmly believe that *Tumbleweeds* will sit you again in the saddle as King of the West," a reporter for the *San Francisco Chronicle* wrote the old star. Yet after the picture had played moderately well in New York, Chicago, and San Francisco, United Artists booked it into second-rate theaters in the rest of the nation's bigger cities. Bill was heartbroken when he learned that *Tumbleweeds* had been transferred from the Mutual Theater in Washington, D.C, to the Howard, which was in the capital's black section. "I have fought fair in my battle for independence," Hart said, "and this is a foul blow."

The movie fared better in small towns, but Hart contended that United Artists had deliberately mismanaged its distribution. "It is an awful black eye for a picture to play second-run houses in the large cities," he said. Without full exploitation and adequate returns from the country's major urban areas, an expensive motion picture had no chance of showing a profit. Hart ultimately filed a lawsuit against United Artists, alleging that *Tumbleweeds* had not been allowed to reach its full commercial potential, and won damages of $278,000.

Hart knew that his career was over. Thwarted by powerful syndicates that were backed by big money, he had no chance of reaching his public. "I have the satisfaction of knowing I made a great picture," he said of *Tumbleweeds*, but his rancor never died. He hated Joe Schenck and made Schenck, whom he called Skunk, the butt of his outspoken anti-Semitism. Hart would spend the rest of his life whining and feeling sorry for himself. "I get so many hard knocks myself that I have worn my teeth smooth gritting them," he said in October 1925. "The game of life would be real sport to any full-blooded man if folks would play fair, but they don't. They hit you right in the belly."

A screen adaptation of *A Lighter of Flames*, which Hart had planned as his next picture, was abandoned. Friends urged him not to quit. "Now for the love of Mike, don't crawl back into your shell again," Western actor Monte Blue wrote Hart in March 1926, "but stay where people can see you, for they love you." Older fans remained loyal to a man they had revered since childhood, and letters poured in every week from all parts of the world, asking him when he planned to make another movie. But Hart had had enough. "The picture industry is so big, so tremendous, and has been established such a short time that it has been impossible to ever get it down to a firm solid business basis," he wrote on October 27, 1925. "I love the picture game. It has made me what I am and it has given me everything that I own." Yet the obstacles and the pain had become too great for him to endure.

In 1939 *Tumbleweeds* was reissued with music, sound effects, and an eight-minute prologue, photographed at Hart's ranch. The old actor, dressed in western attire, spoke to audiences in the movie's prelude for the first and last time, in a bombastic voice better suited to nineteenth-century melodrama than to the sound camera. "The rush of wind that cuts your face," he declaimed, reflecting back on his days in silent pictures, "the pounding hooves of the pursuing posse. . . . Oh, the thrill of it all!"

He was ready at last to build his Valhalla—a Spanish colonial mansion atop a hill, which he called "La Loma de los Vientos" (Hill of the Winds), at his Horseshoe Ranch. Designed by Los Angeles architect Arthur Kelly and not finished until 1928, the two-story home would be finished in white stucco with a red-tiled roof, contain twenty-two rooms, and cost $93,000. Bill would crowd the interior with western art (including a plethora of original Russells and Remingtons), Indian rugs and textiles, antique guns, bows and arrows, wampum belts, buffalo robes, a quirt from Wyatt Earp, and all sorts of other relics from the old West. Notched crossbeams in the house would be painted with Indian designs, and a bearskin rug, a gift from Will Rogers, would be spread in front of a fireplace in the spacious living room on the second floor. A circular stairway would lead from the foyer to the main living quarters, where Mary Ellen would have a bedroom at one end and Bill would have his at the other, with a sitting room in between. A telephone booth, with a window that went up and down for privacy, would be located in the hall between their quarters. (Hart's telephone number was 20.) The house would be furnished simply but comfortably and include a projection room (lined with tin because of the combustible film then in use), a dumbwaiter, an intercom system, seven bathrooms, servants' quarters, and two balconies.

Outside the house was a panoramic view of the smaller surrounding hills, although scrub oak, fir, cypress, sage, and chaparral would eventually cloak the mansion. There was usually a good breeze on the hill, and a garden of desert flowers and cactus would be part of the landscaping. A long, winding road, which passed the cowboys' bunkhouse, would lead up to the main house from the property's entrance, while down below were the old ranch house, the barns, a tack room (with a collection of hand-tooled saddles), and the corral.

Hart kept several horses at Horseshoe Ranch, and after 1925 he would spend most of his time there. He kept the house on DeLongpre, but his solace came from the ranch. He planned to devote his retirement to reading about his beloved West, riding his favorite horse, visiting with friends who shared his views, and writing his memoirs and stories for boys. In 1928 Hart would make a cameo appearance in King Vidor's *Show People*, which starred Marion Davies, but after what he considered "the tragedy of *Tumbleweeds*," he wanted nothing more to do with Hollywood. Acquaintances in the movie business remarked that the Gray Eagle of silent pictures had gone to the Hill of the Winds and perched there. Like the frontiersmen he impersonated, Hart had become part of a vanishing breed.

The stone-faced Hart in a typical studio pose.
Courtesy of Mickell Seltzer.

Jane Novak enjoying a prank between takes on a Hart film. Courtesy of Mickell Seltzer.

Hart and leading lady Jane Novak.
Novak wrote on the back, "a still from
one of our films—but I have no idea of
the title." Courtesy of Mickell Seltzer.

Hart and Jane Novak in costume.
Courtesy of Mickell Seltzer.

Hart and Fritz, inscribed
"To Little Jane In Remembrance of Fritz."
Courtesy of Mickell Seltzer.

A drawing of Hart and Fritz, inscribed to Jane Novak,
"from two who loved her." Courtesy of Mickell Seltzer.

Jane Novak with her daughter, Mickey, on Fritz.
Courtesy of Mickell Seltzer.

Hart and company on the set of *Wagon Tracks*. Courtesy of the Academy of Motion Picture Arts and Sciences.

Hart asleep with Fritz, with the mule Lizabeth (left) and the horse Cactus Kate (standing). Courtesy of Mickell Seltzer.

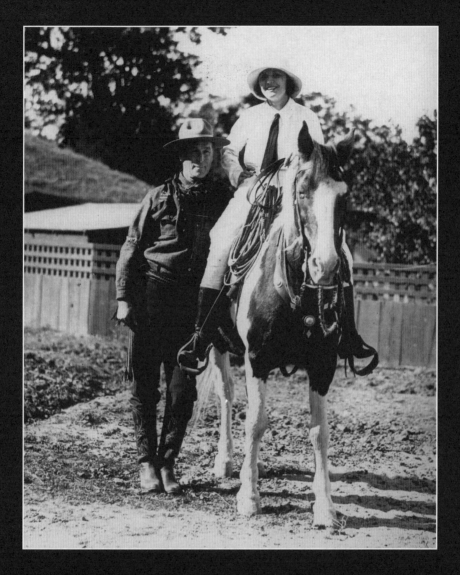

Hart with actress Pola Negri on Fritz. Courtesy of the
William S. Hart Collection, Seaver Center for Western History
Research, Los Angeles County Museum
of Natural History.

 Hart with the former
lawman Bat Masterson
in Masterson's office in New York. Courtesy of the William S.
Hart Collection, Seaver Center for Western History Research,
Los Angeles County Museum of Natural History.

Hart with his friend the artist Charles M. Russell. Courtesy of the William S. Hart Collection, Seaver Center for Western History Research, Los Angeles County Museum of Natural History.

Wagons awaiting the land rush in *Tumbleweeds*.
Courtesy of the William S. Hart Collection, Seaver
Center for Western History Research, Los Angeles
County Museum of Natural History.

Hart and leading lady Barbara Bedford in a clinch in *Tumbleweeds*.
Courtesy of the William S. Hart Collection, Seaver Center
for Western History Research, Los Angeles
County Museum of Natural History.

Hart and Our Gang at the Hal Roach Studio, circa 1930.
Courtesy of the G. J. Mitchell Collection.

Hart's sister, Mary Ellen Hart. Courtesy of the William S. Hart Collection, Seaver Center for Western History Research, Los Angeles County Museum of Natural History.

The living room of Hart's ranch house, with Charles Russell's painting *Buffalo Hunt* to the right of the piano. Courtesy of the William S. Hart Collection, Seaver Center for Western History Research, Los Angeles County Museum of Natural History.

Retirement

Charlie Russell died in Great Falls, Montana, on October 24, 1926. Hart had visited with the artist in California just a few months before his death. "We seldom talked of the old days," Hart said, "but this day we did. We talked a lot." Russell's death seemed to serve as a license for Hart to retreat deeper into the past. "The life on the frontier is a great memory to think back to," the retired actor repeatedly said. "The Sioux tribe taught me much that has been good in my life."

Wyatt Earp, nearing the end of his life, continued to write Hart about getting his story as a frontier marshal presented correctly, either as a book or on film. John H. Flood had written a draft of Earp's life story, which Hart read, but Thomas Y. Crowell rejected the piece for publication. "The manuscript might have proven acceptable had it been written more in the style of a historical narrative," Earp wrote Hart. Then Walter Noble Burns, the author of *The Saga of Billy the Kid*, tracked down the old peace officer and "burst in" on him one day, trying to get information on Earp's adventures in Tombstone for a story Burns was preparing on Doc Holliday. "I enjoyed his *Saga of Billy the Kid* immensely," Hart wrote Earp when he learned of the writer's intrusion. "It was beautifully written. But my dear friend, . . . it was copped bodily . . . from a story published many years ago by Charlie Siringo, called *The Life of Billy the Kid*." In December 1927 Hart read a book review by Bernard DeVoto and recommended the historian to Earp as a possible author for his life story. "He seems to be keenly familiar with Western history," Hart wrote of DeVoto. "He certainly sizes up the Burns book in great shape."

But time was hanging heavily on the old actor. Mary Ellen had not been well after her automobile mishap and suffered frequent colds and minor ailments. "The great trouble is her condition has been so weakened by the long illness that anything that hits her is doubly and trebly hard to shake off," Hart wrote Earp in September 1926. Hart himself was not in the best of health, but his spirits were worse.

He managed a trip to Philadelphia in the fall of 1926 for the Dempsey-Tunney fight. "The big scrap should be immense," Hart wrote a friend. "I cannot see it any other way than what it is—a first-class man against a second-class man. But it will be a fight, you bet!" Jack Dempsey wrote Hart soon after Hart's return home: "The fight certainly was a disappointment, Bill, but there is no use in crying over spilled milk."

Sculptor C. C. Cristadoro made a life-sized bronze of Hart and Fritz, and Hart spent months trying to arrange a proper site to display the statue. "I have an uncontrollable desire to have a reproduction of myself and my horse placed at some lonely spot on the rim of the Grand Canyon of Arizona, far away from crowds and the strife of life," he wrote an acquaintance. "In my eyes the Grand Canyon . . . is a religion symbolically taught." Hart contacted Senator Henry Ashurst of Arizona attempting to get the statue accepted by the National Park Board but had no success. "The artist has caught a look of distance in the eyes that would match the location we seek," Hart told Ashurst in September 1926, "as though the work was modeled on that very spot where God made life in death." In Hart's mind the bronze was not merely a modeling of him and Fritz; it was "a symbolic group of the West—a cowman of the West and his horse." In November he donated the statue, entitled "The Range Rider of the Yellowstone," to the city of Billings, Montana, and in July 1927 he was the guest of honor at its unveiling on Rim Rocks, overlooking the valley of the Yellowstone. "I have just returned from one of the biggest frontier celebrations where western people do congregate," he wrote from Los Angeles.

Bill's ego had grown to the point that he saw himself as an embodiment of America's westward expansion. Curiously enough, countless others seemed to accept the pose. In June 1926 he was the invited guest of the state of Montana at a celebration honoring the fiftieth anniversary of the Battle of Little Big Horn. Indians and whites of advanced age participated in the commemoration, which included a showing of *Tumbleweeds*. "I am just going to come with my friend Standing Bear to meet and enjoy the society of our red and white brothers in this memorable reunion," Bill said before leaving Los Angeles by train. He claimed that he spoke to the Indians who attended the celebration in their own language and told Senator William Borah of Montana that he was doing his best "to represent that West I feel the deepest gratitude." Hart was struck by the beauty of the Custer battlefield and the sight of "hundreds of old warriors" in full regalia who gathered for the occasion. "The volleys fired over the graves of the dead, the soft sound of 'Taps' echoed back by the hills like a benediction, the low, weird death song of the Indian women," he said, filled him with emotion.

After his return home, Hart pontificated more than ever about Indian wars, Native American leaders, and frontier matters outside his scope. "It is a great pity that Crazy Horse was murdered," Hart wrote on July 23, 1926. "He no doubt would have been a great aid to his people. The Indians themselves seem to look upon him as a regular Abraham Lincoln, as in spite of the fact that he was one of their very greatest fighters, he was a very plain man, simple in all his habits, and a great statesman, and always looking out for the Indians and not himself personally. In other words he was directly opposite to the character of Sitting Bull."

The library at the William S. Hart home in Newhall confirms that Hart read extensively on the history and lore of the American West, and undoubtedly he was quite knowledgeable in the field. But his views on the frontier experience had taken on a dogmatic, moralistic timbre that reflected his rigid personality and his cramped view of life. Hart overstated his views and laced them with such unbridled nostalgia that partial truths shriveled into parody. "When a man crosses the Missouri, the West gets into his blood," he was fond of saying. "I reckon the American Indian was the proudest being that ever lived—proud in his tradition, proud in his honor—yet humble in his simple belief in the Great Spirit. . . . The Indians of today are far from being the splendid examples of physical manhood that were their ancestors who lived in the freedom of the Western outdoors."

People from diverse walks of life wrote Hart during his later years as if he were the savant on the American frontier and its native population. "I have a full blooded Ojibway Indian in my church," a minister in St. Louis wrote the actor in November 1925. "I am proposing to spend two months with his tribe in the Canadian woods next summer. What a thrill it would be to have a long visit with you before I go."

Others wrote asking Hart if there were extant photographs of Crazy Horse, what the actor thought really happened at the Alamo or with the Donner party, how far one could shoot with a six-gun, and endless questions about Indian life, cowboys, and western gunfighters. "I have studied those characters so much that I almost feel as though I know them," Hart said in 1924. Some of the letters he received undoubtedly came from fans attempting to strike up a relationship with their favorite movie star, but others were sent by western history buffs who seemed genuinely curious about how William S. Hart viewed certain matters related to the frontier experience.

In 1928 Hart claimed that he spent $15,000 a year on postage, stationery, and a secretary to answer his mail. "Here's a letter from Bombay, India, asking why I don't make any more pictures," he told an interviewer that year. "God knows I'd like to make some." The reporter noted that a blur came into "the indignant eyes of the noblest cowboy of them all" as he spoke about his aborted movie career.

When not busy with correspondence, Bill rode Fritz over the hills of his ranch and sometimes poured out his heart to the horse, seemingly convinced that Fritz understood. Hart struck one Hollywood journalist as a melancholy reflection of the man who had rambled through the untamed West in so many silent pictures. When asked why he did not continue making movies, Hart replied, "[I am doing] what I am forced to do—nothing." He appeared increasingly forlorn and cultivated a tragic pose. About the cowboy stars who had replaced him on the screen, he expressed nothing but contempt. How could audiences take them seriously—decked out as they were in silk shirts, kid gloves, boots with silver spurs, and riding Arabian chargers in saddles of hand-tooled leather and pounds of embossed silver?

For Bill Hart life had stopped, except for the memory of what had been and the adulation he received from a stardom that was gone. He seemed incapable of change. Hart voiced dismay in 1926 when he learned that the police horses in Los Angeles were to be sold at auction. "To my mind," he said, "the mounted officers with their stock saddles and riatas were not only highly efficient and useful in handling crowds but were a distinct asset to our city in helping to perpetuate the picturesqueness of old Spanish California."

He continued to feel put upon, lied to, and attacked from all sides, personally and professionally. "It seems that the fates have decreed to batter me from pillar to post to such an extent that I am dazed," he wrote in August 1926. "It takes every moment of my time to endeavor to straighten out my affairs." Winifred, his estranged wife, accused him of using his name to keep her from working, and Hart still had to answer to the painful charge of being a wife beater. Worst of all, he said of his pending divorce, "is what I . . . feel at being classed as the lowest sort of slime that ever crawled the earth—that which is more crooked and groveling than a rattler with the stomach ache."

He fretted about Mary Ellen's poor health and wrote Mrs. Earp in February 1927 that he was building the new house on top of a mountain at the ranch so that Mamie could "sit out and enjoy the sunshine." Mary Ellen's unhappiness after breaking her neck in an automobile accident had grown fierce. "I wonder if it would help to write," she mused in her diary around 1928, "to write of blankness, . . . for I sense nothing else; of beauty that I cannot touch, of nearness that is far way, of complete bafflement of plans made and dying in stagnation; of lying in bed, hours, days, years."

Bill also turned to writing as a partial release from his cheerless existence. In 1925 he published *The Order of Chanta Sutas*, about a society for boys he had in mind, and he devoted much of his early retirement years to trying to sell stories he had written to magazines. Meeting with little success, he focused on *My Life East and West*, his romanticized autobiography that Houghton Mifflin published in

1929. "It is a record I want to leave behind for my young son," Hart said. "The fates say I shall not have my boy with me. The book is a message from a father to his son." Written with simplicity and drama, the memoir is a highly colored account of the actor's life and travails, more like a fast-paced scenario than a meaningful probing of a man's achievements and personal development. "In more than one sense," Frank Daugherty wrote in *Photoplay*, "Bill wrote that book with his tears." The actor found writing for publication more difficult than turning out screenplays, and he often complained that publishers treated him as shabbily as Hollywood studios had. He admitted to Wyatt Earp that he had had difficulty getting his autobiography accepted, since editors objected to much of the motion picture material "wherein I told the truth." Ultimately he had to take forty-five thousand words out of the book before Houghton Mifflin found the manuscript acceptable.

Hart received offers to appear in vaudeville on the Orpheum circuit, but he was never seriously tempted to accept them. Will Hays urged Hart to maintain his membership in the Motion Picture Producers and Distributors of America, as D. W. Griffith had done when he stopped making movies, but Hart refused even after Hays assured him that he would not be expected to pay dues since he was no longer producing films.

Hart regularly telephoned or wrote Nancy Russell after Charlie's death, and occasionally he visited Trail's End, the Russells' home in Pasadena. "She is bearing up . . . in fine shape," Hart wrote after having dinner with the artist's widow in March 1927, "as when Charlie went, she not only lost a husband, she lost one of the finest men that ever pulled on a pair of boots. We drank a silent toast to Charlie." Rumors of a romance between Hart and Nancy circulated, and there were even suggestions that the old actor had proposed to his friend's widow. Nancy's picture still resides on a table beside Hart's bed in the house in Newhall, but it is unlikely that either of them had serious intentions of remarrying.

Hart saw Will Rogers frequently, appeared with him onstage or at banquets now and then, and repeatedly voiced admiration for the humorist's talent. "He stands absolutely alone in the world today," he wrote of Rogers in 1927. "His humor is the brand that makes people think. Will Rogers is a credit to America." From time to time the two men ran into one another at Harry Carey's ranch, for Bill and Harry got together at least once a year. "Hart used to scare me with his bombastic personality," Harry Carey, Jr., remembered, "but my father genuinely liked him. I thought he was pretty hammy myself."

Bill remained friends with both Charlie Siringo, who lived in nearby Long Beach during his later life, and James Montgomery Flagg, who eventually illustrated five of Hart's books. "I like Bill because he is naive and honest and westernlike," Flagg said. But the illustrator found the retired actor preoccupied with his ranch, his horses and dogs, and his collection of antique guns. When Gatewood Dunston, a motion picture projectionist in Norfolk, Virginia, with whom Bill exchanged letters for years, asked Hart for one of his guns as a remembrance in 1931, the actor responded, "It would be like parting with one of my legs to let one go."

In the spring of 1927 Bill was working hard to get his palatial new house at the ranch in shape so that he and Mary Ellen could move in. "It is running into a great deal of money and requires constant attention," Hart wrote, but "I have what I think is a fine home." The mansion would not be fully ready for occupancy for another year, but the estate already had become Bill's pride and joy.

Hart talked little about his son, although he continued to express sorrow that he could not be with the boy. "He is a wonderful, manly little chap," Hart said. When a reporter, whom Hart claimed was a relative of Adolph Zukor, wrote in 1928 that the former cowboy star told her over the telephone that he had no use for his son, Hart was furious. He detested "sob sisters" and "mud throwers," he said. In January 1930 Bill wrote that he was depressed because his son had asked to see him and a meeting had been arranged at a friend's house. "But at the last minute my son's mother refused to let him come," Hart said. "I would cut the legs off my body . . . if I could have him with me."

During his retirement, Bill saw a great deal of Joe McNinch, a fan whom the actor had met shortly before he started work on *Tumbleweeds*. As their friendship grew, Joe often dropped by the Harts' home for morning visits. Bill would usually be reading when Joe arrived, and after chatting with their visitor for a few minutes, Mary Ellen would disappear. "That's all I'd see of her," McNinch recalled years later. "I don't think there was very much Bill Hart didn't know about the old West. Above everything else, he was a private person. We had many a nice visit, and I enjoyed his friendship for a long time. He called me 'Laddie,' but it took me quite a while to know the man well enough to call him Bill. He was always Mr. Hart."

As Bill grew more reclusive, Mary Ellen became even more so. Psychiatrists maintain that retreating into illness is often a means of gaining a feeling of superiority, and that may well have been the case with Mary Ellen. Certainly sickness brought her much-needed attention. Rambling entries in her diary suggest that she was a person trying to make sense out of her life. "I can see now that I have feared and lost the true [fruits] of my efforts," she wrote on February 11, 1928. "Anger is the resentment of restraint—mental and physical. . . . My physical inaction fills me with rage." She lacked the knack of dealing with her problems, she said, or of turning them over to God. She read a great deal, was concerned with religious and moral issues, and clung to the belief that life had a purpose. "No one is ever satisfied with life," she said. "If we can create a perfect whole of anything, we have achieved the purpose of living. Only some people are unreasonable enough to expect a smile of appreciation. Better be satisfied with the inner satisfaction."

Without exactly saying so, she seemed to be angry at her brother for not fully recognizing the sacrifices she had made for him during the early years. "I always tried to meet the things that were expected of me," she wrote in her scant diary. One pregnant line suggests that Mamie may have resented Bill's celebrity, or perhaps his attitude of self-importance. "There are few people," she said, "great enough to die great." And on another occasion she wrote, "the glare of publicity blinds them."

Most of the time Mary Ellen seemed bored: "[It's] a lovely dull day, even the radio wouldn't answer. I sorted out papers—sent out nine letters. It rained all last night. I tried to straighten out my closet and got all sweaty and chilled—Bed." On January 1, 1931, she wrote:

"I really believe we are only ourselves when we are alone. . . . The world comes very close, but I wonder if as individuals we develop more firmly alone, dig ourselves out into the light. But my digging is over."

In the summer of 1928, as the new house at the ranch neared completion, Mary Ellen's health took a sudden turn for the better, but the improvement was only temporary. Both Bill and his sister were wedded to negativism, and they often internalized bad news and let their pain manifest itself in aches and symptoms of physical malady. Mary Ellen would be a semi-invalid for the rest of her life, and she spent her later years with a wheelchair in arm's reach.

In March 1928 the area that included Newhall and Saugus was threatened when a 180-foot dam in San Francisquito Canyon gave way, sending an enormous wall of water cascading down the narrow valley of the Santa Clara. "None of us was hurt," Hart wrote from Horseshoe Ranch, "but hundreds and hundreds of little boys and girls and their fathers and mothers were killed—and hundreds of animals too! . . . Only those who were in it or near it can realize how tragic it all was." At one point there were seventy-eight bodies in the shack at Newhall designated as a morgue. A boy in Hart's employ at the ranch lost his father, two elder brothers, and two elder sisters and their husbands and children. Only half of the bodies of the youth's relatives were ever recovered.

Talking pictures had become a reality in 1928, and Bill longed for an opportunity to make his Patrick Henry story or a yarn about Davy Crockett into a sound movie. "I was supposed to have one of the finest voices on the speaking stage," he wrote in May 1928. The next year Hal Roach, a well-known independent film producer, approached Hart about starring in a sound Western. A contract was signed, but six days later Nicolas M. Schenck, president of Loew's Incorporated, the parent company of Metro-Goldwyn-Mayer, which released Roach's films, wired the producer that MGM would not be interested in handling a Hart movie. Hart agreed to the cancellation of his contract with Roach, but he was deeply hurt and complained that he was "automatically barred" from an industry he had helped launch. "I do not measure up," he said. "Someone wants to keep me out of pictures."

Hart felt helpless, a lone man at odds with the corporate structure. "There is nothing I can do about it," he said. "They tell me Western pictures are no longer popular. They told me that when I first came to Hollywood in 1914. I didn't believe it then, I don't believe it now. . . . These past five years of mine should have been the best, the crowning working years of my life. No matter what turn the Wheel of Fortune may take now, I can never be given back time. I am nearing the end of the trail."

In 1928 and 1929 the aging silent picture star became involved with helping Wyatt Earp find an author to write the life story he wanted done before his death. Earp received a letter in January 1928 from Stuart N. Lake, who lived in San Diego, asking for the rights to his story. "He writes in a modest and unassuming manner," Earp wrote Hart. "Will you kindly advise me in this?" Hart responded that he did not know Lake, nor had he ever heard of him.

Hart had been criticized for placing Wild Bill Hickok in Dodge City in his movie, and he reminded Earp in his letters that both he and Bat Masterson had spoken as if Hickok were there. "Those historians gather so much material on hearsay," Hart wrote Earp in May 1928, "then suddenly they commence to state it all as fact." An old newspaperman named Wilstach had given Hart a few hairs that Wilstach claimed came from Hickok's head. "I hope they did," Hart wrote Earp, "but I am not making any affidavit that they did."

Stuart Lake visited Earp early in June 1928, and the two had an enjoyable chat. The old gunman found the writer a "nice, modest young fellow" and felt confident that Lake was up to the task of writing his story in a truthful manner. In November Earp wrote Hart that Lake was making progress on the book and doing a thorough job of research. "[H]e has written everyone whom I ever have known," Earp said.

Charlie Siringo had recently died, and in a letter to Hart, Earp called Siringo "one of the great scouts in the advance of civilization and the subduing of the frontier." "Isn't it sad that, during this great era of prosperity, life was so ungenerous to him? . . . Just one more riddle in the great mystery of life . . . ; we must carry on." Hart had written Siringo shortly before his death, "[The] Charlie Siringos and

Wyatt Earps are very few and soon no message can be had from the last of such gallant frontiersmen. I only hope that every word you write . . . will be published, so it may always stand as a record and true guide to those to come who will want to know of the West." Hart felt the same about Lake's biography of Earp.

In poor health, Earp suggested that Hart take over an offer he had received to write an article about the old West for the *Los Angeles Evening Express*. Hart found the idea preposterous. "I might even take a stab at substituting for President Coolidge at a cabinet meeting," he replied, "but I will be damned if I'd ever have the nerve to substitute for Wyatt Earp in talking of the frontier. . . . I would not attempt it for a million dollars. . . . I cannot tell you how glad I am to be considered your friend."

In December 1928 Earp wrote Hart that he was flat on his back with illness and that Lake promised to have his manuscript finished soon after Christmas. On January 7, 1929, Earp wrote Bill again, shortly after his brother Newton and fight promoter Tex Rickard had died, in a despondent mood. "All of [this] reminds us that the world moves on," the old sheriff said, "and age must make way for buoyant, bubbling youth. . . . I can't plan anymore to climb the hills and hit the drill."

Wyatt Earp died six days later. "I have just returned from the funeral services of a very dear friend of mine, who has crossed the Big Divide—Wyatt Earp, the last of the really great gunmen–peace officers of the frontier," Hart wrote Joe McNinch. Hart and Tom Mix were both pallbearers at Earp's burial, a singular blend of myth and reality.

Shortly after the funeral Hart began a lengthy correspondence with Stuart Lake, who wrote Hart how much he had admired Earp's "modesty of spirit and his great strength of soul." Lake informed Hart that the gunman had told him things that he never told anyone else—"not even to his own brothers or, for that matter, to Mrs. Earp." Hart agreed to talk to Houghton Mifflin about publishing Lake's book. Mrs. Earp soon proved an obstacle, however, for she insisted on the right to approve the manuscript before Lake submitted it to editors. "The memory of her husband is so dear and vital to her that there is bound to be considerable anxiety," Hart wrote the frustrated biographer on January 21. But the obstacles the widow posed were deeper than Hart realized. "Her interest is not historical accuracy," Lake told the actor; "she wishes to make sure that I tell what she calls 'a nice, clean story.' . . . I have tried to explain to Mrs. Earp that the saloons were merely incidental spots in the landscape, gambling was in the relationship of latter-day golf, but God knows I lack the temerity to try to gloss over the shooting." Earp had anticipated his religious wife's scruples about a realistic treatment of his days as a frontier sheriff and had assured Lake that he could handle her objections when the time came for publication. "Now that he cannot," Lake told Hart, "there is the additional stimulus to sentiment which his memory will give."

Hart remained confident that Mrs. Earp would come around to a sensible view of her husband's experiences in Dodge City and Tombstone. "It is frontier history," Hart wrote Lake. "It cannot be changed." But Josephine Sarah Earp persisted in thwarting Lake's efforts to get his biography published, rebuking the writer for not keeping her informed of his actions and demanding that he make incessant revisions. Lake held to his belief that the book must tell Wyatt's story accurately. "It means the whole difference between a successful book and a flat failure," the author wrote Earp's widow.

By January 1931 Lake's restraint had been shattered. "I shall continue to carry out my end to the best of my ability," the thwarted writer wrote Josephine Earp, "and that task has been made no easier for me by constant heckling and interference which is in no way warranted. I have been patient, tolerant, sympathetic, and understanding; I have wasted hours of time trying to explain and re-explain things which have been misconstrued and distorted. . . . The patience that I own is being strained close to the breaking point." Lake's *Wyatt Earp, Frontier Marshal* was published by Houghton Mifflin later that year and judged by historians to be a mixture of fact and fiction.

Meanwhile Nancy Russell was contemplating a book about her husband and wrote Hart asking for his impressions of Charlie. Bill responded with a full account of his relationship with the cowboy artist, but the widow's biography never materialized. Nancy Russell died in 1940.

Hart himself kept busy turning out stories for boys. *Hoof-Beats*, advertised as a Western thriller set in the 1870s before the Custer massacre, was published by Dial in 1933 and was dedicated to Bill, Jr. According to the book's dust jacket, "Indians, cowboys, hidden treasure, troopers, mustangs, guns, love, and life and death make up as fast-moving and enthralling a tale as one could wish." Middie, a horse, becomes a real character with a tender personality in *Hoof-Beats*. Indians are muscular and bronze, and all braves are great horsemen. There is a search for gold and attempts to locate a lost canyon in the book, all written in a western vernacular. "The lack of the conventional craftsmanship of story-telling in *Hoof-Beats* is an assurance of the authenticity of its authorship," the *New York Sun*'s reviewer said. "No one can read it and harbor a thought of the possibility of its having been 'ghost-written.'" *Law on Horseback and Other Stories*, which Hart published himself, appeared two years later.

Bill attended rodeos from time to time, always sensitive to the possibility of cruelty to animals in some of the events. Calf- and goat-roping contests, he thought, should be eliminated. "The nearer I approach to gray hairs," he said, "the more it hurts me to see any animal harassed in any manner." In most rodeo contests he felt that the humans who participated were in greater jeopardy than the horses and steers involved.

Hart recorded *Pinto Ben* for Victor in 1928, made radio appearances with singer Rudy Vallee from time to time, and periodically traveled to New York, where he enjoyed seeing Broadway shows. "Every time I appear in public," he said in 1933, "it is worked as news that I am returning to the screen. The fan letters pour in and I have to do all the explaining, which puts me in the same old hole." Hart saw few films and avoided movie premieres and Hollywood social life altogether. He wanted no part of an industry dominated by "the evils of the motion picture magistrates." By 1935 he had moved out of his house on DeLongpre and leased it to actress Kay Francis.

He did visit the set of *Billy the Kid*, which King Vidor directed in 1933 with Johnny Mack Brown in the title role. Part of the movie was filmed in the hills around Newhall, and the production crew had built a little town there for the picture. Moving around and shooting from different angles, Vidor and Brown noticed a horse and rider off in the distance. "Every once in a while we'd have to change angles to get him out of the scene," Brown remembered. The rider turned out to be William S. Hart. "All he wanted to do was come out and look me over," Brown said, "because his favorite character was Billy the Kid." Hart showed the picture's director and star the revolver he claimed had belonged to the famous New Mexico outlaw, and he taught Brown how to turn his body so that his heart was away from a gunman shooting at him, which Hart said was more authentic than the way most movie cowboys stood. "I don't think he knew any more about Billy the Kid than we did," Vidor said. "By then I'd done a lot of research." But Johnny Mack Brown and Hart developed a lasting friendship, and when Brown called on the retired actor at his ranch, they sometimes ran one of Hart's old movies.

Harry Carey, Jr., remembered Hart bringing *Tumbleweeds* to the school in Newhall, where young Carey was a student for a time, and showing the film in the school's auditorium. The youngsters found the old man terribly theatrical and laughed at his movie. "Hart liked kids," the younger Carey said. "One day I was in the drugstore in Newhall, waiting for my mother to pick me up after school, and Hart came in and bought me and my friends each a big ice cream soda. We thought he was a helluva guy."

Later, when young Carey was enrolled in Foxe Military Academy, he and his father visited Hart at Horseshoe Ranch and sat around the breakfast room table talking. "Young man, do you know your Shakespeare?" Hart asked the boy in his pompous, declamatory manner. The youth, dressed in his military uniform, admitted that the only thing he knew about Shakespeare was that Romeo was in love with Juliet. Hart dropped the subject and returned to ranting about how the Hollywood Jews had ruined him. "Well, Bill," the elder Carey said with a chuckle, "the Jews bought you this goddam ranch."

Hart was delighted that many of his fans stayed so loyal, yet he seldom missed a chance to tell them how powerless he was to return to the screen. "I fought cleanly, without rancor or malevolence," he told a reporter who asked why he had abandoned his career. "I was whipped. . . . Every inch of me is sore—and not from physical blows." In 1933 he said that he would never have dreamed ten years before that he could "be persecuted for all time" because he fought for his rights, and he characterized himself as "a living chain gang fugitive."

Visitors to Horseshoe Ranch noted a grayness in Bill's face, as if he had spent too many hours indoors, and a softness they had not expected. The big house on the hill seemed silent, and Mary Ellen was usually nowhere in sight. Hart's dogs and horses appeared to be his kith and kin, but even they caused him grief. In 1933 Cactus Kate was kicked by a mare, suffered a broken leg, and had to be destroyed. "I did it myself," Hart said, "but God how it hurt. However I couldn't let anyone else do it."

Hart claimed not to understand the Great Depression, yet he said the slump in the motion picture business was no mystery to him. "I bought and paid for my knowledge," he wrote a friend in May 1931. Jane Novak and her daughter, Mickey, lived in a small house on the Carey ranch for two years during the hard times. Despite the breakup of their romance, Bill harbored a fondness for Jane and wished her to be happy. With her mother's film career over, teenage Mickey came to Hart during the worst of the depression and asked him for money. He gave her a hundred dollars to tide them over until things got better.

In the spring of 1933 Bill suffered a bad cold on a return trip from making personal appearances with Johnny Mack Brown in New York and Chicago. "I just must take care of myself," he said. That summer Bill had an operation for an abdominal ailment and was in the hospital for several weeks. He regained his strength enough to eat Thanksgiving dinner with Will Rogers and his wife but spent months convalescing at his ranch.

Gatewood Dunston saw some newsreel footage taken of Hart around 1935 and wrote the actor that an acquaintance with him had remarked that the old cowboy star looked so good that he must have had cosmetic surgery. "If anyone else ever inquires about my having my face lifted," Hart replied, "tell them that as yet I have never needed to have it done, and if I live to be a thousand years of age, I never would have it done." Hart surmised that the film Dunston had seen had been taken at a recent rodeo in Newhall, where he appeared with singer Alice Faye. "If I can sit alongside a pretty girl like that and photograph well, I consider it a great compliment," he said.

Mary Ellen was quite ill in the spring of 1935, and her spirits fell to a low ebb. "I'm out of breath with living," she wrote in her diary in May, "and find so much of what I've written dull. . . . Not for worlds would I go back and detail these past years—too searing. Just forget and hope there will be a few growing days left. . . . The why of things is too puzzling."

By 1936 Bill admitted that he was too old to do the stunts for the camera he had once done. Besides, he said, he was too busy with his ranch to attempt a comeback. "The motion picture has lost all its motion," he said. "The motion pictures of today are merely photographs of shows on the stage, with the lines spoken through a machine instead of directly by the actors." Hart thought Cecil B. DeMille's *The Plainsman* was "an awful mess," and three years later he found fault with John Ford's *Stagecoach*, pointing out that the Indians would have been smart enough to shoot the horses and end the long chase toward the end of the picture. He disliked Twentieth Century-Fox's *Jesse James*, which starred handsome Tyrone Power, and said that Jesse James, Jr. and his family, who visited him from time to time, were "despondent about the whole affair." Hart swore that he would never see another Western because current filmmakers were apparently incapable of doing anything right. He had sold the rights to *O'Malley of the Mounted* to Twentieth Century-Fox in the early 1930s and complained that the studio had butchered his original treatment in the remake that starred George O'Brien. "How they can deliberately cut the guts out of a story is beyond my comprehension," Hart said. "They murder the story and use my name to pull in the public."

Hart felt that he had been treated fairly by most Hollywood reporters, even though interviewers were inclined to twist facts a little in their desire to dig out something sensational for their story. Hart said that he had been lucky because there was little that was sensational about him. He continued to believe that the public wanted Westerns that were properly made. "Barbed wire hasn't killed the West," he told a fan magazine writer, "nor drugstore cowboys either."

The old star maintained that he would have liked to be more charitable to worthy boys' organizations, but his enforced retirement had restricted his finances and limited his generosity. He claimed that he willingly lost $25,000 a year on Horseshoe Ranch but complained that lawyers' fees and doctors' bills had depleted the rest of his cash reserve. He made little or no money on his books and gave away hundreds of copies to libraries and friends.

In December 1937 Hart was back in the hospital for a month, this time with pleurisy and a set of fractured ribs. He added another bedroom onto the ranch house that year and converted his former bedroom into what became known as the "dogs' room." That was Hart's favorite place to sit and visit with friends. "I don't recalled being in the living room more than four or five times," Joe McNinch said. "We always went in the back door and sat in the corner of the dogs' room to visit."

In his later life Hart had two Great Danes that were his closest companions aside from Fritz. Prince Hamlet, one of the Danes, died in late January 1938. Fritz died ten days later, an even bigger blow to the old star. "I'd give both my shoes—with my feet in them—to have him back," Hart said. Letters of condolence poured in from fans when they learned of the pony's death, but the sympathy offered only temporary relief to Hart's sad heart. He dug a grave for Fritz at the foot of the hill near the old ranch house. A string band from San Fernando played at a short burial service for the horse, with the ranch hands, a few friends, and some local children standing by. Hart erected a stone monument over the grave, with a bronze tablet on which was inscribed, "To Bill Hart's Pinto Pony Fritz, Age 31 Years, A Loyal Comrade." Cactus Kate and Lizabeth were also buried at the ranch, and up the hill a few feet, toward the bunkhouse, Hart created a dog cemetery. A picture of Fritz hangs over Hart's bed to this day.

Heavy with grief, Bill wrote his friend Gatewood Dunston in June 1938, "The old customs are fast disappearing." He had not been well and had a trained nurse with him all winter. He seemed preoccupied with preserving his image and talked of creating a museum at the ranch. "It is my intention to keep my films in good shape," he wrote Dunston, "and before I kick off I shall give them to the government to keep as illustrations of the old frontier as I knew it to be." Yet he wanted his father's papers destroyed and told Mary Ellen that whichever one lived longest must see that they were burned. "They are too sacred to fall in other's hands," he said.

His court battle with United Artists was not fully resolved until 1938, and Hart spent several months that fall in the East. If anything, his hatred for studio executives, particularly the Schencks, had grown. "The ones who control the industry are not only ignorant, but choke full of egotism," he wrote Dunston. "I am not going back into pictures under any circumstances."

Bill published *And All Points West* in 1940, coached actor Robert Taylor in the art of the fast draw for Metro-Goldwyn-Mayer's 1941 version of *Billy the Kid*, and continued to answer scores of letters from the "wonderful grown boys and girls that have never forgotten me." But his eyesight was failing. "At times my eyes slump terribly and I can scarcely see at all," he wrote Dunston in May 1941. In November he entered Columbia Presbyterian Medical Center for the removal of a cataract.

Devastating rains earlier in 1941 had ruined some negatives and prints Hart kept in his film vault. He moved them to the old ranch house and tried to salvage what he could. "The Museum of Modern Art has been begging for them for years," he said. "Now I'm afraid they are past saving." However, he was able to donate nineteen complete negatives and some posters to the museum in 1942.

Jane Novak came to visit Hart with Joe McNinch in May 1941. Joe followed Jane into the house and remembered that Hart stood silent for a minute looking at her, then held out his arms. "She looks grand," Bill wrote Martha McKelvie after Jane's visit. "Doggone her, I nearly made a meal from her face. I haven't kissed a gal so hard for twenty years. Did she back up? No, she didn't—not an inch! Bless her heart, I think she edged forward a bit."

Warner Bros.' *One Foot in Heaven* in 1941 contained a memorable scene in which a young minister sees his first movie, a William S.

Hart Western. The attention the sequence received sparked another round of speculation that the old cowboy star might return to the screen. Gene Autry supposedly wanted Republic to costar him in a picture with Hart, but Hart pointed out that it had been sixteen years since he had made a film and that he was enjoying retirement.

December 7, 1941, brought the news of the Japanese bombing of Pearl Harbor. "All radio programs interrupted by war chaos," Mary Ellen wrote in her diary. "Will thinks Japanese move will be followed by a German move." Hart was in New York at the time but left for California the next day. "Trust no future, however pleasant," Mamie wrote in her diary the day of the attack on Honolulu.

Mary Ellen died less than three years later. With her death Hart lost any zest for living he had left. "The better part of my life has gone from me," he wrote Dunston shortly after his sister's death. His own health soon suffered a serious decline. "There is nothing I can attribute my illness to," he wrote Dunston, "except that I believe it is caused by the deep grief I feel over the loss and absence of my darling sister. At times it seems to be too great a burden to carry. She was in all reality the better part of my existence."

*Chapter
Eleven*

The Final Reel

Although Bill and Mamie had lived with tension between them, part of Bill died with his sister. Mary Ellen had been his constant partner for thirty years. Without her the mansion on the Hill of the Winds became a tomb. Soon after her death, Bill invited Ann Lendt, the nurse who had cared for Mary Ellen and him earlier, to take up residence in the house. "She was more of a companion than a nurse," Joe McNinch said, "but Ann was there quite a while."

Hart was sick during most of 1944 and in bed a good part of that time. He read a great deal, despite his failing eyesight, and particularly enjoyed Gene Fowler's biography of John Barrymore, *Goodnight, Sweet Prince.* "It holds me as no book has done for years," Bill wrote McNinch. "It brings out human nature as biographies seldom do. I knew the man Jack Barrymore. I realize now I never knew him. Yet I can see nothing but stark truth in every word of the author."

The old actor drew up a new will that year, leaving the bulk of his estate to Los Angeles County to be preserved as a museum and public park. "I am only trying to give back to the American public some part of what the American public has already given to me," he said. "When I was making pictures, the people gave me their nickels, dimes, and quarters. When I am gone, I want them to have my home."

Hollywood gossip columnist Hedda Hopper wrote that Bill Hart must be terribly lonely up at the ranch without his beloved sister. "It would be the same on any foot of ground that surfaces the earth, dear Hedda," Hart replied, "and will be the same when my ashes go underneath this earth by her side." Bill filled the void by devoting hours to closing Mary Ellen's estate. "No one knew my darling sister's wishes but myself," he wrote Gatewood Dunston in February 1945.

Hart corresponded with Jane Novak sporadically, and Jane occasionally came to visit him with Joe McNinch, usually finding the feeble star in bed. Once she and Joe gave Hart a small birthday party, and Jane made him a cake with rope around the side and figures of cowboys on top. "Sometimes when I'm sitting by myself I think of Bill," Novak said years later, "and I feel like he's talking to me. I think about him a lot."

When oil was discovered on property near Horseshoe Ranch, Hart refused to permit any drilling on his land. After several oil promoters had tried to convince him to change his mind, he reportedly got out a bullwhip and barked that he would use it on the next one who set foot on his ranch. He did not want his view cluttered with derricks, he said.

During his last illness, Bill emerged from a coma and told how he had crossed over to "the other side," where he heard beautiful music and saw green fields, open ranges, towering mountains, and bright sunshine. Ann Lendt had left the ranch by then, and the actor's final days were spent in misery. William S. Hart, Jr., arrived at the house in the early summer of 1946 and claimed that he found his father strapped to his bed, drugged, and left to the care of a drunken male nurse. Young Bill dismissed the nurse and took his father to California Lutheran Hospital. The old cowboy star died there in a coma on Sunday, June 24, 1946, at 11:20 P.M., with his son by his bedside. Hart was eighty-two. "His ailment was nothing you could give a name to," a hospital official said. "It was just the result of growing old."

"The gaunt and strong man of the silent flickers, dies with his boots off in a hospital bed," the *New York World Telegram* reported the next day. "And many a spreading middle-ager pauses in his worries about atomic social problems to recall the boyhood thrills of the Saturday matinee performances of that hero of mesa and canyon, sagebrush and cactus, whose steel nerves, granite countenance, and ambidexterity with shootin' irons gave always the triumph of might and right over cattle-rustlin', bank-robbin' villains."

Funeral services were held at Hart's home in Newhall and in Forest Lawn Memorial Cemetery in Glendale. At the latter, which was open to the public, Rudy Vallee sang "Home on the Range" and "The Long, Long Trail," and the Reverend George Davidson of St. John's Episcopal Church delivered the eulogy. "His life was a pattern any wholesome boy might well covet and follow," Davidson said. "He lived cleanly, fought valiantly." Hundreds of fans, veteran actors, and grizzled cowhands crowded the little church at Forest Lawn to pay their last respects, and many more stood outside on the lawn. An Indian blanket made of red roses and white daisies covered the coffin, which was opened at the end of the service, and mourners filed past in silence. Hart's body was cremated, and the ashes were sent to Greenwood Cemetery in Brooklyn, where they were placed beside the graves of his parents, Mary Ellen, his baby brother, and his youngest sister.

The actor made no provision for his twenty-four-year-old son in his will, since, he claimed, he had amply provided for the boy during his lifetime. He bequeathed a sum of $50,000 to the Society for the Prevention of Cruelty to Animals. The ranch, the splendid house there, and its artwork and furnishings became the property of the County of Los Angeles. The home at the foot of Sunset Strip in Hollywood was left to the Los Angeles Park Commission, in exchange for a pledge to construct a fountain on the property and maintain the estate as a monument in Hart's honor. "After all, the public made me a star and gave me my wealth," Hart had told actor Joel McCrea. "I want to show how grateful I am for what they did for me."

When William S. Hart, Jr., learned the contents of his father's will, he was so distressed that he charged that the old man had been mentally incompetent at the time the document was drawn up and demanded that an autopsy be performed on his father's brain. Microscopic tests were made to determine the mental responsibility of the late actor, a process that took weeks to complete.

Bill Hart, Jr., then went to court to contest the will, and a four-month legal battle ensued over control of property estimated to be worth $1,170,000. After five days of deliberation, a jury of nine women and three men decided that the late cowboy star's mind was sound in

1944 when his final testament was signed. Bill, Jr., attempted to break his father's will again in 1950 and filed another lawsuit against the estate in 1955.

Hart's acquaintances had mixed reactions. Joe McNinch and his wife, Virginia, appeared in court to testify that their friend was lucid at the time his will was drawn up and felt that he had the right to do what he wanted with his property. Olive Carey, Harry's wife, never forgave Bill for ignoring his son's and ex-wife's welfare in the distribution of his estate. "The old bastard didn't leave anything to Winifred and Bill, Jr.," Olive fumed. "Hart built a monument to himself, and it made my mother madder than hell," Harry Carey, Jr., said.

For more than a decade Horseshoe Ranch, with the W S brand on the front gate, remained sealed, with a barbed-wire fence around the acreage to keep out intruders. William S. Hart Park in Newhall was dedicated on September 20, 1958, and visitors began to trickle through. The home has never become a huge attraction, although picnickers use the lower area of the property, and the expense of maintaining the buildings has grown exorbitant over the years. Hart stipulated in the bequest that no fee could be charged to patrons who tour the ranch, and the financial burden on the county, especially with periodic earthquake damage, has become a drain.

In 1962 Walt Disney gave the park eight buffalo, and through the decades the herd there has grown. The corrals at the ranch are stocked with animals, and Fritz's grave and the dog cemetery are enclosed and nicely kept. The interior of the main house is much as Hart left it, with his clothes still in the drawers, a mass of buffalo robes still in a closet, his shaving mug and toothbrushes still in the bathroom, and his hand-tooled boots and broad-brimmed hat in his bedroom, as if awaiting his return. Mary Ellen's wheelchair is still in her room, her bath salts are on the lavatory, and her personal effects remain largely in place. Bookcases are filled with volumes on the American West, and the actor's frontier artifacts and movie memorabilia are on display along with his remarkable collection of western paintings. In the entryway stands a bronze of Hart by C. C. Cristadoro, the actor crouching forward, dressed in cowboy regalia and holding a pistol in each hand.

William S. Hart, Jr., matured into a large man, gentle in disposition, who shunned the Hollywood scene except for infrequent visits to director John Ford's Field Photo Farm in the San Fernando Valley, where Western actors and stuntmen used to congregate. For a while young Hart worked on a book about his father and hoped to sell the motion picture rights, but the story was never published, and no movie of the old cowboy star's life has been made.

Winifred Westover died in 1978, bitter to the end over Hart's treatment of her and Bill, Jr. Jane Novak, who maintained fond memories of her former costar and sweetheart, lived until 1990, having accepted years before that William S. Hart lived too prim a life for marriage.

The high school in Newhall is named for Hart, but most of the visitors to Horseshoe Ranch would have trouble naming a single title of the old cowboy star's movies. Hart's Westerns are shown occasionally at retrospectives attended by diehard film buffs, and festivals celebrating his career have been held from time to time in Newburgh, where he was born.

The Hart ranch and the museum-like home on the promontory of La Loma de los Vientos stand as the old star's personal monument, and his presence there, especially when the house is viewed alone as the sun sets, is haunting. Volunteers who conduct tours of the mansion claim that they have actually seen the old man sitting in the easy chair in his bedroom. One of the docents, Frank McKendall, was showing a man from Oregon through the house in September 1990 when McKendall claimed he saw Bill as he turned from the gun case to enter Bill's bedroom. "Bill Hart was sitting in the chair next to the bed," McKendall said. "I was startled and took a deep breath. His image disappeared. . . . A cold chill came over me, and I then moved to the Dogs' Room."

Lucille Evenson, another docent at Horseshoe Ranch, professed multiple sightings of the silent movie star. The first was on a Sunday afternoon, when Evenson felt "a presence" at her side on the second floor of the house and unexplicably started moving her hand back and forth as if stroking something. She later concluded, "I had been stroking the back of one of Mr. Hart's beloved dogs." On another occasion, during the last tour of the day, Evenson suddenly did an about-face, returned to Hart's bedroom, and stopped, facing the actor's chair, in front of which were his boots. "This time," she said, "the boots were very much filled with The Man himself. Standing motionless, I continued to look at him, with a mutual stance from him. After a brief moment of shared silence, I turned and left, not so affected as I had been at my first encounter with a pleasant, if intangible, presence that I believe remains after all these years."

For a generation William S. Hart personified the untamed West for silent picture audiences around the world. Millions idolized the screen's sad-faced cowboy, who vowed vengeance with clenched fists and set jaw, turned evil into good, and cleaned the rowdy frontier to make it a fit place for chaste women and innocent children to live. Hart was the first in a long line of sexless he-men in Western films who seemed to love their trusty steeds more than their leading ladies, battled villains and baser instincts, and emerged victorious in the final reels of countless pictures, usually by riding into the landscape alone but exonerated.

Although Bill Hart gained wealth and international fame, he confronted more than his share of dark canyons in his private life and seemed helpless to sustain intimate relationships or much lasting joy from the career that made him a star. His love affairs—whether with women, his country, or the American West—were best in the abstract or kept at a distance, while his hatreds were vehemently personalized. Self-absorbed and pessimistic, Hart let rancor, prejudice, and self-pity triumph over happier, more positive thinking. Far from the column of strength he impersonated on the screen, Hart could be wimpish and petty in his personal affairs. The West that he portrayed in movies was drawn from a nostalgia for his romanticized boyhood that in reality was troubled and peripatetic. Yet his early experiences in the West served as a moral and emotional anchor for the actor's retiring personality, as well as the inspiration for his unique contribution to American motion pictures. Future generations would remember William S. Hart as the silent screen's greatest exponent of the frontier West, and even professional historians acknowledge an authentic quality in his Westerns. "Hart's commitment to realism coupled with his love for the Old West aided in the development of . . . a fictional type that some consider America's unique contribution to story-telling," Richard Etulain wrote in *The Hollywood West*. Yet Hart viewed life through the eyes of an actor steeped in nineteenth-century melodrama and was steadfast in his allegiance to Victorian virtues. His "real" West on film came more from appearances and trappings than from complex characterizations or discerning social commentary. Although his career lasted little more than a decade, Hart remains the screen's first important cowboy star and a harbinger of Hollywood's Western tradition.

Filmography

Films are listed in chronological order within each year.

1914

His Hour of Manhood (two reels). New York Motion Picture Company. Director: Thomas Chatterton. Cast: William S. Hart, Clara Williams, Thomas Chatterton, Gertrude Claire.

Jim Cameron's Wife (two reels). New York Motion Picture Company. Director: Thomas Chatterton. Cast: William S. Hart, Clara Williams, Thomas Chatterton, Thelma Salter, Lewis Durham.

The Bargain (five reels). New York Motion Picture Company. Director: Reginald Barker. Cast: William S. Hart, Clara Williams, J. Barney Sherry, J. Frank Burke, James Dowling.

On the Night Stage (five reels). New York Motion Picture Company. Director: Reginald Barker. Cast: William S. Hart, Robert Edeson, Rhea Mitchell, Herschel Mayall, Gladys Brockwell, Shorty Hamilton.

The Passing of Two-Gun Hicks (two reels). New York Motion Picture Company. Director William S. Hart. Cast: William S. Hart, Leona Hutton, Arthur Maude, J. Barney Sherry, M. Willis.

In the Sage Brush Country (two reels). New York Motion Picture Company. Director: William S. Hart. Cast: William S. Hart, Rhea Mitchell, Herschel Mayall, Thomas Kurihara.

1915

The Scourge of the Desert (two reels). New York Motion Picture Company. Director: William S. Hart. Cast: William S. Hart, Rhea Mitchell, Gordon Mullen, Joseph Dowling, Dr. Beasling, Mr. Thompson, Roy Laidlaw.

Filmography

Mr. "Silent" Haskins (two reels). New York Motion Picture Company. Director: William S. Hart. Cast: William S. Hart, Rhea Mitchell, J. Barney Sherry.

The Sheriff's Streak of Yellow (two reels). New York Motion Picture Company. Director: William S. Hart. Cast: William S. Hart, Jack Nelson, Gertrude Claire, Bob Russell.

The Grudge (two reels). New York Motion Picture Company. Director: William S. Hart. Cast: William S. Hart, Charles Ray, Margaret Thompson, Thomas Kurihara, Ernest Swallow.

The Roughneck (two reels). New York Motion Picture Company. Director: William S. Hart. Cast: William S. Hart, Enid Markey, George Fisher, Howard Hickman, Roy Laidlaw.

The Taking of Luke McVane (two reels). New York Motion Picture Company. Director: William S. Hart. Cast: William S. Hart, Enid Markey, Clifford S. Smith. S. C. Smith, Ernest Swallow.

The Man from Nowhere (two reels). New York Motion Picture Company. Director: William S. Hart. Cast: William S. Hart, Margaret Thompson, J. P. Lockney, Alfred Hollingsworth.

"Bad Buck" of Santa Ynez (two reels). New York Motion Picture Company. Director: William S. Hart. Cast: William S. Hart, Fanny Midgley, Thelma Salter.

The Darkening Trail (four reels). New York Motion Picture Company. Director: William S. Hart. Cast: William S. Hart, George Fisher, Enid Markey, Louise Glaum, Nona Thomas, Milton Ross, Roy Laidlaw.

The Conversion of Frosty Blake (two reels). New York Motion Picture Company. Director: William S. Hart. Cast: William S. Hart, Louise Glaum, Charles Ray.

Tools of Providence (two reels). New York Motion Picture Company. Director: William S. Hart. Cast: William S. Hart, Rhea Mitchell, Frank Borzage, Walter Whitman.

Cash Parrish's Pal (two reels). New York Motion Picture Company. Director: William S. Hart. Cast: William S. Hart, Clara Williams, Robert Kortman, Lewis Durham.

The Ruse (two reels). New York Motion Picture Company. Director: William S. Hart. Cast: William S. Hart, Clara Williams, Jack Davidson, Fanny Midgley, Gertrude Claire, Robert Kortman.

Pinto Ben (two reels). New York Motion Picture Company. Director: William S. Hart. Cast: William S. Hart, Fritz.

Keno Bates, Liar (two reels). New York Motion Picture Company. Director: William S. Hart. Cast: William S. Hart, Herschel Mayall, Margaret Thompson, Louise Glaum, Gordon Mullen.

A Knight of the Trails (two reels). New York Motion Picture Company. Director: William S. Hart. Cast: William S. Hart, Leona Hutton, Frank Borzage.

The Disciple (five reels). Triangle Film Corporation. Director: William S. Hart. Cast: William S. Hart, Dorothy Dalton, Thelma Salter, Robert McKim, Charles K. French, Jean Hersholt.

Between Men (five reels). Triangle Film Corporation. Director: William S. Hart. Cast: William S. Hart, Enid Markey, House Peters, J. Barney Sherry, Bert Wesner, Robert McKim.

1916

Hell's Hinges (five reels). Triangle Film Corporation. Directors: William S. Hart and Charles Swickard. Cast: William S. Hart, Clara Williams, Jack Standing, Louise Glaum, Alfred Hollingsworth, Robert McKim, J. Frank Burke, Robert Kortman, John Gilbert, Jean Hersholt, Leo Willis.

The Aryan (five reels). Triangle Film Corporation. Director: William S. Hart. Cast: William S. Hart, Gertrude Claire, Charles K. French, Louise Glaum, Herschel Mayall, Ernest Swallow, Bessie Love.

The Primal Lure (five reels). Triangle Film Corporation. Director: William S. Hart. Cast: William S. Hart, Margery Wilson, Robert McKim, Jerome Storm, Joe Goodboy.

The Apostle of Vengeance (five reels). Triangle Film Corporation. Director: William S. Hart. Cast: William S. Hart, Nona Thomas, Joseph J. Dowling, Fanny Midgley, John Gilbert, Marvel Stafford.

The Captive God (five reels). Triangle Film Corporation. Director: Charles Swickard. Cast: William S. Hart, Enid Markey, Dorothy Dalton, Robert McKim, P. D. Tabler, Dorcas Matthews, Herbert Farjeon, Robert Kortman.

The Dawn Maker (five reels). Triangle Film Corporation. Director: William S. Hart. Cast: William S. Hart, Blanche White, William Desmond, J. Frank Burke, Joe Goodboy.

The Return of Draw Egan (five reels). Triangle Film Corporation. Director: William S. Hart. Cast: William S. Hart, Louise Glaum, Margery Wilson, Robert McKim, J. P. Lockney.

The Patriot (five reels). Triangle Film Corporation. Director: William S. Hart. Cast: William S. Hart, Georgie Stone, Francis Carpenter, Joe Goodboy, Roy Laidlaw, Milton Ross, P. D. Tabler, Charles K. French.

The Devil's Double (five reels). Triangle Film Corporation. Director: William S. Hart. Cast: William S. Hart, Enid Markey, Robert McKim, Thomas Kurihara.

Truthful Tulliver (five reels). Triangle Film Corporation. Director: William S. Hart. Cast: William S. Hart, Alma Rubens, Nina Byron, Norbert A. Myles, Walter Perry, Milton Ross.

1917

The Gun Fighter (five reels). Triangle Film Corporation. Director: William S. Hart. Cast: William S. Hart, Margery Wilson, Roy Laidlaw, Joseph J. Dowling, Milton Ross, George Stone, J. P. Lockney.

The Square Deal Man (five reels). Triangle Film Corporation. Director: William S. Hart. Cast: William S. Hart, Mary McIvor, Joseph J. Dowling, Mary Jane Irving, J. Frank Burke, Darrel Foss, Thomas Kurihara, Milton Ross, Charles O. Rush.

The Desert Man (five reels). Triangle Film Corporation. Director: William S. Hart. Cast: William S. Hart, Margery Wilson, Buster Irving, Henry Belmar, Milton Ross, Walter Whitman, Josephine Headley, Jack Livingston.

Wolf Lowry (five reels). Triangle Film Corporation. Director: William S. Hart. Cast: William S. Hart, Margery Wilson, Aaron Edwards, Carl Ullman.

The Cold Deck (five reels). Triangle Film Corporation. Director: William S. Hart. Cast: William S. Hart, Alma Rubens, Mildred Harris, Sylvia Breamer, Charles O. Rush, Edwin N. Wallock, Joe Knight.

The Narrow Trail (five reels). William S. Hart Productions for Paramount-Artcraft release. Director: Lambert Hillyer. Cast: William S. Hart, Sylvia Breamer, Milton Ross, Robert Kortman, Fritz.

The Silent Man (five reels). William S. Hart Productions for Paramount-Artcraft release. Director: Lambert Hillyer. Cast: William S. Hart, Vola Vale, Robert McKim, Harold Goodwin, J. P. Lockney, George P. Nichols, Gertrude Claire, Milton Ross, Dorcas Matthews.

Wolves of the Rail (five reels). William S. Hart Productions for Paramount-Artcraft release. Director: Lambert Hillyer. Cast: William S. Hart, Billy

Elmer, C. Norman Hammond, Vola Vale, Thomas Kurihara, Melbourne MacDowell, Fanny Midgley.

1918

Blue Blazes Rawden (five reels). William S. Hart Productions for Paramount-Artcraft release. Director: Lambert Hillyer. Cast: William S. Hart, Maude George, Gertrude Claire, Robert McKim, Robert Gordon, Hart Hoxie.

The Tiger Man (five reels). William S. Hart Productions for Paramount-Artcraft release. Director: Lambert Hillyer. Cast: William S. Hart, Jane Novak, Robert Lawrence, Milton Ross, Charles K. French.

Selfish Yates (five reels). William S. Hart Productions for Paramount-Artcraft release. Director: Lambert Hillyer. Cast: William S. Hart, Jane Novak, Ernest Butterworth, Bertholde Sprotte, Harry Dunkinson, Thelma Salter.

Shark Monroe (five reels). William S. Hart Productions for Paramount-Artcraft release. Director: Lambert Hillyer. Cast: William S. Hart, Katherine MacDonald, Joe Singleton, George McDaniel, Bertholde Sprotte.

Riddle Gawne (five reels). William S. Hart Productions for Paramount-Artcraft release. Director: Lambert Hillyer. Cast: William S. Hart, Katherine MacDonald, Lon Chaney, Gretchen Lederer, Gertrude Short, E. B. Tilton, Milton Ross, George Field, Leon Kent.

The Border Wireless (five reels). William S. Hart Productions for Paramount-Artcraft release. Director: Lambert Hillyer. Cast: William S. Hart, Wanda Hawley, Charles Arling, James Mason, E. von Ritzen, Bertholde Sprotte, Marcia Manon.

Branding Broadway (five reels). William S. Hart Productions for Paramount-Artcraft release. Director: Lambert Hillyer. Cast: William S. Hart, Seena Owen, Arthur Shirley, Andrew Robson, Lewis W. Short.

1919

Breed of Men (five reels). William S. Hart Productions for Paramount-Artcraft release. Director: Lambert Hillyer. Cast: William S. Hart, Seena Owen, Bertholde Sprotte, Buster Irving.

The Poppy Girl's Husband (five feels). William S. Hart Productions for Paramount-Artcraft release. Director: Lambert Hillyer. Cast: William S. Hart, Juanita Hansen, Walter Long, Fred Starr, David Kirby, Georgie Stone.

Filmography

The Money Corral (five reels). William S. Hart Productions for Paramount-Artcraft release. Director: Lambert Hillyer. Cast: William S. Hart, Jane Novak, Herschel Mayall, Winter Hall, Rhea Mitchell, Patricia Palmer.

Square Deal Sanderson (five reels). William S. Hart Productions for Paramount-Artcraft release. Director: Lambert Hillyer. Cast: William S. Hart, Ann Little, Lloyd Bacon, Frank Whitson, Andrew Robson, Edwin Wallach.

Wagon Tracks (five reels). William S. Hart Productions for Paramount-Artcraft release. Director: Lambert Hillyer. Cast: William S. Hart, Jane Novak, Robert McKim, Lloyd Bacon, Leo Pierson, Bertholde Sprotte, Charles Arling.

John Petticoats (five reels). William S. Hart Productions for Paramount-Artcraft release. Director: Lambert Hillyer. Cast: William S. Hart, Walter Whitman, Winifred Westover, George Webb, Ethel Shannon, Andrew Arbuckle.

1920

Sand (five reels). William S. Hart Productions for Paramount-Artcraft release. Director: Lambert Hillyer. Cast: William S. Hart, Mary Thurman, G. Raymond Nye, Patricia Palmer, William Patton, Lon Poff, Hugh Jackson, Fritz.

The Toll Gate (six reels). William S. Hart Productions for Paramount-Artcraft release. Director: Lambert Hillyer. Cast: William S. Hart, Anna Q. Nilsson, Jack Richardson, Joseph Singleton, Richard Headrick, Fritz.

The Cradle of Courage (five reels). William S. Hart Productions for Paramount-Artcraft release. Director: Lambert Hillyer. Cast: William S. Hart, Ann Little, Thomas Santschi, Gertrude Claire, Francis Thorwald, George Williams.

The Testing Block (six reels). William S. Hart Productions for Paramount-Artcraft release. Director: Lambert Hillyer. Cast: William S. Hart, Eva Novak, Gordon Russell, Florence Carpenter, Richard Headrick, Ira McFadden.

O'Malley of the Mounted (six reels). William S. Hart Productions for Paramount-Artcraft release. Director: Lambert Hillyer. Cast: William S. Hart, Eva Novak, Antrim Short, Leo Willis, Bertholde Sprotte, Alfred Allen.

1921

The Whistle (six reels). William S. Hart Productions for Paramount-Artcraft release. Director: Lambert Hillyer. Cast: William S. Hart, Myrtle Stedman, Frank Brownlee, Georgie Stone, Will Jim Hatton, Richard Headrick, Robert Kortman.

University in Dallas; tapes of the remaining interviews are in the author's possession.

Douglas Bell's extensive oral history with Eugene Zukor (May 7, 1992–December 30, 1993) for the Herrick Library was helpful in understanding Hart's position at Artcraft. Other data came from interviews with Gilbert M. (Broncho Billy) Anderson (1958), Johnny Mack Brown (1971), Jean Dalrymple (1979), and Louella Parsons (1959), housed in the Columbia University Oral History Collection; and sessions with Ted French (1971 and 1972), Ann Little (1971), Mr. and Mrs. Jim Rush (1972), and Irvin Willat (1971), transcribed and deposited in the Mayer Library at the American Film Institute in Los Angeles, give insights into the making of Hart's films. A conversation about Hart with Jane Novak and Joe McNinch (March 3, 1989) was taped, transcribed, and edited by Carol Sandmeier and loaned to me by Mickey Seltzer.

The actor's perceptions on his craft and descriptions of his love for the West are revealed in the prefaces to his books, particularly *Pinto Ben and Other Stories* (New York: Britton, 1919) and *Hoofbeats* (New York: Dial, 1933), and in magazine articles published under his byline, notably "Living Your Character," *Motion Picture Magazine* 13 (May 1917): 71–72; "And They Are All Beautiful!" (about his leading ladies), *Motion Picture Magazine* 18 (August 1919): 38–39; and "The Compleat Cowboy," *The Picturegoer* 2 (September 1921): 12–13.

Contemporaries' written memories of Hart are offered by Karl Brown, *Adventures with D. W. Griffith* (New York: Farrar, Straus and Giroux, 1973); Harry Carey, Jr., *Company of Heroes* (Metuchen, N.J.: Scarecrow, 1994); Charles Chaplin, *My Autobiography* (New York: Simon and Schuster, 1964); Jesse L. Lasky with Don Weldon, *I Blow My Own Horn* (Garden City, N.Y.: Doubleday, 1957); Jesse L. Lasky, Jr., *Whatever Happened to Hollywood?* (New York: Funk and Wagnalls, 1975); Francis Marion, *Off with Their Heads!* (New York: Macmillan, 1972); Pola Negri, *Memoirs of a Star* (Garden City, N.Y.: Doubleday, 1970); Adela Rogers St. Johns, *Love, Laughter and Tears* (Garden City, N.Y.: Doubleday, 1978); and Adolph Zukor with Dale Kramer, *The Public Is Never Wrong* (New York: Putnam's, 1953). Also worth noting are Hedda Hopper with James Brough, *The Whole Truth and Nothing But* (Garden City, N.Y.: Doubleday, 1963); Lee Shippey, *Personal Glimpses of Famous Folks* (Sierra Madre, Calif.: Sierra Madre Press, 1929); and "William S. Hart, as He Is to Those Who Know Him," in *The Little Movie Mirror Books* (New York: Ross Publishing Company, 1920).

White Oak (seven reels). William S. Hart Productions for Paramount-Artcraft release. Director: Lambert Hillyer. Cast: William S. Hart, Vola Vale, Alexander Gaden, Robert Walker, Bertholde Sprotte, Helen Holly, Standing Bear.

Travelin' On (seven reels). William S. Hart Productions for Paramount-Artcraft release. Director: Lambert Hillyer. Cast: William S. Hart, James Farley, Ethel Grey Terry, Brinsley Shaw, Mary Jane Irving, Robert Kortman, Willis Marks, Fritz.

Three Word Brand (seven reels). William S. Hart Productions for Paramount-Artcraft release. Director: Lambert Hillyer. Cast: William S. Hart, S. J. Bingham, Jane Novak, Gordon Russell, George C. Pearce, Colette Forbes, Ivor McFadden, Herschel Mayall, Leo Willis.

1923

Wild Bill Hickok (seven reels). Famous Players–Lasky for Paramount-Artcraft release. Director: Clifford S. Smith. Cast: William S. Hart, Ethel Grey Terry, Kathleen O'Connor, James Farley, Jack Gardner, Carl Gerard, William Dyer, Bertholde Sprotte, Leo Willis, Naida Carle, Herschel Mayall, Fritz.

1924

Singer Jim McKee (seven reels). Famous Players–Lasky for Paramount-Artcraft release. Director: Clifford S. Smith. Cast: William S. Hart, Phyllis Haver, Gordon Russell, Edward Coxen, William Dyer, Bertholde Sprotte, Patsy Ruth Miller, George Siegmann, Baby Turner.

1925

Tumbleweeds (seven reels). William S. Hart Company for United Artists release. Director: King Baggott. Cast: William S. Hart, Barbara Bedford, Lucien Littlefield, Gordon Russell, Richard R. Neill, Jack Murphy, Lillian Leighton, Gertrude Claire, George Marion, Captain T. E. Duncan, James Gordon, Fred Gamble, Turner Savage, Monte Collins.

Notes on Sources

For the early years of William S. Hart's life, the primary source remains his autobiography, *My Life East and West* (Boston: Houghton Mifflin, 1929), although his memories are highly romanticized. The actor's later life and career are solidly documented in the William S. Hart papers at the Seaver Center for Western History Research in the Natural History Museum of Los Angeles County. Most of the Hart material in the Seaver Center consists of correspondence, business records, publicity releases, newspaper and magazine clippings, and canceled checks, but the collection also includes such miscellaneous items as Mary Ellen Hart's scant diary.

More Hart letters exist in the Gatewood W. Dunston Collection at the Library of Congress and the Martha Groves McKelvie Collection at the Nebraska Historical Society. The Dunston Collection also includes production material on the actor's films and newspaper clippings. Further insight into the cowboy star's movie career may be found in the Jimmy Starr Collection in Haden Library at Arizona State University and in the Gladys Hall, Hedda Hopper, and Adolph Zukor Collections in the Margaret Herrick Library of the Academy of Motion Picture Arts and Sciences in Beverly Hills. Hart's exchange of letters with Stuart N. Lake, concerning the latter's biography of Wyatt Earp, is preserved in the Lake Collection at the Huntington Library in San Marino, California. Copies of the actor's love letters to Jane Novak, written during April and May 1921, are in the possession of Novak's daughter, Mickey Seltzer, who lives in Sherman Oaks, California. Hart's friend, Joe McNinch, now deceased, shared with me letters he received from the silent picture star, as well as related memorabilia McNinch had in his home.

Personal recollections of Hart were given in interviews taped by author with Gene Autry (July 24, 1984, in Los Angeles), Harry Carey (December 28, 1998, in Durango, Colorado), Diana Serra Cary (August 1997, in Glendale, California), Joe McNinch and Mickey Seltzer (both 28, 1997, in Sherman Oaks, California), King Vidor (August 4, 1975, erly Hills), and Eugene Zukor (July 31, 1975, in Los Angeles). Transcripts most of these sessions are in the DeGolyer Library at Southern Methodist

The best fan magazine articles on Hart include Henry Carr, "Bill Hart Comes Back," *Motion Picture Magazine* 24 (September 1922): 25, 94–96; Maude Cheatham, "And They Live Happily," *Motion Picture Magazine* 23 (June 1922): 36–37, 88–89; Maude Cheatham, "Desert Heart," *Motion Picture Magazine* 21 (April 1921): 58, 90–91; Elsie Codd, "Good Man–Bad Man," *The Picturegoer* 3 (February 1922): 16, 59; Elsie Codd, "The Retirement of Bill Hart," *The Picturegoer* 1 (April 1921): 12–13; Frank Daugherty, "Ol' Bill Hart Is Coming Back!" *Photoplay* 39 (December 1930): 50–51, 132; Adele Whitely Fletcher, "Out from the West," *Motion Picture Magazine* 23 (February 1922): 22–23, 84; Gertrude Gordon, "William S. Hart, the Man of the West," *Motion Picture Magazine* 12 (November 1916): 117–123; Helen Ogden, "Concerning Bill–and Jane," *Picture Play* (August 1921): 44–45; Adela Rogers St. Johns, "Bill Hart's Bride Has Him Thrown, Tied, Branded, and Feeds His Bulldog Caramels," *Photoplay* 21 (April 1922): 46–47, 106; and "William S. Hart Speaks the Sioux Language," *Motion Picture Magazine* 16 (September 1918): 44.

Later articles related to Hart and his career include James Card, "The Films of William S. Hart," *Image* 5 (March 1956): 60–63; Katherine H. Child, "Two-Gun Bill: The Story of William S. Hart," *Terra* 26 (November–December 1987): 20–25; Bruce Firestone, "A Man Named Sioux: Nostalgia and the Career of William S. Hart," *Film and History* 7 (December 1977): 85–89; Tom and Jim Goldrup, "Filmed in These Here Hills," *Western Clippings*, no. 23 (May–June 1998): 24; George Mitchell, "Thomas H. Ince," *Films in Review* 11 (October 1960): 464–84; George Mitchell, "William S. Hart," *Films in Review* 6 (April 1955): 145–54; George J. Mitchell, "The William S. Hart Museum," *Films in Review* 13 (August–September 1962): 401–6; George Pratt, "The Posse Is Still Ridin' Like Mad," *Image* 7 (September 1958): 152–61; Julio J. Pro, "The Legacy of a Friendship," *Southwest Art* 16 (August 1986): 22–23; and "The Stage Career of William S. Hart, 1898 to 1912," *Silent Picture*, no. 16 (Autumn 1972): 17–20.

Newspaper clippings on Hart exist in the Seaver Center at the Natural History Museum of Los Angeles County, the Herrick Library of the Academy of Motion Picture Arts and Sciences, in the theater section of the New York Public Library, and in the film and television archives of the Doheny Library at the University of Southern California.

For a sketch of Hart's life and analysis of each of his movies, see Diane Kaiser Koszarski, *The Complete Films of William S. Hart* (New York: Dover, 1980).

Notes on Sources

Among the better books dealing with motion pictures during the time Hart was active in Hollywood are Kevin Brownlow, *The Parade's Gone By* (New York: Knopf, 1969); Kevin Brownlow, *The War, the West, and the Wilderness* (New York: Knopf, 1979); James Card, *Seductive Cinema: The Art of Silent Film* (New York: Knopf, 1994); William K. Everson, *A Pictorial History of the Western Film* (New York: Citadel, 1969); George N. Fenin and William K. Everson, *The Western* (New York: Bonanza, 1962); Leatrice Gilbert Fountain with John R. Maxim, *Dark Star* (New York: St. Martin's, 1985); Nils Thor Granlund with Sid Feder and Ralph Hancock, *Blondes, Brunettes, and Bullets* (New York: David McKay, 1957); Arthur Knight, *The Hollywood Style* (London: Macmillan, 1969); Frank Manchel, *Cameras West* (Englewood Cliffs, N.J.: Prentice-Hall, 1971); George C. Pratt, *Spellbound in Darkness* (Greenwich, Conn.: New York Graphic Society, 1973); Terry Ramsaye, *A Million and One Nights* (New York: Simon and Schuster, 1926); and Jon Tuska, *The Filming of the West* (Garden City, N.Y.: Doubleday, 1976). Also worth consulting are Michael K. Schoenecke, "William S. Hart: Authenticity and the West," in Archie P. McDonald, ed., *Shooting Stars: Heroes and Heroines of Western Film* (Bloomingon: Indiana University Press, 1987), 1–19, and Richard W. Etulain, "Broncho Billy, William S. Hart, and Tom Mix: The Rise of the Hollywood Western," in Richard W. Etulain and Glenda Riley, eds., *The Hollywood West* (Golden, Colo.: Fulcrum, 2001): 7–13.

Reviews of Hart's plays and movies abound in the clippings in the Seaver Center and the Hart files in the theater section of the New York Public Library. More readily available are those in the *New York Times* and *Moving Picture World*.

Chapter 1

The chronology of this chapter and the bulk of the narrative were shaped by the first 102 pages of Hart's autobiography, *My Life East and West* (reissued in 1968 by Benjamin Blom). Those pages comprise 29 percent of the actor's memoirs, which indicates the importance Hart placed on his boyhood in formulating his views and exposing him to America's last frontier. I have tried to cut through the cowboy star's mawkish narrative and synthesize what his actual experiences in the West were.

Information about Hart's boyhood in the Fox River Valley of Illinois was supplemented from newspaper articles in the *Aurora Beacon News* dated June 30, 1929, August 4, 1929, August 11, 1929, August 25, 1929, September 1, 1929, May 20, 1945, December 30, 1945, January 13, 1946, January 20, 1946, and July 31, 1971, sent to me by the Aurora Public Library. These items include letters from Hart commenting on his boyhood, as well as correspondence from people who knew him as a boy in the Fox River area, namely John Parker and John Scheets, both of whom extend Hart's recollections of that period and give a clearer picture of Nicholas Hart's work as a miller. A letter from Nellie W. Herren of Oswego, published in the *Aurora Beacon News*, May 20, 1945, provides a description of the Parker Mill, which stood on her land. Mary Ann Pirone of the Genealogical Reference Service of the Aurora Library provided me with data from the 1870 Illinois Federal Census and the Edwards Aurora Census Report of 1872.

The Hart papers in the Seaver Center at the Natural History Museum of Los Angeles County do not hold much on the actor's childhood, although letters from Hart dated July 20, 1920, September 7, 1926, and May 25, 1927, add glimpses into his boyhood years. An article in the *New York Evening Herald*, October 1919, offers quotes from the cowboy star about his grandfather's legal career in England and his father's oratorical ability.

Clipping files in the local history department of the public library in Newburgh, New York, contain data on Hart's birth and youth there. Background data on Newburgh during the time Hart and his family lived there was provided by Patricia A. Favata, *Newburgh: Her Institutions, Industries and Leading Citizens* (Newburgh, N.Y.: Pat's Paper Potpourri, 1992): a reprint of a volume compiled by John J. Nutt in 1891.

Chapter 2

The major source for Hart's early years on the stage remains chapters 8 through 11 of *My Life East and West*, although there are abundant reviews of the actor's plays in the Hart collection at the Seaver Center and in the theater files of the New York Public Library, many of which are duplicates. The cowboy star subscribed to a clipping service, so his press coverage is well represented in his personal papers.

Hart's respect for Charles M. Russell is revealed in a letter the retired actor wrote Nancy Russell on January 22, 1929, and the artist's response to Hart, dated June 29, 1902, confirms Russell's favorable impression of Hart after their introductory meeting in Montana. Both letters are preserved in the Seaver Center. Secondary sources on Hart's relationship with Russell include Brian W. Dippie, *Charles M. Russell, Word Painter, Letters 1887–1926* (Fort Worth, Tex.: Amon Carter Museum, 1993), and John Taliaferro, *Charles*

Notes on Sources

M. Russell: The Life and Legend of America's Cowboy Artist (Boston: Little, Brown, 1996).

Hart told of his meeting with Al Jennings in Elsie Codd's "Good Man— Bad Man," published in *The Picturegoer,* February 1922, p. 59; and Jennings's career as an outlaw is discussed in Richard Patterson, *Train Robbery* (Boulder, Colo.: Johnson Books, 1981).

The actor's engagement to play opposite Helena Modjeska is fleetingly treated in Marion Moore Coleman's *Fair Rosalind: The American Career of Helena Modjeska* (Cheshire, Conn.: Cherry Hill, 1969).

Chapter 3

Hart's Western roles on the stage are discussed in chapter 12 of his autobiography, although he also reflects on them in his book *Pinto Ben and Other Stories*. Reviews of the shows are abundant in the Hart papers and the files at the New York Public Library. Of special interest might be those that appeared in *The Stage* on November 4, 1905, which comments on Hart's rendition of Cash Hawkins in *The Squaw Man*, and the September 10, 1912, issue of *Variety*, which voices disappointment over the performer's vaudeville act "Moonshine." The actor's reservations about the character of the Virginian and Owen Wister's limitations as a western writer are discussed in Bruce Firestone's article "A Man Named Sioux," published in the December 1977 issue of *Film and History*.

Information on the 101 Ranch Show is supplemented by Ellsworth Collings and Alma Miller England, *The 101 Ranch* (Norman: University of Oklahoma Press, 1937), and Hart's relationship with Bat Masterson is discussed in Robert K. DeArment's *Bat Masterson: The Man and the Legend* (Norman: University of Oklahoma Press, 1979), 393–96. Hart's remark to Louella Parsons about Masterson appeared in the *New York Morning Telegraph* on October 30, 1921, and his regard for the former frontier gunman is revealed in a column in that newspaper on October 9, 1921.

The future cowboy star's return to Aurora, Illinois, during his tour with *The Virginian* is described in an article by Lutz White, "'Two Gun' Bill Hart Product of This City," in the *Aurora Beacon News*, June 30, 1929, which includes quotations from an interview with John Scheets soon after the publication of the star's autobiography.

Hart's reaction to seeing his first Western movie and his introduction to Inceville are remembered on pages 198–202 of *My Life East and West*.

Chapter 4

Most of the information on Inceville came from Kevin Brownlow's *The War, the West, and the Wilderness* and George C. Pratt's *Spellbound in Darkness*, although Ann Little's and Irvin Willat's oral histories in the American Film Institute offer firsthand accounts. My interview with Diana Serra Cary provided insights into the Hollywood cowboys' attitude toward Hart, and Cary's *The Hollywood Posse* (Boston: Houghton Mifflin, 1975) discusses that group's views and subculture at length.

Hart's recollections of his early film work are recorded best on pages 202-15 of *My Life East and West*, but the actor also commented on his first year at Inceville in *Pinto Ben and Other Stories*, letters to Gatewood W. Dunston on January 8 and August 30, 1938, the December 5, 1914, issue of the *Moving Picture World*, and in Maude Cheatham's article "Desert Heart" in *Motion Picture Magazine* of April 1921. Data on Fritz appeared in the *Saugus Enterprise* on February 10, 1938.

Diane Kaiser Koszarski discusses each of the cowboy star's movies, including a plot summary and production details, in *The Complete Films of William S. Hart*. The Dunston Collection in the Library of Congress also contains a wealth of production data, and the *New York Dramatic Mirror* of November 18, 1914, offers a cogent evaluation of *The Bargain*.

Chapter 5

Hart's work for Triangle, his troubles with Thomas Ince, and his bond tour during World War I are discussed in chapters 13, 14, and 15 of *My Life East and West*, although a great deal of press coverage of his bond tour in May and June 1917 exists in the Hart papers and in the clipping files at the New York Public Library.

A Triangle house paper, dated March 25, 1916, gives insights into the studio's atmosphere during Hart's time there, and George Fenin and William Everson's *The Western* and Frank Manchel's *Cameras West* proved particularly helpful in understanding this period. An English journalist's observations about life in Hart's production company while on location are reprinted in Kevin Brownlow's *The War, the West, and the Wilderness*.

Gertrude Gordon's assessment of the actor's stature as a Western star appeared in "William S. Hart, the Man of the West," published in *Motion Picture Magazine*, November 1916, pages 117-23.

Production data from Hart's Triangle films are chronicled in Diane Kaiser Koszarski, *The Complete Films of William S. Hart*, and confirmed by material in the Dunston Collection at the Library of Congress. The actor's penchant for melodrama and religious symbolism is revealed in the *New York Times* review of *The Disciple* on October 18, 1915, and his growth as a delineator of Bret Harte–like characters is extolled in the *Times* review of *The Return of Draw Egan* on October 2, 1916.

Hart's dissatisfaction with Triangle is referred to in a telegram dated September 30, 1916, and his continuing disgust with the exhibition of his Triangle pictures under different names is clear from his letter to Gatewood Dunston of June 13, 1931.

Jean Dalrymple's childhood admiration for Hart and her attempt at a scenario for the cowboy star are remembered in Dalrymple's oral history for Columbia University. The same collection contains Louella Parsons's recollections of her meeting with the actor in Chicago.

Adolph Zukor recalls his association with Hart and the actor's awkward appearance astride Fritz in *The Public Is Never Wrong*. Famous Players' negotiations with Hart are revealed in an exchange of letters between Zukor and Cecil B. DeMille on March 22 and March 23, 1917, both in the Zukor papers at the Herrick Library.

Chapter 6

The cowboy actor's work under his early Artcraft arrangement is remembered in chapter 16 of *My Life East and West*, although the Hart papers in the Seaver Center are extensive for the period after November 1918, when the star's studio underwent reconstruction. Production material from 1919 on is far more plentiful than earlier, with frequent memos and press releases issued by Hart's director of publicity, Paul Conlon, preserved in the Seaver Center.

Numerous pieces of Hart correspondence throughout the first six months of 1919 detail his work on *The Poppy Girl's Husband* and *The Money Corral*, his location experiences in the Mojave Desert during the filming of *Square Deal Sanderson* and *Wagon Tracks*, and his trip to New Orleans for work on *John Petticoats*. Mrs. Jim Rush discusses her experiences on the Western star's pictures in her oral history for the American Film Institute, and Hollywood cowboys' speculation that Hart ate alum to make his lips tight before close-ups was recalled in a telephone conversation with Diana Serra Cary, daughter of one of the wranglers who knew the cowboy star.

Hart states that actors said lines during the making of his pictures but that music was seldom played on his sets in a letter to Gatewood Dunston on December 5, 1938. He tells of his quarrel with Ince over Fritz in his autobiography and in a letter to Dunston of February 14, 1942.

A newspaper item, dated April 8, 1919, describes Hart's serving as referee for a boxing match between a fighter and a kangaroo.

The actor's role in the formation of United Artists is told in his memoirs and supported by Charles Chaplin's *My Autobiography* and Adolph Zukor's *The Public Is Never Wrong*.

Hart discusses his leading ladies in "And They Are All Beautiful!" and extols the virtues of Jane Novak in a letter to Martha McKelvie dated May 5, 1919. Louella Parsons speaks of the actor's appeal to women in her oral history for Columbia University.

The actor's travels in conjunction with the Third and Fourth Liberty Loan Drives are covered city by city in clippings on file in the Seaver Center, and Hart's encounter with a Sioux Indian at city hall in New York is recorded in Harry Carr's "Bill Hart Comes Back." The star's mock holdup of a train to publicize the Victory Loan Drive was reported by the Associated Press on April 17, 1919.

Hart's relationship with Bat Masterson is recounted in DeArment's *Bat Masterson: The Man and the Legend,* and his admiration for Theodore Roosevelt is stated in a letter to Charles W. Barrell on January 2, 1918. Hart discusses his views on George Armstrong Custer in Gertrude Gordon, "William S. Hart, the Man of the West," and in several letters from November 1916.

The actor's concern over his nation's current domestic troubles fills a letter written on August 22, 1919, and his patriotism and suspicion of aliens is revealed in correspondence dated December 22, 1919.

Woodrow Wilson's fondness for Hart's films is described in a press item from July 18, 1920, and an article in the *Los Angeles Evening Herald,* July 2, 1918, proclaims the actor a "true man of the plains."

Chapter 7

Hart discussed the films he made under his second Artcraft contract in chapters 16 and 17 of his autobiography, and memos issued by the actor's publicist, located in the Seaver Center, cover that work in detail. The star's correspondence from this period is also extensive. He wrote of his attitude toward Mexicans (August 5, 1919), his unmarried status and rented apartment (November 26, 1919), the amount of fan mail he received and the length and popularity of his movies (January 7, 1920), his longing to retire

(March 21, 1920), that Charlie Russell had not changed (April 28, 1920), his court battles (July 28 and September 4, 1920), his progress in writing short stories and his vague political views (August 26, 1920), his objection to his pictures being shown under different titles (October 30, 1920), and the $87,779 he received from Thomas Ince (December 1, 1920).

In letters to Adolph Zukor, Hart warned about Ince's scheming (January 3, 1920), wrote of the overhead at his studio and the consistent quality of his pictures (January 7, 1920), and complained about the release of his films during the summer months (January 19, 1921).

The actor's letters to Gatewood Dunston mention his use of a Colt 36 in pictures set before 1865 (April 11, 1931), the release of *White Oak* under different names (June 23, 1933), that the star was not hurt in the jump off a cliff in *Toll Gate*, that he did not use the Running W in his pictures, and Fritz's skill in doing stunts (May 1, 1939).

Hart outlined his goals in writing stories for boys in a letter, dated October 30, 1919, to the Britton Publishing Company. More thoughts on his writing appeared in the *Oakland Tribune* of March 12, 1920.

The statement that no horse was too wild for Bill to ride accompanied a photograph of the star on the cover of *Boy's Cinema*, December 13, 1919, and Hart is referred to as a man who represents humanity in the *Picture Show*, March 13, 1920. The *Newsboy's World* of September 15, 1920, hails the actor as a man who knows the West and could be elected sheriff should he care to run for that office. Hart's nomination for sheriff on the Democratic ticket in Hood River country, Oregon, is referred to in a press release dated May 30, 1920. All of these items are in the Seaver Center.

The star's comment that he would rather buck a bronco than try to talk about women is quoted in "And They Are All Beautiful!" Maude Cheatham related her observations of the location work on *White Oak* in "Desert Heart."

The neighborhood around Hart's house on DeLongpre Street in Los Angeles was described in my interview with the star's longtime friend Joe McNinch. Harry Carey, Jr., gave me his recollections of Hart and the cowboy actor's visits to the Carey ranch during our visit in 1998. Eugene Zukor discussed Hart in his oral histories for both Southern Methodist University and the Academy of Motion Picture Arts and Sciences.

Adolph Zukor recalls in his autobiography Hart's mock train holdup, the star's gift of a silver-mounted bridle to the mogul's daughter, his western affectations, and his amusement at being assigned the "bridle" suite in the

Ritz Hotel. Pola Negri remembered her Sunday visits to the Hart ranch in *Memoirs of a Star*.

The cowboy star's relationship with Wyatt Earp is documented at length in the correspondence between the two men in the Seaver Center.

Hart is compared with Buffalo Bill as a symbol of the frontier West in the *Portland Oregonian* on March 21, 1920, and his ability to show the struggle between good and evil in his movies is extolled in a letter, dated March 8, 1920, that he received from a New York fan.

Chapter 8

Hart does not mention his romance with Jane Novak in *My Life East and West*, and his marriage to Winifred Westover, the birth of his son, and his divorce are covered in just five lines.

The most intimate data on the actor's courtship of Novak came from letters that Hart wrote the actress during April and May 1921, loaned to me by Mickey Seltzer, Novak's daughter. Novak discussed her life and relationship with the cowboy star and his sister Mary Ellen in a taped interview with Joe McNinch in March 1989, and Mickey Seltzer shared her memories with me on repeated occasions, as did McNinch and Harry Carey, Jr. Hart praised Jane to Adolph Zukor in a letter dated January 19, 1921, and discussed the ardor of his romance with Jane in correspondence with Martha McKelvie. Bill's teasing of Jane and the actress's observation that the star had grease spots on his vest and tie were remembered in Zukor's autobiography. Helen Ogden's "Concerning Bill—and Jane" gives insights into how the liaison was reported to fans.

Hart's marriage, separation, and divorce were detailed in contemporary Associated Press items, and the actor mentioned his marital troubles in letters dated September 16, 17, and 24, 1922, located among his personal papers. Maude Cheatham's "And They Live Happily" and Adela Rogers St. Johns's "Bill Hart's Bride Has Him Thrown, Tied, Branded, and Feeds His Bulldog Caramels" described the couple's brief marital bliss for fans. Hart wrote the elder Zukor that he and his wife had taken separate residences on June 14, 1922, and he voiced distress over his marriage in letters to Martha McKelvie. Adela Rogers St. Johns, who was close to Winifred Westover, refers to "the brutal way Bill Hart let his sister drive [Westover] out of the house" in *Love, Laughter and Tears*.

Hart's reference to Will Rogers as the greatest humorist since Mark Twain appears on page 309 of his autobiography, and the actor's visits with

Rogers, Bat Masterson, and Jack Dempsey are recalled on adjacent pages. The actor's belief that Masterson and Wyatt Earp were "the last of the greatest band of gunfighters" was quoted in the *New York Morning Telegraph* on October 9, 1921. More information on his friendship with Will Rogers may be found in Richard M. Ketchum, *Will Rogers: His Life and Times* (New York: American Heritage, 1973), and Betty Rogers, *Will Rogers, His Wife's Story* (Indianapolis: Bobbs-Merrill, 1941).

Andy Adams wrote the cowboy actor on June 27, 1921, about their similar views on the frontier West, and J. C. Miller approached Hart about coming to the 101 Ranch in a letter dated July 14, 1921.

Paramount's concerns over the star's continuing box office appeal is documented in letters from Jesse Lasky in the Zukor papers and in Lasky's autobiography, *I Blow My Own Horn*. Hart wrote Zukor on January 19, 1921, that he intended to take a long rest after completing his next picture. Elsie Codd discusses the qualities the actor's successor in Western movies will need in "The Retirement of Bill Hart."

Chapter 9

The cowboy star recalled making his last films, the split with Famous Players, and various writing projects in chapters 18 and 19 of his autobiography.

Hart and Jesse Lasky exchanged telegrams and letters in late November and early December 1923 regarding controls the actor would have to accept if he continued working under the Paramount banner. Lasky wrote Hart on December 15, 1923, that *Singer Jim McKee* would be the star's last picture for the company, and Hart notified Lasky on December 28 that he would move out of the studio as quickly as possible. On that same date, Hart wired his lawyer that it looked to him as though Lasky and Zukor were "determined not to do business with anyone they can't control."

A great deal of production material on the filming of *Tumbleweeds* exists in the Seaver Center, and letters in the Hart papers dated August 1, 1925 (regarding the start of the picture), October 15, 1925 (stating the movie's size and high cost), and October 22, 1925 (confirming that postproduction work was about to begin), are particularly revealing. Hart stated in a letter on October 27, 1925, that he did not intend to make many more films. On March 9, 1926, he recounted having seen *Tumbleweeds* for the first time with an audience, and on June 9, 1926, he wrote about his disappointment that the movie had been transferred to a lesser theater in Washington, D.C. On November 15, 1926, he wrote that he expected to lose $75,000 on the

picture, and on March 26, 1927, he complained about the film's poor distribution. Correspondence to Hart from the New York office of United Artists,
dated August 19 and September 16, 1925, assured the actor that massive
exploitation of the picture had been planned.

Sid Grauman wrote on November 20, 1923, that *Wild Bill Hickok* had
played to capacity audiences at his Metropolitan Theater, and Courtland
Manning wrote Hart on February 4, 1924, his recollections of seeing Hickok
with Buffalo Bill and Texas Jack in *The Scouts of the Prairie* in Buffalo, New
York, during the 1870s. On March 5, 1926, Monte Blue wrote Hart from
Warner Bros., begging the star not to retreat into his shell and offering assurance that the public still loved the old actor.

A letter from Colt's Fire Arms Company on February 20, 1922, asked
Hart's permission to use his image on advertising posters, and the actor
wrote his acceptance on March 1. The agreement between Hart and the
Kingfisher Company to use his name on boys' clothing was signed on
October 20, 1922. Grosset and Dunlap sent regrets on February 5, 1926, that
A Lighter of Flames, which the company had published, was not going to be
made into a motion picture.

Hart wrote that he had broken his foot and that Mary Ellen was ill on
October 2, 1924, that he owned forty or more buffalo coats and robes on
May 26, 1925, that Mary Ellen was then in her ninth month in bed on June
16, 1925, about the hard knocks life had dealt him on October 19, 1925, and
about the impossibility of dealing with the consolidated movie industry on
October 27, 1925. To Gatewood Dunston, the actor wrote that his father
had spoken of Wild Bill Hickok (June 24, 1932) and of the "tragedy" of
Tumbleweeds (January 7, 1942). To Thomas Ince, he wrote of the "wonderful sensation" of being a dad (October 2, 1924).

Wyatt Earp wrote Hart on July 7, 1923, regarding his desire to correct
wrong impressions about his life as a western peace officer. Mrs. Earp wrote
the actor on December 18, 1923, saying how much she had enjoyed *Wild
Bill Hickok*. The retired frontier sheriff also wrote Hart on November 18,
1924, April 11 and 16, June 6, and July 3, 1925, and the actor sent replies on
July 7 and October 21, 1925. Background material on Earp may be found in
Stuart N. Lake, *Wyatt Earp, Frontier Marshal* (Boston: Houghton Mifflin,
1931) and Casey Tefertiller, *Wyatt Earp: The Life Behind the Legend* (New
York: John Wiley, 1997).

The Starr Collection at Arizona State University includes press releases from
Adam Hull Shirk, one of Hart's publicists, covering the actor's appearance at

the Lambs Club, George Bernard Shaw's comment that Hart had "done everything that can be done in dramatic dumb show," the Western star's advice to boys to "work hard and play hard," and his contention that historians have missed much that was characteristic of the West. All of these items are dated 1925 and are located in Haden Library's Special Collections.

Susan E. Meyer's *James Montgomery Flagg* (New York: Watson-Guptill, 1974) discusses the circumstances surrounding the portrait that Flagg painted of Hart on Fritz.

Buster Keaton's parody of Hart in the movie *The Frozen North* (1922) is described by Rudi Blesh in *Keaton* (New York: Macmillan, 1966) and by Marion Meade in *Buster Keaton: Cut to the Chase* (New York: HarperCollins, 1995).

George Mitchell provides background on Hart's ranch and examines the contents of the actor's home there in "The William S. Hart Museum," although most of my information came from an after-hours tour of the property in 1999 conducted by Zandra Stanley, then director of the Hart Museum.

Chapter 10

Hart sketches his life during the late 1920s in the final chapter of his autobiography, and newspaper items and letters covering his retirement years are abundant in his papers. Rumors of his return to the screen, his infrequent public appearances, his court battle with United Artists, and his travels and illnesses were all reported in the press and sent to Hart by a clipping service. Frank Daugherty recounted a visit he made to Horseshoe Ranch in 1930 in "Ol' Bill Hart Is Coming Back!" and Lee Shippey referred to the actor as "the noblest cowboy of them all" in *Personal Glimpses of Famous Folks*.

Among the Hart correspondence are letters in which the cowboy star wrote about the current plight of Native Americans and the statue Cristadoro had made of him (October 22, 1925), that when "a man crosses the Missouri, the West gets into his blood" (November 4, 1925), that Wyatt Earp was "the last of the great Gun Men Peace Officers of the American Frontier" (February 22, 1926), that he was doing his best "to represent that West I feel the deepest gratitude" (June 18, 1926), that he had attended the fiftieth anniversary of the Custer defeat and his dismay that police horses in Los Angeles were to be sold (July 1, 1926), his idea for placing his statue on the rim of the Grand Canyon (July 8, 1926), that moviemakers no longer knew how to make Westerns (July 20, 1926), his appraisal of Crazy Horse (July 23, 1926), that the fates seemed to "have decreed to batter" him (August 16, 1926), his regret that he was no longer working (August 17, 1926), his denial that he was keeping his wife from making movies (October 23, 1926), that the Alamo was one of his pet subjects (December 29, 1926), that he addressed the Sioux in their own language at a ceremony in Billings (January 14, 1927), that he had made a stage appearance with Will Rogers (March 10, 1927), that he had had Nancy Russell to dinner (March 14, 1927), that he wished Jane Novak supreme happiness (April 7, 1927), his resignation from the board of the Motion Picture Producers and Distributors (April 7, 1927), his dislike of the syndicate that controlled most of the moneymaking theaters in America (June 22, 1927), his efforts to sell stories he had written (September 2, 1927), his love of boxing (October 12, 1927), construction on his ranch house (February 17, 1928), the collapse of the dam in San Francisquito Canyon (March 12 and 16, 1928), the arrival of talking pictures (May 22, 1928), that Charlie Siringo and Wyatt Earp were among the last of the "gallant frontiersmen" (July 6, 1928), making records for Victor (November 27, 1928), his contract with Hal Roach and its cancellation (June 12, 1929), a trip to New York (January 17, 1931), that he had written *My Life East and West* for his son and his failure to understand the Great Depression (May 27, 1931), the large number of fan letters he received and his continued persecution by Nick Schenck (January 18, 1933), his convalescence from a recent illness (November 28, 1933), his desire to create a Hart museum (February 1, 1939), and the damage rains had caused in his film vault (February 7, 1941).

Wyatt Earp wrote Hart on October 19, 1925, September 6 and December 14, 1926, May 4, July 4, November 13, and December 29, 1928, and January 7, 1929. The actor replied on June 3 and September 9, 1926, February 26 and December 16, 1927, and May 8, July 6, November 16, and December 28, 1928. Hart wrote Mrs. Earp on February 3, 1927. Originals or copies of these letters are in the Hart papers. Correspondence between Stuart Lake, Hart, and Mrs. Earp is dated January 17, 18, 19, 21, 25, 28, and 29 and March 12, 1929, and November 12, 1930. All of the biographer's letters are in the Lake Collection at the Huntington Library.

Nancy Russell wrote Hart on January 15, 1929, asking the actor's impression of her husband, and Jack Dempsey wrote Hart on October 8, 1926, expressing his disappointment over losing the fight with Tunney. The cowboy star mentioned having been at Wyatt Earp's funeral in a letter to Joe

McNinch on January 16, 1929, and he wrote Gladys Hall on January 10, 1930, that he would cut his legs off to have his son with him.

To Gatewood Dunston, the actor wrote about the loyalty of his fans (December 24, 1929), that there was no present prospect of his returning to work (April 21, 1930), that he could not part with one of his guns (March 16, 1931), the great extent of his correspondence (June 24, 1932), that he had had to destroy Cactus Kate (January 1, 1933), his suit against United Artists (April 25, 1931), a 60,000-word western story he had written (June 24, 1932), his recent return from the hospital (September 19, 1933), the evils of motion picture magistrates (February 28, 1934), his denial that he had had a face-lift (March 4, 1935), his forthcoming book, *The Law on Horseback* (July 22, 1935), that DeMille's *The Plainsman* was "an awful mess" (April 7, 1936), his disgust with the sound remake of *O'Malley of the Mounted* (May 29, 1936), his decent treatment by newspapers (August 17, 1936), that he had had a trained nurse with him for ten days (January 8, 1938), the death of Fritz (February 21, 1938), that old ways were fast disappearing (June 28, 1938), his intention to keep his films in good shape (July 14, 1938), that he had just returned from New York (December 5, 1938), that Jesse James, Jr., was unhappy with the Fox film about his father's outlawry (February 14, 1939), his determination not to make any more movies (May 13, 1939), that he had appeared on radio with Rudy Vallee (July 24, 1939), that grown boys and girls had not forgotten him (October 16, 1940), the failure of his eyesight (May 28, 1941), and that "everything has gone" for him (December 19, 1943). All of these letters are in the Dunston Collection at the Library of Congress.

The actor wrote Martha McKelvie about Mary Ellen's improved health on July 17, 1929, and that his eyes were failing on May 31, 1941. The McKelvie letters are in the Nebraska Historial Society.

Fritz's death and burial were described in the *Saugus Enterprise* on February 10, 1938.

Mary Ellen's musings about the meaning of life came from her diary, preserved in the Seaver Center.

Hart's visit to the set of King Vidor's *Billy the Kid* was remembered in the oral history Johnny Mack Brown taped for Columbia University and my interview with Vidor for Southern Methodist University.

Personal insights into Hart's life and character were supplied in my interviews with Harry Carey, Jr., Joe McNinch, and Mickey Seltzer.

Chapter 11

Hart made his remark to Hedda Hopper about the loneliness he felt after Mary Ellen's death in a letter to the columnist dated February 1945, now in the Hopper Collection at the Herrick Library. The actor praised Gene Fowler's *Goodnight, Sweet Prince* in a note to Joe McNinch, which was in McNinch's possession at the time of our interview.

Adolph Zukor tells in his autobiography of the cowboy star's refusal to allow drilling for oil on his land and recalls Hart's description of crossing over to "the other side" while in a coma. Hart's continued affection for Jane Novak is evident from a letter he wrote her on August 6, 1945.

To Gatewood Dunston, Hart wrote of his failing health and despondency over Mary Ellen's death (July 15, 1944) and the job of closing his sister's estate (February 23, 1945). Newspaper items regarding the actor's death, the tests made on his brain to determine his mental condition at the time his will was signed, and William S. Hart, Jr.'s attempts to break his father's will exist among the Dunston papers in the Library of Congress.

Young Hart's discovery of his father drugged and strapped to his bed was reported in *Newsweek*'s obituary of the actor. Other obituaries of the actor appeared in the *New York Times* and the *New York World Telegram* on June 25, 1946. A copy of Hart's will may be found in the Hart papers.

William S. Hart, Jr.'s intention to write a book about his father was rumored in a newspaper article on August 21, 1947. Other press items regarding the Hart property were among the items in Joe McNinch's scrapbook. Olive Carey's anger at the cowboy actor's exclusion of his son and ex-wife from his property settlement was remembered in my conversations with Harry Carey, Jr.

Signed statements by Lucille Evenson and Frank McKendall describing what they perceived to be appearances of Hart's apparition in the home at Horseshoe Ranch are on file in the William S. Hart Museum in Newhall, California.

Index

Index